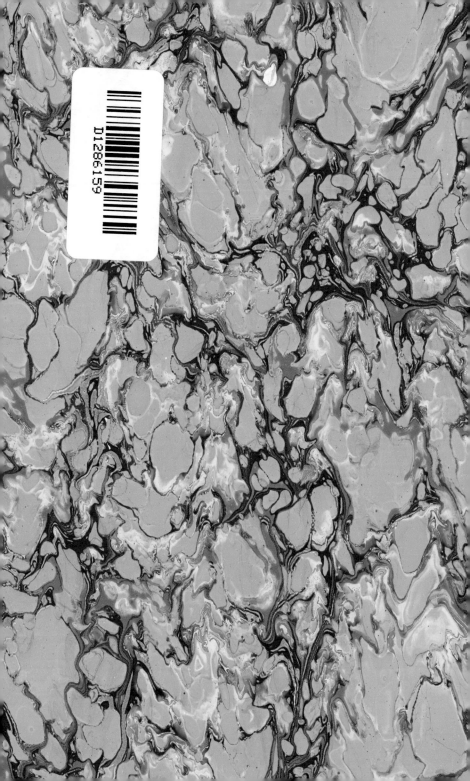

BRIGHT WATERS

There is not in the wide world a valley so sweet
As that vale in whose bosom the bright waters meet
Oh! the last rays of feeling and life must depart
Ere the bloom of that valley shall fade from my heart.

from *The Meeting of the Bright Waters* by Tom Moore (c.1807)

BRIGHT WATERS

A Celebration of Irish Angling

Chosen and edited by
Niall Fallon & Tom Fort

MERLIN UNWIN BOOKS

First published by Merlin Unwin Books, Ludlow, in 2002

Merlin Unwin Books
Palmers House
7 Corve Street
Ludlow
Shropshire SY8 1DB

ISBN 1 873674 49X

Typeset by Merlin Unwin Books, Ludlow.
Printed and bound in Great Britain by Biddles Ltd

Many of the game fishing pieces in *Bright Waters* are reprinted from Niall Fallon's *Irish Game Anglers' Anthology* (originally published in 1991). The editor, Tom Fort, and the publishers of this volume are especially grateful to Niall's widow, Patricia, for her support and encouragement of this publication.

Contents

To the Fallons

To Niall Fallon's widow, Patricia
and to his surviving brothers,
Brian, Conor, Ivan and Padraic.

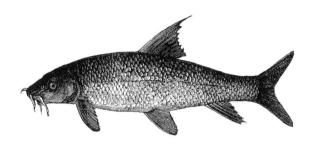

Preface

I last saw Niall Fallon in December 1995, a month before his shockingly sudden death at the age of 54. He had expressed a desire to catch a barbel, never having even seen one. We went to the Kennet, but the day being numbingly raw, we gave the barbel a miss, and pursued pike with deadbaits. It was a mode of fishing which aroused him, a fly fisherman to his core, to much scoffing, and his disdain was but little relieved by a handsome five pounder which impaled itself in the mill pool.

That evening we went to the Fishermen's Dinner, an annual fixture at which I and two of my brothers and sundry angling chums and wives are wont to meet, eat to excess, drink just short of it, and make a good deal of noise – not all of it concerning fish. Niall seemed in good fettle, for a man who had suffered a serious heart attack the previous summer. He proposed a toast to his doctor, and as the night wore on, we savoured in anticipation of the expeditions of the coming year: the Suir (again), the Eden (again), maybe Sheelin or Ennell this time, maybe the Conon.

I never spoke to him again in the flesh, though I continue to in spirit whenever I am on any of the waters we fished together. A couple of days after his death, I wrote this tribute for the *Financial Times*:

News from Ireland made a bitter January night seem more bitter still.

My friend Niall Fallon, who taught me everything I knew about Irish lakes and rivers and Irish trout, was dead. The last time I had seen him, we had planned excursions for the coming year. It would be a year of fishing for him. Not now.

He was a fine and honourable man, incapable of mean-mindedness or malice. He was also a fine fisherman, which is why I write of our friendship here. In fishing, as in other matters, Niall kept his quality quiet.

He was nothing much to look at on the water, a barrel-shaped man of medium height, in a shabby Barbour, a shapeless piece of Irish tweed jammed over his snowy hair. Not for him the long, elegant cast. His fishing was severely practical, wholly concentrated. He got close to the trout, wading if possible, then cast a short line, over and over again. His maxim, vastly valuable to me, was to keep at them.

Niall was a scholar of Irish fishing, as of Irish history and culture. He had a vast library of Irish fishing books, and had fished in every county of the island. He had spent five years living beside Corrib in the far west, writing his book about the Armada and tutoring himself in the ways of the trout of the great lake, and of the seatrout which in those blessed days still thronged the rivers and loughs of Connemara.

It was to the west that he took us on our first visit. We drifted Corrib and lovely Tawnyard, and were mightily buffeted on Shindilla and Ballynahinch. In truth we caught precious little, for we were pretty inept and the wind was awful. But we delighted in that bare, boggy, watery landscape, and in the love that our guide had for it.

We went again a few years later, and were slightly more successful. We stayed first in Cong, the village between Mask and Corrib. I caught my first salmon on fly from the river there, and we had an intriguing day boating over the white sand of Lough Carra. The highlight, though, was a magnificent trout which Niall took where the waters of Mask dash down the Cong Canal towards Corrib. He caught that fish on a wet fly while the rest of us were confounded by the conditions. We ate it in our fingers as the fire died down and the sun sank over Joyce's Country.

From Cong we journeyed to a very different landscape: soft, green Tipperary, and the Suir, which I think Niall loved best of any river away from his home. He winkled out a few, but the rest of us caught nothing, for the trout were simply too clever to be duped by our clumsy ways.

It is the Suir which has drawn me back to Ireland year after year; that, and the Blackwater near Mallow, where one of Niall's brothers has a tempting stretch; and of course the Deel and the Boyne, which meander through the fields near his home in County Meath – superb limestone streams whose blighting by the dredgers Niall railed against so eloquently, and whose faltering rebirth gave him such pleasure.

One memorable September we rented Careysville, the Duke of Devonshire's lodge on the Blackwater. The fishing was superb, the best we ever had; the eating, and drinking and gaiety were on the epic scale.

One night he subsided to the floor under the gaze of the great Irish moose whose head stood over the snooker table. Next morning he told us how he had woken in the night convinced that he had lost his false teeth, and how he had searched for them in the dark (he couldn't explain why he hadn't turned on the light), even exploring the hidden recesses of the lavatory in the hope that he had vomited them away; and how at length he had located his gnashers where he had left them, beside his bed.

He loved English fishing, too. He came each summer to join his brothers on the Kennet. And with us, there was a succession of trips to the Eden in Cumberland, all of them enriched by Niall's wisdom and humanity. He showed us aspects of the river which had escaped us: the hatch of the blue-winged olive and the fall of the hawthorn and where the big trout lay in the currant bush run.

Niall was chiefly responsible for turning me from tyro into the middle-ranking journeyman fly-fisher which is all I shall ever be. He showed me how to catch trout on the Suir, which convinced me I might stand a chance of catching them anywhere. And it was on the Suir that we last fished the fly together.

During daylight hours I did better than him, for the first and only time. Come evening and we fished at Drangan, above Cahir. It was warm and still and the surface was molten gold as the trout chased the blue winged olives. Niall caught fish after fish, he couldn't remember how many, but enough to make it a grand evening, the latest – and last – of so many.

Many years ago he gave me a copy of his first-rate book, *Fly Fishing for Irish Trout*. After I heard of his death, I looked it out. He had written in it an Irish exhortation, translated as: 'To the good man of the rivers, the trout, and plenty of whiskey.' It seems a fitting epitaph.

Niall's funeral was held in the hideous church just down the road from his house. I had never been in Ireland in winter before. The cold was bitter, and there was snow on the ground. A huge congregation turned out, for he was a man with a vast circle of friends. An atrocious sound system rendered most of the priest's comment inaudible; which may have been as well, for Niall was a firm non-believer. One of his four children gave a simple and intensely moving address, then we gathered by the graveside, overcoats flapping in the wind. My brother Matthew and I, and our friend Stevie, adjourned to an extraordinarily simple and basic bar in Longwood, where the Bushmills and the recollections of the friend we had lost drove out the chill, replacing it with the warmth of love and shared happiness.

But I felt the loss keenly, and still do. Was it the next summer, or the one after, that I was back on the Suir? Wherever I went, I felt his shadow across my path, heard that soft insistent voice, with its recurrent stammer. Yes I felt sad – but hugely grateful, too, that I should have been with him on this magical river, and listened to him, and learned from him.

My last evening I intended to fish at Swiss Cottage, just below Cahir, which was Niall's favourite stretch. But when I arrived there was a diagonal line of fishermen across the river, shouting at each other in French. I hastened upstream, to Ballycarron. I had fished there once before, with Niall, on a wild June day, and the high banks had afforded us protection from a blasting wind. This time, there was no breath of wind, and the sky was afire with the declining sun. It shouted evening rise, blue winged olive.

Sure enough, the olives were hatching, and it seemed that every fish was on the move. I did not need my departed chum to tell me to tie on the Orange Quill. Awash with confidence, I waded forth, and began covering feeding fish. And I covered them, and I covered them, and not one would look at it. Despair mounted. What would Niall have done, I moaned. He would have stopped, assessed the situation. I did. I stared at the water. The olives were coming down, in squadrons, but undisturbed. I dipped my hand, and my fingers came up papered with minute flat-winged creatures. Caenis!

Ha, I thought! Niall would be proud of me. For I had with me, acquired that morning, a caenis imitation tied on a size 28 hook. I managed somehow to attach this particle of fluff, and laid it accurately enough in front of a mighty fish which was growing mightier still as a result of gorging a couple of dozen of the tiny insects each time it opened its gob. I was just wondering how long the odds must be against one artificial being taken among such a host of naturals when the gob opened, and my little fly vanished. I lifted the rod tip, a massive tail cleaved the water, and my leader snapped. I went back to my B&B, the sound of Niall's hilarity booming in my ears.

Niall lived in a rambling old house on a crossroads about an hour's drive from Dublin, where he had worked for many years for the *Irish Times*. Despite its proximity to the capital, the area is Ireland at its greenest and most deliciously rural. Across the road, a pair of fine gates leads to a grand Georgian mansion, the drive crossing the little River Deel by a brick bridge. Thus Niall had dry fly fishing five minutes from his front door. He cherished that stretch, even one year paying £50 to the former owner of the mansion to rent it – until he discovered that it was already rented to the Deel Anglers, and was open to him on his £3 annual subscription.

I stayed at his home for a few days in the summer of last year, being looked after by his widow, Patricia, while I trawled through his fishing library to collect the material for this book. The work was arduous (of course) and the weather vile – but nevertheless, I managed, somehow, to squeeze in a few hours by and in the river. I had four nice trout on the Boyne, and was reminded yet again (as if I needed it) by the tiny Stoneyford that wild trout of no great size will generally take a great deal more deceiving than the fat, farm-fed stockies of the chalkstreams of southern England.

But the best of it was on the Deel, a good many miles upstream from Niall's home. I had been joined by Stevie, who borrowed our absent host's waders, and the stiff little Daiwa carbon rod made to look like imitation cane, which Niall inexplicably preferred to the authentic Chinese bamboo which we waved about. In its upper reaches, the Deel is really tiny; keeping itself to itself as it chatters its way through slumbrous farmland, almost hidden below tangled banks and ivy-clad miniature bridges. But, heavens, it is full of fish – bright, dashingly spotted, buttery little beauties – which were guzzling away at a sparse but constant smattering of olives in a manner that gladdened our hearts, and would have made the old man's face crack into a grin of pride.

Such fishing can be had only in Ireland, and it was just one of the treasures of his country that Niall so cherished. He was steeped in its history, its literature, its peculiarities, its traditions of learning and hospitality. To travel with him from Meath down to Cork or Cahir, or across to Galway or County Clare was to receive an education in the beauties, and oddities, and blessings and sufferings of this singular island. He seemed truly to know every lough and every river, to have fished most of them or know someone who had, or have it on authority that to do so would be a waste of time. That was but one of the qualities which made him such an entertaining and irreplaceable companion.

It was inevitable that Niall would become a collector of books on Irish fishing. The love of writing on the sport was another bond between us, and we each took a keen pleasure in introducing the other to some new book or author, or abusing a volume recom-mended with excessive keenness. I remember boasting to him about my discovery of the fishing adventures of Zane Grey, only to find that he had had a battered copy of the great man's *Tales of Freshwater Fishing* for years. Similarly, when he urged me to find the two little books by G.D. Luard which both of us regarded as containing some of the most delightful accounts of fishing anywhere published in the last half century, I was able to tell him that I already regarded Luard as a familiar friend.

He was proud of his collection, and jealous of rivals. He would mutter darkly about his one serious competitor, a shadowy figure encountered occasionally around the salerooms and secondhand shops, speculating hopefully on the possibility of some accident befalling this fellow, and his hoard of books coming onto the market. Niall himself wrote disappointingly little about the sport he loved so much, although his book *Fly Fishing for Irish Trout* is a treasure trove of wisdom and insight, enlivened by some sparkling story-telling. He was a severe self-critic, and dispensed praise with a cautious hand. I still cherish the few words of congratulation he had for my book, *The Far From Compleat Angler*.

The *Irish Game Anglers' Anthology* was Niall's last book. After its publication in 1991, he did occasionally refer to 'work in progress' on an autobiographical angling book, but I do not know how far he got. The demands of his job at the *Irish Times* left him little enough time for writing of his own, and when he left the paper to pursue a new career as a freelance, his pathological tendency towards taking on an excessive work load left him equally deprived.

Apart from the occasional foray to the local canal after pike and rudd, Niall had virtually no experience of coarse fishing, and I doubt if he ever thought of extending the ambit of his anthology to cover either that branch, or sea fishing. But I have long thought that it would be a fitting tribute to him, and to Irish fishing, to reprint the bulk of what he chose as being the best of writing about salmon, trout and sea trout; and to add to it a limited selection from the comparatively small body of work on coarse and sea fishing.

It is inevitable that, in a country with such a wealth of magnificent game fishing, the emphasis should have always been on the salmonids, rather than on the coarse and sea fishes; inevitable, too, that most of the writing should have come from English writers. Angling as a diversion had been enjoyed in England for centuries before the island of Ireland was properly subjugated and its remoter fisheries made available to the colonising power. Even so, there is evidence that salmon were being caught on the fly on the Galway river well before the end of the 18th century; while Daniel's *Rural Sports* of 1807 contains a tempting advertisement: 'The waters of Ireland abound in all that can invite the angler to their banks.' The plate of James O'Gorman's *The Practice of Angling* – which was first published in Dublin in 1845 and is the first authentic and readable Irish fishing book – shows flies tied by the Ennis craftsman Corny Gorman in 1791.

There is the odd bow towards pike fishing in O'Gorman's thoroughly diverting two volumes, and also in the earlier – and much inferior – *Angling Excursions* of Gregory Greendrake, and *The Sportsman in Ireland* by 'Cosmopolite,' otherwise one R. Allen. Bickerdyke's *Wild Sports in Ireland* – a book which I have never seen anywhere other than on Niall's shelves, even though the writer's other fishing books are comparatively common – is a true all-rounder's book, and a wonderfully evocative account of a life of enviable leisure in a bygone age. Barker's terrific *An Angler's Paradise* contains nourishing chunks on pike and perch fishing, even though it is the trout of Inchiquin and the other lakes of Clare which hold unchallenged sway.

The paucity of material is even more acute in sea fishing – a sorry state of affairs, considering the incomparable sport available and enjoyed at almost every point around the coast. Here, that great periodical of the 1960s, *Creel,* came to my aid. Even though I am not a sea fisherman, and have never so much as tangled with a flounder in Irish waters, I had vivid memories of being thrilled to the core in my youth by the accounts of Clive Gammon, Leslie Moncrieff, Bernard Venables, Des Brennan and others of fantastic sport in Dingle Bay, off Achill Island, and in other wild waters; battles with bass, tope, porbeagle, skate and other species equally obscure to me, illustrated with astonishing colour pictures of true rod-bending action. So I went up to my attic, to my piles of old *Creels*, and dug them out, to see if they were as good as I remembered. And they were.

So here are the fruits of my own, somewhat haphazard, labours; and of my old friend's lifetime of acquisition and exploration. I have slightly trimmed his selection – partly to make more space, occasionally where I felt the extract was below par, or his own comments merely repeated material from his introduction. I hope and believe that Niall would have approved of what I have done, and might even have had something guardedly pleasant to say about the result. And I trust that this collection will remind those who know that lovely land and its fishing of the pleasure they have had; and stimulate those who do not, to do something about it before long.

Tom Fort
April 2002

Lough Glencar, County Sligo

Introduction

The history of Irish literature is a strange one. Whereas other angling countries have made something of a fetish of their angling writers, we in Ireland do perversely the opposite; we hide them, we publish them sparsely, and then secrete their books so that only the most persistent of searches can discover them.

It is difficult to say how much of this is due to a sense of self-effacing inferiority. but I have little doubt that my own case is more or less typical. I had read the works of Skues, Halford, Sheringham and J.W. Hills before I had ever heard of O'Gorman, Peard or Kingsmill Moore. To my shame, I even fished with Kingsmill Moore in Connemara, unaware of his fame, or that he had written a book on fishing in Ireland. It was years before I realised that my late uncle's good friend, Dick Harris, crustily benevolent behind the counter of that wonder and now vanished tackle shop, Garnett & Keegan, was none other than J.R. Harris of *An Angler's Entomology*.

In my formative years as an angler during the fifties, the angling literature I read was predominantly English, topped up now and then with scraps from America. The *Angling Times* was a weekly event in our household and therein I drank deeply of a strange mixture of floats and gentles, long-trotting, Allcock Aeriels and Mr Crabtree. I grew familiar with the great coarse waters of Britain – the Hampshire Avon, the Norfolk Broads, the Ouse and the Stour. I could discourse knowledgeably on bleak, dace, carp and chub, none of which I had ever seen, let alone caught. In short, while my practical angling education was wholly Irish, the academic side of that education was ineluctably British.

Irish angling writers came to me at a slow crawl. Occasionally I came across fleeting, but tantalising references to O'Gorman, Barker or Peard. I became intrigued. Like a prospector for gold, I scented a fortune of delight. I began to dig.

Slowly the nuggets began to reveal themselves. Kingsmill Moore was the first (and, in many ways, the best). Then came Luce, strangely under-rated. A friend bought a copy of Barker for me, and gradually but inexorably, the other authors seeped into my life.

And what is it like, this corporate body of angling writers? For one thing, it is sizeable. How sizeable I cannot say with finality; but there are certainly well over one hundred books which deal wholly or partially with angling in Ireland. A high proportion were not written by Irish anglers, but by authors from England, and further afield, who spent fishing holidays in Ireland. However, the solid heart of our angling literature is indisputably Irish – O'Gorman, Kingsmill Moore, Dick Harris, Luce, Gwynn, Greendrake, Gaffey.

If the heart of our angling literature is Irish, the body is not wholly so. It is composed largely of English anglers who came principally to fish the western rivers and lakes, primarily for salmon, but also for brown trout and sea trout. In many ways, this well-trodden route has given rise to equally well-trodden experiences; as a result, there is a certain repetitive quality in many of the accounts.

But there is extreme richness too, much of it little-known and thus neglected as angling literature. Dr Walter Peard's *A Year of Liberty,* which describes a spring, summer and autumn tour of the cream of Ireland's fisheries in 1867, is relatively well known but still mostly unavailable. It remains a lively, well-written, diverting and revealing account of Irish angling in halcyon times. Some of the fishing which Peard enjoyed verges on the outrageous, almost the unbelievable; in particular, the trout fishing was of majestic quality and proportion.

F.D. Barker, born and brought up with a variety of fishing in America, discovered County Clare when living in England and thus began a love affair which lasted for many years and culminated in a rare and delightful angling classic *An Angler's Paradise,* published in 1929. Barker concealed the object of his particular angling affection, the region around the town of Corofin and Lough Inchiquin, by giving fictitious names and altering maps. He had as his boatmen and advisers the famous Egan family of Corofin, headed by the wonderfully drawn Patsey, who boated for him on 'Inchicrag' for many years. Later on, in his declining years, Barker built himself a house beside Inchiquin. A true love affair.

Barker, like Peard, enjoyed wonderful fishing. Then as now Inchiquin, its surrounding lakes and River Fergus, could be dour, but the quality of the fish caught then could not be repeated today. Inchiquin is still an excellent fishing lake and the Fergus is one of our finest limestone streams, but some of the days and nights which Barker and Patsey experienced are mere dreams for the rest of us.

G.D. Luard had something of Barker's instinct for secrecy (how like an angler not to give away his best fishing). His *Fishing Fact or Fantasy* and *Fishing Fortunes and Misfortunes* are by no means great literature but they paint a lovingly evocative and accurate account of fishing in deepest rural Ireland during the first half of this century. As with Barker and his 'Inchicrag,' Luard christened his anonymous angling kingdom 'The Big River' and 'The Little River.' On both, he spent many years' holidays, from a schoolboy to an old man, with 'Dick,' his great friend and owner of 'The Big House, Ballyhimmock.'

Curiously enough, the location and characters of Luard's books remained a mystery for many years until Dr Jean-Pierre Poux, that fine French angler, member of the eccentric and exclusive Fario Club of the late and great Charles Ritz and, not least, lover of the difficult trout of the Tipperary Suir, persuaded me to solve it.

In the the end, it proved simple enough: 'Dick' turned out to be one Richard Grove Annesley, landed gentleman, gardener, angler, hunter and shot; 'The Big River' and 'The Little River' became the Cork Blackwater and its lovely tributary, the Awbeg, where Edmund Spenser once lived. And Ballyhimmock, cleverly disguised by Luard, was the beautiful Annesgrove near Castletownroche, Co.

Cork, whose woodland gardens were created by 'Dick' and which are now open to the public to wander in and admire.

Luard's writing has a quality of involved belonging, a running thread of enthusiastic and simple love of angling and the places it brings the angler; this sense permeates his books much as it does those of BB (Denys Watkins-Pitchford). The two Luard books – and he wrote another very good one on his angling experiences in North America – remain for me at the centre of Irish angling writing, evoking that indefinable and loose quality of Irish fishing, where organisation is absent, where nothing ever turns out as planned, where fun is forever threatening the serious.

On a higher plane of literature, however, is my own personal favourite: Stephen Gwynn, Member of Parliament, writer and lover of Ireland. Gwynn, let it be said at once, had severe shortcomings as an all-round game angler. The art of dry-fly fishing for trout remained always at a distance from his sphere of angling accomplishment, which is hardly surprising in one whose fishing was learned amongst the spate streams and hill loughs of Donegal, where a half-pound trout was a triumphant crown to a day on the water. By his own account, he was clumsy with fish and tackle, so much so that he referred always to himself as being a duffer; and indeed based perhaps his best book, *Duffer's Luck,* on his own evaluation of himself.

But what a writer Gwynn was! – lyrically descriptive, sparely dramatic, hysterically funny. Three extracts in this book, picked almost at random, illustrate to perfection those distinct traits; 'A Connemara Twilight' is a simple account of an idle row in the gloaming of western Ireland; 'The Sway of Corrib' describes an intense and absorbing battle with a great trout; and 'Sprite on the Slaney', though I have read it a hundred times, still makes me laugh.

Like Luard, Gwynn remained emotionally rooted in Ireland. Both men had travelled, fished and lived elsewhere; they must have been entirely opposite characters, yet their books have a curious linking of mutual love of Ireland and its fishing, and a keen sense of the ridiculous. They can, and do, laugh at themselves as anglers must.

Humour was a quality shared by two of the earlier writers on Irish angling. O'Gorman and Greendrake (sometimes known as Greydrake) wrote two seminal works which, although showing wide differences in knowledge, approach and experience, nevertheless harmonise well together in giving us a strong taste of what angling was like in Ireland in the early part of the 19th century. O'Gorman's *The Practice of Angling* and Greendrake's *Angling Excursions* are rarely met with these days and cost a small fortune from antiquarian booksellers; but they remain as charming and lucid descriptions of a bygone age. We do not know who they were; even O'Gorman's first name is a mystery, while Greendrake and Greydrake were, we know, pseudonyms for one J. Coad. There is much to research here.

Although first published as late as 1931, and lately republished through the enthusiasm of Colin Laurie McKelvie, S.B. Wilkinson's *Reminiscences of Sport in Ireland* again is notable for its vivid portrayal of the 19th century and the early part of this century. Wilkinson was an engineer whose job took him to the more remote and wild parts of the west of Ireland, particularly to the north-west. There was little for him to do other than shoot and fish, and luckily for him he loved both. He enjoyed a quality of sport which we can only envy; his book is filled with tales of battles with big salmon and great bags of birds, of day after day of superb sport sustained by whiskey and peat fires. Wilkinson was no writer but his energy and vivacity shine through every page of this splendid book.

Much the same love of sport, the same ability to laugh at one's misfortunes, the same modesty, are displayed by Laurie Gaffey, who wrote two little-known books some fifty years ago. *A Freelance Angler in Ireland* and *Freshwater Fishing in Ireland* are over-ambitiously titled; they are, in fact, descriptions of Gaffey's own fishing days, most of them spent within a few miles of Dublin. What makes them memorable in some minute but unmistakable fashion is the love which runs through them like a vital vein of life. This lends Gaffey's otherwise flat and jumpy writing a liveliness and interest, and more especially a humour best expressed perhaps in his description of a day when everything went wrong – a day that every angler knows full well.

T.H. Kingsmill Moore, judge, angler, writer, humanitarian, is widely and properly regarded as the finest writer on Irish angling. I am perhaps the sole exception to this popular opinion, for I feel that Stephen Gwynn was a man whom angling had to some extent humbled; he could make mistakes and admit to them; he had short-comings and he knew it. Kingsmill Moore was a great man and a great angler but he did not suffer fools at all, let alone gladly, and there are in his book few instances of the failures and the foolish-nesses which beset all anglers.

But what an angler and a thinker Kingsmill Moore was – an Irish Skues who brought a similarly acute and logical mind to the proper analysis of angling problems. His knowledge of seatrout angling and of that strange fish and its ways was as comprehensive as it was illuminating; he appeared to have a facility for seeing into the mind of the seatrout, of divining their quirky whims. And he wrote divinely well, almost as well as Stephen Gwynn.

Where Kingsmill Moore surpasses Gwynn, however, is in a superior analytical way. Gwynn was robust and honest, an old-fashioned angler who rarely theorised but got on with what he was doing and enjoyed it hugely. Kingsmill Moore, on the other hand, approached the problems of angling determined to solve them through logic and invention. That he succeeded is evident; his sea trout flies are amongst the finest and most successful still used – the Kingsmill, the Bruisers, the Bumbles. His writings on the fisheries of Connemara remain definitive blueprints.

I fished a couple of times with Kingsmill Moore, both times by accident. The first time was on the Corrib, when he arrived to find no boat awaiting him. I was nearby, a young man with a boat but without either boatman or partner. 'Partner?' said the Judge. 'I'll partner you – and you boat me.' So he did and I did. I had never, to my shame, heard of him as an angler but knew of his public reputa-tion as a humanitarian, espousing all sorts of good causes. We fished and he talked; he was a good and kindly man.

The second time was at Delphi, a few years later. I had dropped by in the hope of a day on Doolough but the fishery was booked out. Kingsmill Moore was on his way out the door to fish Finlough. He recognised me and as he was short of a partner we fished together. He was older and noticeably more frail, but the talk was as stimulating and ceaseless as ever. All I remember of the angling was that I used a small Claret and Mallard to greater effect than he used his own creations; but he could not change.

We never met again, other than once or twice socially, but before his death our paths crossed in a curious way. I was fishing the Corrib with a boatman who is now dead and for one reason or another, the talk came around to Kingsmill Moore. Did he know him? Begod he did – sure didn't the Ould Judge give him a reel, and didn't he have the same reel with him in the boat that day. He produced it, a well-worn Hardy salmon Uniqua, and I bought it from him on the spot for a fiver. I have it in my study and I like to think it was the same reel that the great man used to catch four salmon one after the other from the Fairy Seat on the Slaney – that very incident described in this book.

A.A. Luce's *Fishing and Thinking* is not half as well known, nor indeed all that highly esteemed, yet I find it one of the best books on Irish angling that I have read. There is admittedly much in it which is philosophical and even obscure, but this should not be allowed to hide the fact that it is filled with close observation, shrewd analyses and diverting tales. Luce loved Lough Conn particularly and *Fishing and Thinking* contains the finest writing on that lake ever published.

Although it is not *per se* an Irish Book, J.R. Harris' *An Angler's Entomology* is as good as being Irish. For years I had heard of 'Dick' Harris as a good friend of my angling uncle Leo Maher, and had met Harris many times across the counter of that now defunct angling emporium, Garnett and Keegan of Dublin. But for some odd reason it took me years to connect that gruff but kindly presence with the man who wrote what is still the definitive work on angling entomology.

It is nearly forty years since his book was published, but Harris remains indomitably alive in every sense, a man whose knowledge of fishing in Ireland is unequalled. Here is a real Skues and a Sawyer combined; sitting by the window of his house in Dublin, where he ties flies without the aid of glasses, he has solved my fishing problems with an almost dismissive ease. What a pity it is that Harris has not written a book on Irish fly-tyings, for no one knows more about the subject*.

While these men comprise the body of those who have written more or less exclusively about Irish fishing, there is an even bigger body of angling writers who have included Ireland as a smaller part of their books. Both Sir Edward Grey and Maurice Headlam have written beautifully of the Suir and its difficult trout and I could omit neither of them from this anthology. Negley Farson dropped in to Ireland once or twice in his world travels, while a rarely seen work of John Bickerdyke's, *Wild Sports in Ireland,* deals almost entirely with fishing and shooting on the Shannon – if you ever see a copy, buy it and treasure it.

Sir Thomas Grattan Esmonde was an international sportsman who caught salmon in British Columbia, shot moose in Alberta, wolves in Romania and kangaroo in Australia. He lived in Co. Wexford, my own home county, and owned a fishery on the Slaney, of which he wrote well and lovingly. His two books, *Hunting Memories* and *More Hunting Memories* have excellent bits and pieces in them, not the least of them concerning Lough Derg, where he dapped for many years for the great trout which are, alas, now very scarce there.

More centrally Irish are the works of the Rev. Henry Newland and of Cosmopolite, otherwise R. Allen. The latter made a trip to Ireland during the 19th century and later wrote of it cantankerously, outrageously and inaccurately in *The Sportsman in Ireland.* I find it amusing, annoying and entirely unbelievable – but read it you should. The Rev. Newland's book *The Erne, its legends and its Fly-Fishing*, is entirely different, dappled with the nostalgia of those great years before the Erne was ruined in the cause of progress. A fine and romantic book, as is William Hamilton Maxwell's unforgettable *Wild Sports of the West* which, although it holds little enough of fishing, has enough to bring the reader back to it again and again.

Many anglers have sampled Irish fishing and written briefly of it before moving on. Edward Durand *(Wanderings with a Fly Rod)* wrote of the bog rivers of the midlands, still almost as unknown as

* He died in 1994

they were in his time; British Army man Arthur Mainwaring was stationed in Ireland for a while and showed that he enjoyed thoroughly its fishing and its women, and not least its drinking (*Fishing and Philandering*); James Dickie in *From Tyrone to the Test* wrote perceptively of fishing both in the north and south of Ireland. There have been many others – Francis Francis, W. Belton, Frederick Halford, Philip Green, Joseph Adams, J.B. Drought, A.W. Long, Sidney Spencer, Brian Clarke, Sir Humphrey Davy, Hugh Falkus, J.W. Hills, and in latter years, David Street. And, I have no doubt, many more I've neglected.

Many are guide-type books, technical and topographical. They are too numerous to list but they include Edward Fahy, Colin Laurie McKelvie, Peter O'Reilly, Ken Whelan, Peter Brown, Michael Kennedy, T.J. Hanna, Hi-Regan (J.J. Dunne), William Matson, Augustus Grimble, W.E. Frost and M.E. Brown, E.J. Malone (the definitive work on Irish flies, *Irish Trout and Salmon Flies*). There have been others also, including some indescribably inaccurate so-called 'guides' – pity the angler who might use them as such.

From them all, I have culled the meat of this book. If they have proved one thing to me at least, it is that Irish angling has had its chroniclers, perhaps not as many as in other countries but collectively managing to impart a good deal of the unique flavour of fishing in Ireland. Together they give a diverting and interesting view of a nation by lake and river, a nation in whose bountiful waters the salmon and trout continue to thrive. May future writers of these riches continue to thrive and give us more of the same.

Niall Fallon
Hill of Down
Co. Meath
Ireland
1991

Playing a salmon on the river Bush, below the Leap, c.1900.

PART ONE: GAME FISHING

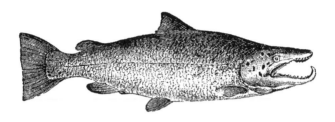

Verbum Sap

Watching the river one sultry summer's day, it occurred to me that the reason fish refused to take in such weather might be because they were all half asleep like myself, and that possibly a brick-bat or two in their midst might make them sit up and take notice. This theory I ventilated in *The Field*, incurring the usual derision that invariably greets any novelty of ideas.

On the day in question the Colonel and I started fishing in the Quarry Pool. For a quarter of an hour we fished most carefully, but then we had to stop, for a workman came to tell us they were about to explode a charge of dynamite in the quarry. Watching the blue smoke curling away from the fuse, I found myself wondering what the fish would think of the concussion, and remembered my own remarks on stirring them up. Now, whether the workmen had put in an extra charge for our benefit I do not know, but the explosion seemed a mighty one as the huge rocks, riven from their hold, rose slowly into the air only to descend again into the field with a mighty thud. One block, at least twice the size of a man's head, fell with a thundering splash into the very middle of the river, not forty yards from where we had been fishing.

'Now is the time,' quoth the Colonel, 'to prove your precious theory.' The ripples caused by this bolt from the blue had barely subsided as I made my next cast, and felt a pull at the shrimp. In another cast or two he came again, and I killed a fifteen pounder! *Verbum sap.*

A Mainwaring, Fishing and Philandering.

The Fisherman

'Although I can see him still,
The freckled man who goes
To a grey place on a hill
In grey Connemara clothes
At dawn to cast his flies,
It's long since I began
To call up to the eyes

This wise and simple man.
All day I'd looked in the face
What I had hoped 'twould be
To write for my own race
And the reality;
The living men that I hate,
The dead man that I loved,
The craven man in his seat,
The insolent unreproved,
And no knave brought to book
Who has won a drunken cheer,
The witty man and his joke
Aimed at the commonest ear,
The clever man who cries
The catch-cries of the clown,
The beating down of the wise
And great Art beaten down.

Maybe a twelvemonth since
Suddenly I began,
In scorn of this audience,
Imagining a man,
And his sun-freckled face,
And grey Connemara cloth,
Climbing up to a place
Where stone is dark under froth,
And the down-turn of his wrist
When the flies drop in the stream;
A man who does not exist,
A man who is but a dream;
And he cried, 'Before I am old
I shall have written him one
Poem maybe as cold
And passionate as the dawn.'

W.B. Yeats, *The Wild Swans at Coole*

A Little Swim

When fishing in Connemara, in the summer of 1869, I started one morning very early from Glendalough Hotel, our headquarters, for the Snave Beg ('The Little Swim'), so called because it is the narrowest part of Ballinahinch Lake, in fact little more than a strait joining the upper to the lower lake. My wife and two children were, after their breakfast, to meet me there. By half-past nine I had killed two salmon, and in order to cast my fly over a fish that was rising a long way out, I stepped out from stone to stone on some slippery rocks. Just as I reached the point I was making for, my feet went from under me, and I fell flat on my back into the lake. All my clothes, I need not say, required drying, so, as the sun was hot, I spread them on the rocks and ran about the across the heather to warm and dry myself. While I was still in this unusual fishing costume I heard the

5

sound of a car rapidly approaching, and saw, to my horror, that not only were my wife and children upon it, but also another lady. Fortunately there was a large rock close by; behind this I carefully concealed myself, and despatched one of my boatmen to stop the car, and to ask them to send me a rug and as many pins as they could muster. The rug was pinned round me, my arms left free, and my legs sufficiently so to allow me to walk, and thus attired I fished for three full hours, until my clothes were dry.

William Le Fanu, *Seventy Years of Irish Life*

The Inside Cast

As befitted his position and generation, the squire set great store by etiquette. 'Always remember there is another angler in the boat.' He taught us to imagine that there was a high perpendicular sheet of glass fixed athwart the boat, and extending out for some distance from the sides. This marked out the areas proper to each rod, both in the forward and backward casts, and if flies did not trespass outside their own areas there could be no tangling. A simpler way to avoid any possible tangling is to use a switch cast, which ensures that the flies never cross the line of the boat and has the further advantage that the flies are longer in the water. The only time when experienced fishermen occasionally get their lines tangled is when fishing a dry-fly in the twilight, and when this happens it is well to remember how far sound travels over water.

Consideration for the other angler also requires the direction of the boat's head to be changed frequently, especially when fishing a shore. Most anglers prefer to cast forehanded, with their arm free of the boat, and the cast nearer the shore is usually the better. I once asked the squire what he thought of a famous classical scholar who came from the neighbourhood. 'Not much,' he replied. 'He always tried to take the inside cast.'

T.H. Kingsmill Moore, *A Man May Fish*

6

The Duke's Dinner

With reference to these black fish, writing of them recalls an amusing incident which happened to us some years ago, when, having brought home a gentleman of 42lb, who for reasons best known to himself had gone into the deepest mourning, our host packed him off to a well-known owner of racehorses. The gift was warmly acknowledged, and in return we were sent the winner of the Cesarewitch, which happened to be in the stable of our friend. So far so good, for a few days later all of us were a little the richer. Now the big fish had been sent by our host because he knew his friend was not an angler, and would not attach much importance to the colour of the gift. Neither did he; but to our dismay, later on we heard that as he was leaving home, and could not eat it himself, he had presented it, 'as one of the finest and best-conditioned fish he had ever seen,' to a royal duke, who, well knowing all about salmon, was much too clever to eat it. Now, although the duke had also backed the winner of the Cesarewitch, he nevertheless vowed we had conspired to make an attack on his digestion, and that this was a matter that could only be put right by a meeting round the royal table under a solemn promise that we would drink as much 'forty-seven' as the big fish would have wanted of water for him to swim in.

Augustus Grimble, *The Salmon Rivers of Ireland*

A Careless Angler

A letter has been sent me by the gentleman to whom it had been addressed; I give it without note or comment:

STAMER PARK, ENNIS. April 20th, 1838

My dear sir
I find that O'Gorman is writing a treatise on angling, and has taken on himself to give prudential directions to the lovers of the delightful

7

sport. Now, you shall see how well-qualified this Nimrod of the rivers and lakes has proved himself to direct or advise. What I am about to state, has occurred within a few days, and to my own knowledge.

He had killed a large salmon on the Upper Fergus, which encouraged him to put a boat on it; his first day in the boat was dead fine, yet he had not fished long when he rose a large salmon (not a breath of wind!). 'Oh,' said he, 'he won't take, but I will try him with a single-gut fly;' on looking at which, he observed the noose a little faulty; the rower desired him to retie it; – 'No,' said he, 'if he even rises, he will not take,' and down he threw the fly most exactly, and on raising his hand, had him fast. Away the fish went, showing himself, and shortly ran back. On wheeling up, the handle of the wheel turned on the axle, and now he is regularly beat; but he pulled in the line through the loops, which, when again running out, hitched; the salmon sprang out of the water, unravelled the noose, and took away the fly, which a few rounds of silk would have saved, as the link was not broken, but slipt – and the top of the rod was also smashed on the occasion. Here is a fellow to talk of Franklin's advice! Well, sir, the next day I met him with a broken rod, not spliced, only lapt together – the same wheel put in some way to rights. And here I must remark that he has two or three pet rods and wheels intended for an expedition somewhere that I can't guess at; but away he went with a fry to look for pike, not a mortal with him, and he had not been long out, when he got hold of a very large salmon, which quickly abstracted about ten yards of his line, which was actually cut by an old top loop which he neglected replacing by a new one. The day after, I went with him, and rowed him up the river; still the same lapt rod, the same wheel, but a new top loop, and nothing but a slated fry for a bait. We had not got to the upper part of the river, when he called out – 'I have him!' – thinking him a large pike; but to my great delight, after a long race, it proved to be a very fine spring salmon, which we killed after great play. Then he says, – 'If there is a salmon in this next ford, I will rise him with a fly;' which he did, but for want of wind, the fish would not take.

Now, sir, here is your famous angler, having good rods, using bad ones, not even spliced; bad wheels, bad lines, old sharp top loops, from sheer laziness not even tying or even knotting the noose of his fly; and I have learned from a bystander, that he lost, after sunset one day last week, another large fish and his fly, by some like neglect. I request you may show this letter to Counsellor Henn, who will be sure to abuse him as he deserves; and I hope you will not be wanting on the occasion; to conclude, he is a very neglectful, careless angler, though possessing great perseverance, with a very impatient, bad temper: indeed, I think he is the worst tempered angler I ever met.

Believe me, my dear sir,
Yours truly,
M. Finucane.
The Hon. John Plunkett.

O'Gorman, *The Practice of Angling*

Sprite on the Slaney

Another episode – but it has not the authentic touch of fame because I am the sole articulate witness – was the adventure of Sprite, the dog. Sprite was Michael Sweetman's Sealyham, and we met when I first came down to fish on Michael's water, and renew a friendship made in France. I suppose I was introduced to Sprite at the station, but I first became seriously aware of him when I hooked a salmon about the third or fourth cast. Nobody expects things to happen quite so quickly, and Michael and his gilly were gravely concerned about my methods, which they thought too drastic; while I was priding myself on bringing the fish to the gaff inside of a minute or two. Then suddenly there was a flop, and Sprite had gone for the salmon which I was heading to the bank.

Normally, the duty of any looker-on was to hold Sprite: I have gaffed a fish for Michael with him under my arm, palpitating like a motor car, and screaming like a soul in pain because he was not allowed to go and bite the salmon. When there was no spare hand on the bank, Sprite always went in. Once I believe in his zeal he bit through Michael's line, and more than once he caused the loss of fish. He was beaten, but the instinct was too strong: besides, Michael fostered it. He had brought back from India one of the fish wrought in brass scales which writhe all over when you shake them, and it was a regular game to make Sprite attack it when it wriggled. Once it lay still and dead on the floor he took no further interest: nor did he in your dead salmon, except that he would guard what had been caught under his auspices. But while the fish was still plunging, Sprite desired passionately to get his teeth in. Once, Michael, gaffing a fish for me, let it slip from the gaff on the bank, and hurriedly seized it by the tail. Sprite had the same idea an instant later, and it was Michael's finger that he bit. Michael, who was a just man, did not beat him then; he said it was his fault, and Sprite was within his rights. Indeed I am a little doubtful whether he ever really beat Sprite, and he never really had the heart to leave him behind.

I had, though, and used to shut him up when I went down by myself, but more than once he dodged me and sneaked along under cover. It happened so one day when there was a little flood on the river, but so late in August that one did not take fishing seriously. I saw him stealing down on the far side of a hedge, but thought no more and proceeded to fish Synott's stream without any expectation – using light tackle and a very small fly, as one would in Donegal. And when the fish took, it was pretty far down and he was fairly heavy; still I got him in to the bank and was getting my gaff out, when splash! there was a small white object also in the water; Sprite in the midst of his rabbit-hunting had heard my reel go and seen the rod bent, and came valiantly to my assistance.

Now there was a pretty strong stream, and just below where I stood trying to gaff my fish, was a line of alder bushes, perhaps fifty yards long, with branches into the water, and the fish, scared by Sprite, had retired towards them. Even without the dog, I should have had difficulty in getting him up stream unless he wanted to come, and I saw no means at all to get hold of Sprite. Remonstrance was useless, Sprite was out to enjoy his hunt. So I took a resolution.

The main stream ran a little outside the alders, and I turned the fish into it, and when he got out a few yards, I lifted to make him wallop on the top, and he did, and Sprite of course made straight for him. Equally of course, the fish headed fast down stream away from this new variety of otter. The alders had been cut, I held my rod high, and down we went in procession: the salmon with my fly in him, heading it, Sprite a couple of yards behind, paddling fiercely, and I legging it along the bank inside the bushes. There was a stile to climb, but I got over, and in that order we continued till the alder bush ended, and there was, as I knew, a back-water on my side. Into this I pulled the fish when he reached it. Sprite, carried by the stream, went away past us, and landed twenty yards farther down, and by that time I had whipped out my salmon. Undoubtedly the dog felt he had been done. He walked up the bank past me, and affected not to know there was a salmon there. Michael averred that Sprite did not like that matter mentioned to him for at least a fortnight.

Stephen Gwynn, *Duffer's Luck*

A Dog's Life

He would dive down, too, after salmon fry caught and thrown back when trout-fishing, till only the stump of his tail was visible, and where the water was deeper he was sometimes completely submerged, remaining under for quite a long time, and hunting eagerly with wide open eyes beneath the water. Sometimes he caught one that was feeble, and then I regret to say he at once proceeded to scrunch and eat it. I'm afraid his tastes were a bit crude; certainly he thoroughly enjoyed a meal of raw fish fresh from the river, and probably this added to his sporting interest in them.

Once I made good use of this habit of his. One rather heavy and thundery day I was keeping an eye on the men haymaking by the side of the river, when I noticed several nice trout rising in the flat that bordered the meadow. Luckily I had my rod with me, but I had forgotten my landing-net.

I put on a biggish olive, and began with the lowest of them. He took it at once. The question was how to land him, for there was a line of rushes growing in the water about two yards out. Then I bethought me of Jock – I called to him and showed him the fish, now swaying on the top of the water, a nice trout of about three-quarters of a pound.

He caught on at once, plunged into the stream, seized the fish neatly in his teeth, and brought it ashore quite uninjured and without touching the cast, though I confess that once on shore I had to extract the fish from his jaws to prevent his making a meal of it. Three more he landed for me and then the rise was over.

G.D. Luard, *Fishing Fortunes and Misfortunes*

The Water-Keeper's Wife

In the year 1908 I went over to Newport for a few days, and with the exception of the railway everything appeared just the same as when I left the place some thirty years before. I walked out one morning to see the spot from where I had hooked a fine sea trout; this was while I was living here and the tale is worth recording, showing how I gained by having a water keeper's wife on my side! I had got up early as there had been a nice spate and everything was perfection. About the second cast I was 'in him,' the trout making several desperate leaps and runs getting over a ridge of gravel into another pool and from which I felt I could never get him back and knew that he had me beat! The road and the river abutted and, just at this time, a country woman came along and 'bid me the time of day' and after looking at me playing the trout saw the predicament that I was in, she said it was a bad business and asked if the fish was any size. I told her, as far as I could judge, from three pounds to four pounds – 'a murdering pity' to lose such a good trout. Then she made this proposal: that she would take the rod and play the fish and when he was beat I might get a chance at him with the landing net. That was agreed to at once; it was the only chance and not much of a one at that. The woman took the rod out of my hands and I saw at once it was not the first time that she had played a trout. I proceeded to drop down from the wall about ten feet into about three feet of water running pretty swiftly, wading across to the far side of the stream. The fish could see me quite plainly and every time I approached it fled from one end of the pool to the other in very heavy water, making most determined rushes and 'leps'. The trout was now showing signs of being tired, and his big golden-looking body shining through the brown peaty water made me think that he might be a bigger one than I thought at first. After another run and jump it had shifted into another stream. Here the good lady 'stuck the butt' well into the fish and led it beautifully up to and into the net. Such a beauty! I had to wade back to the river wall; everything my lady friend did was with precision: the way she wound up the line and laid the rod on the top of the wall, reel up, then reached down for the handle of the landing net, pulling it up safely to the road; while I got out of the river bed, climbing up to the top of the wall in time to give a tap on what Dr Peard in the 'Year of Liberty' calls the 'occiput.' I had not scales with me, but on my return to my rooms was able to record that this sporting fish pulled the scales at five pounds good!

I thanked the good woman for having helped me and made her come in and have some breakfast and congratulated her on the masterful manner in which she had killed the fish. In reply she said: 'Your honour, what about it? I have killed scores and scores of them in my time. Shure isn't me husband head water-keeper up by,' meaning of the district. If all the water-keepers and their wives were such good sportsmen and women, using rod and line only (and no dragging of the pools with nets), there would be better fishing and I would never begrudge them a fish killed fairly.

S.B. Wilkinson, *Reminiscences of Sport in Ireland*

The Worm's Turn

Oh! those Irish similes: if one could but remember them all or even a quarter of them. There was that prince of fishermen, Jack Douane, of Fermoy. I asked him to get me some worms to go salmon fishing. On going down to the stable yard over which he presided to get them, he turned them out for my inspection, as miserable a lot of gudgeon bait as ever I saw. 'Why, Jack,' said I, 'what's the use of these wretched microbes; they're no use.' 'No use?' he exclaimed in a most aggrieved tone, as though I had asked him to lend me a shilling. 'No use? I declare to goodness if ye don't get behind a bush when you're puttin' them on, the trout'll lep out and ate ye.'

A Mainwaring, *Fishing and Philandering*

Wiping the Eye

By three o'clock I had not seen a quiver of a decent trout. I had thrown back three or four of the variety called 'tiddlers' and the breakfast mood of depression again had me in its grip. I vented it on Johnnie.

'Where are all these fine fish you were telling us about?' I asked. 'I don't believe there's a decent fish in the river.' He looked at me in pained surprise. 'There's grand fish does be in it,' he said. 'It's no lies I'm telling ye, for I seen them same. Come with me and I'll put yez where ye'll play Puck with them.' He discarded my flies for some home-made manufacture of his own, led me half a mile down stream to a natural dam above a long, dark pool and bade me cast across 'the way the trouts would be coming up to meet ye.'

Well, I did. I fished the pool, and several other pools as well, until my arms ached as severely as my temper. And I caught exactly three trout which, placed head to tail, might possibly have measured thirteen inches. Then from a little copse near by came Joan with what appeared to be the top and middle joints of an old salmon rod, spliced together with strong wire. In lieu of a reel, from the top joint hung a length of stout blind cord, to which was appended a salmon cast and a hook, baited with a peculiarly revolting worm.

'Hello,' I said, 'Where have you sprung from? You can't possibly fish with that contraption.'

'Sez you!' replied the damsel in the disgusting vernacular of the rising generation. 'You watch.'

She dropped her loathsome bait into the water, squatted on her haunches on the bank and waited. But only for an instant. There was a boil in the water; a heavy splash, and the child sprang to her feet clutching the rod tightly in both hands, while almost simultaneously something described a parabola and hit the bank with a resounding smack six inches from my face. It was well both rod and tackle were of salmon-breaking strain, for that trout (and I lie not) turned the spring balance at an ounce under three pounds.

Johnnie once again had told the truth by accident; his wizened face was wreathed in smiles, though the fisherwoman was the least concerned of anyone. 'I've caught them here before,' she said, 'but only little things. I dare say I shall never catch another quite as big as that.' I shouldn't wonder if she spoke the truth. But when she pattered off, doubtless to dig up another close relation of that most disgusting worm, I laid down my rod gently, lit a pipe, and brooded darkly on the uncertainty of earthly things.

J.B. Drought, *A Sportsman Looks at Eire*

Mr O'Sullivan

The six years when I was never in any one country for over six months, when I was living in Wagon-Lits and Ritzy and non-Ritzy hotels; when I was arguing with customs officials, concierges, and foreign chancelleries around the world; when about the only things that ever caught up with me were my bills, were years, you would think, that held little chance for sport. Yet I saw to it that they provided just that thing. I believe that you do not learn much about any country by sitting in its capital. I had been some four months knocking about remote parts of Spain before I went to Madrid to see Primo de Rivera – and fishing with the Shetland drifters or over at Stornoway in the Hebrides taught me much more about the plight of the British herring industry than I could ever have dug out of the Ministry in London. So when I suggested to my paper that it would be a good thing to take my small round-nosed car and drive around the perimeter of Ireland – both the Free State and Ulster – so that the Irish in the States might have some first-hand impressions of what it was like these days, my paper, being far-sighted, snapped at it.

It was not my fault that the Punchestown races were at Naas; that the Shelbourne in Dublin was full of perhaps the gayest collection of sporting people on earth; that I lost heavily on the races, and, in remorse, left the flesh-pots of Dublin – and poached every stream that I could, driving up the west coast of Ireland. In Connemara and in the Joyce country I got some most useful Irish politics that way. (But I got amazingly few fish!) At Dingle I lay over a few days to go off with the Irish 'nobbies' trawling in Bantry Bay. I lived with the captain of the little *Mary Immaculate*, and at night both he and his wife told me what the big steam trawlers were doing to all the little Irish fishing villages: 'Ruining us, they are!' said Captain O'Flaherty. 'Mind you,' said his wife, 'if it wasn't for the remittances coming back from America – sure Dingle itself wouldn't be here!' All the way out to the fishing grounds in the 'Nobby' Old John was down on his knees in our cabin, praying and counting his beads, for luck, and against the physical ordeal that lay ahead of him; for he was an old man, and he hung as if crucified on the warp getting in the trawl. The last day when a fog came down we saw the big grey shape of an Atlantic liner, her horn blowing, feeling her way past through the murk.

It was raining all the time, and the old man at the tiller waited until he got thoroughly drenched before he put on his yellow oilskins. 'Ah,' he said, 'I knew a man that trolled naked. Galway, he was. He took off his clothes and put himself into a bag. It had holes for his arms and legs.'

Commissioned by the *New York Sun* in 1919, to write some articles on Sinn Féin, I deliberately used my trout rod as a bit of camouflage. At Killarney I got Mr O'Sullivan, the butcher, to give me the lie of the land; where, in his judgment, was the best place to fish – were there streams handy? He took me out in his car, where he fell into a dissertation about trout.

'A delightful subject!' said Mr O'Sullivan. 'It holds so many contradictions!'

'Are you one of those men who carry every fly in the world in their book – or do you chance it with just six or seven kinds?' I asked.

Mr O'Sullivan stopped his car: 'I belong to the latter school. And I'll tell you why....'

'Is it true,' I asked, 'that some of the lads were going to ambush a British lorry on its way to the Gap of Dunloe yesterday – only, the British took the wrong road by mistake?'

'Sure! and how the divvle did you hear about that? Mind you now... they were only Black and Tans... t'would have been no loss.'

'I think I must have driven right past the lads in ambush?'

'Well, if you took that road younder to the Gap of Dunloe – you certainly did. They was lying there all day. The British always take the wrong road.'

'I was lucky.'

'Twas not luck! Ye had the Major with ye. Nobody'll touch him. And you tell the Major we'll allow none of those Sinn Feiners from Cork to come over and burn down Flesk, either.'

'Suppose you're reserving the burning for yourself?'

'Ah, shame on you. The Major's a Unionist – we know that better than he does. But he's no.....absentee. Tell me (suspiciously) I thought you were talking about trout?'

'Personally,' I said quickly, 'I think a 9ft. 3in. rod is quite long enough. And a two-piece rod gives you a better action, doesn't it?'

'Ay – that's true. But you'll not be carryin' a two-piece rod about with you in a car.'

'No, you can't carry a two-piece rod about with you in a car.'

'And especially in railway trains! Do the IRA drill much in these parts?'

'I'll be getting back now,' said Mr O'Sullivan; 'it's not trout ye have on your mind at all at all.'

Negley Farson, *Going Fishing*

Thim Salmon

An Englishman who goes over every year and rents a beat on the Lee was fishing below the Inniscarra weir one Easter holiday. Ardent and earnest fisherman as he was, his luck was out and he had not 'met

17

with fish' for several days and was getting slightly annoyed with the lack of sport, also with the endless succession of trout anglers coming along the banks from the city of Cork, on whom he looked with no sort of favour.

Presently one of these gentlemen strolled up the bank and stopped to watch him casting for a time.

'Would ye be tellin' me, sor, where I could be fishin' not to be pestered by thim salmon?'

'What do you mean, pestered by salmon?'

'Well now, sor, it's the wan day of the year I do be fishin' and I started out with three casts; thim dam salmon have the two of thim whipt off me, and if they takes the other it's home I'll have to be going with niver a trout in me bag.'

I leave you to imagine the Englishman's feelings, but I hope the recording angel was looking when he supplied the man with another cast, and a couple of trout flies, and told him to get on with the job.

W. Durand, *Wanderings with a Fly-rod*

An Angler in School

In the year 1826, my father having been appointed Dean of Emly and Rector of Abington, we left Dublin to live at Abington, in the county of Limerick. Here our education, except in French and English, which our father taught us, was entrusted to a private tutor, an elderly clergyman, Stinson by name, who let us learn just as much, or rather as little, as we pleased. For several hours every day this old gentleman sat with us in the schoolroom, when he was supposed to be engaged in teaching us classic lore, and invigorating our young minds by science; but being an enthusiastic disciple of old Isaak, he in reality spent the whole, or nearly the whole, time in tying flies for trout or salmon and in arranging his fishing gear, which he kept in a drawer before him. Soon after he had come to us, he had wisely taken the precaution of making us learn by heart several passages from Greek and Latin authors; and whenever our father's step was heard to approach the schoolroom, the flies were nimbly thrown into the drawer, and the old gentleman in his tremulous and nasal voice, would say, 'Now, Joseph, repeat that ode of Horace,' or 'William, go on with that dialogue of Lucian.'

As soon as our father's step was heard to recede, 'That will do,' said our preceptor; the drawer was reopened, and he at once returned, with renewed vigour, to his piscatory preparations, and we to our games. Fortunately my father's library was a large and good one; there my brother spent much of his time in poring over many a quaint and curious volume. As for me, under the guidance and instructions of our worthy tutor, I took too ardently to fishing to care for anything else. I still profit by those early lessons. I can to-day tie a trout or salmon fly as well as most men.

William Le Fanu, *Seventy Years of Irish Life*

Brown Caughlans

He told me that it was quite a common thing for Lee salmon to take a trout fly. 'When me ould dad was tying flies for ould Mister Haynes in Pathric Street, wasn't it the grand fly he was after inventing that would catch a salmon or a throut ondiscriminate: the 'Mystery Fly' he would bet calling it. It's well I remember the time I was working in the shop with him as an errand boy, and me only knee-high to a shnipe. The English officers from above in the town would be coming in every day to be having a crack with him. Those were the days and thim were the lads; it's a sad day for Cork it was when thim same left.

'The ould dad was fond of his joke and the officers would be liking to hear the yarns he be telling them, and one of the lads would always be teasing the ould man about the flies he tied. 'Why can't you be tying them natral like?' says he. 'Them things aren't like anything that moves in the air above or in the waters beneath.'

'Well now, it's not much good the captain was at the trout fishing, and he would be blaming it all on the flies. One day he gives an order for half a dozen 'Brown Caughlans.' 'And tie them natral like so the throuts will be taking them.' The dad niver says a word to him then, but that evening I sees him tying thim same and muttering to himself: 'Natral! I'll be larnin' him what's natral.'

'The next day the dad slips out for his pint of porther just whin the officers would be coming, and sure enough they comes in and starts asking for the ould man when I was minding the shop. Presently in he comes and 'Good morning, Sean,' says the captain. 'Have ye the 'Brown Caughlans' tied for me?'

'I have so,' sez he. 'They be hanging on a string in the window already for ye.' And himself walks over to get thim. 'Paddy,' sez he, 'have ye been moving thim flies I left here last night?'

'I have not,' sez I.

'Well now,' sez he, 'and that's the quare thing. I had thim same tied all ready overnight, and it's hanging on this string they were,' sez he, pointing to a bit of string across the window. 'Who has thim moved on me?' and he starts hunting all over the shop for thim same. The captain goes over to the window to help him look.

'Is that one?' says he, pointing to an ould cobweb in the corner.

'Musha now, and it is, and here's another and another.' And he picks all six of thim flies from off the webs.

'The ould dad chuckles, 'Isn't it thim spiders that have the flies whipt of me? Now will ye be telling me thim same are on-natral?

And the spiders thimselves not know the differ.'

W. Durand, *Wanderings with a Fly-rod*

Pay Nobody

Another local legend which I heard was a story of the late John Bright and his old fishing crony, Peabody, the philanthropist. They used to fish the Shannon, at Castle Connell, and one day they came up for a turn on the lough. Two of the chief boatmen of Killaloe joined forces, and did themselves the honour of rowing these distinguished visitors. And a severe day's work these rowers had, for their patrons trailed persistently for eight mortal hours, and 'never a drop of the cratur had they brought with them!' Arrived at the landing-stage, late in the evening, there was the inevitable policeman on the bank. John Bright, accosting him, said, 'What is the proper price to pay these boatmen, constable?' He replied, 'Seven-and-sixpence, your honour; but some gentlemen give them ten shillings.' John Bright, turning to his chum, said, 'I have no change, Peabody; have you three half-crowns?' The millionaire produced the coins, and gave them to the boatman nearest to him. Holding them in the open palm of one hand, whilst slowly scratching his head with the other, he said, 'And they calls ye Paybody, don't they? Well, I calls ye Paynobody.'

C.W. Gedney, *Fishing Holidays*

CHAPTER TWO: THE GENUS GILLIE

Miley Costello

River fishing is a one-man pursuit, lake fishing a partnership. There may be a partnership of three, if the second rod is a friend with similar views, but the ideal is two: the angler and his boatman. The boatman supplies the knowledge of local conditions while the angler decides the method of fishing. It takes time to perfect such a partnership, for every angler has his own theories and methods, which necessitate the boat being handled in the way which suits his style, and the boatman must learn to do this without continual direction. Some boatmen will not learn and some try to dictate. The wise angler will accept suggestions from an intelligent boatman but he must never tolerate dictation.

I have had many fruitful partnerships but none so ideal as with Miley Costello of Fermoyle. Speech was unnecessary, and indeed Miley seemed to have a mistrust of speech, doling out his rare remarks as if he was dispensing a dangerous medicine. It was a point of pride with him to be able to read the mind of his angler and take the appropriate action before he was told. Nothing escaped his observation. A turn of the head, a glance at the sky, a shift of position, the opening of a fly box, these gave him the clues to what was going on in my mind. Yet there must have been something more than quick observation. I would think 'I wonder, is the salmon which I saw move by the big rock last Saturday still in the same place?' and Miley would take up the oars and row me to the most favourable point for drifting the big rock. To fish with Miley was to have four eyes. Battling up against half a gale he would suddenly stop the boat and point out a direction for me to cast and as often as not the flies would be taken by a fish whose movement he had spotted despite the roughness of the wave. I can recall his making only one error, and then the real fault was mine. While he was away gathering heather for the luncheon fire the wind died and I changed to a thin and rather worn cast, but kept on the same flies. I was so accustomed to Miley seeing everything that I forgot to tell him about the change when he came back. As soon as we started again after lunch, a big white trout took the tail fly and charged straight in towards the boat. The orthodox counter is for the boatman to pull half a stroke, allow the fish's rush to take him past the stern and so avoiding the danger of a dropper catching on the keel. With any other angler Miley would have done this automatically, but he knew that with a cast of normal thickness I preferred to take in line with my hand and direct the fish by side pressure clear of the stern. The weak cast did not take the strain of so large a fish, and parted. Miley picked up the broken end, examined it and flushed. 'To think I never noticed,' was all he said.

T.H. Kingsmill Moore, *A Man May Fish*

The Ould Earl

'Sure now, and wasn't the ould earl the darlin' man, when so be it wasn't riled he was feeling. If it was so, glory be to God, but he had the words that would scald the feathers off a crow's back. It's well I remember the time when himself had the temper lost entirely, and thanks be to hivin it wasn't meself or the dad, who was with him, that he'd be cursing, but the salmon thimselves that wouldn't be after taking anything all that day.

'There they were leppin' and flappin' in the water for ivery wan to be seeing, and divil the taste of a fly, or a shrimp, or even a worm, would they be taking for a whole week, and it's meself had all the three tried by the same token. Well now, the earl wouldn't be fishing with anything but a fly at all, it's poaching he'd be calling the others, but if so be the fish weren't rising bould, wouldn't he be telling the dad or meself to be putting up the spinning rod and trying the 'Colley' or the shrimp down the water behind him.

'He'd been after throwing the fly all morning, and it's himself could put a fly on the water fit to tempt an angel from hivin, but divil a fish could he meet with in any of the pools he tried. The dad had been watching him careful like, and he says to me: 'No ye young omadhaun, ye be kaping out o'sight of himself, or it's withered ye'll be with the tongue of him. And don't ye be showing yerself 'till he has a fish cot, and by the hair of St. Padhraig it's careful ye'd better be after being with the gaff. By the houly saints, if ye miss your sthroke or break him, the Lord forgive you, cos himself won't and it's murther there'll be.'

'So I hides meself behind the bank the whilst he's fishing down 'Hall's Turn' and 'Parker's Gut;' and the language of him would have shut the mouth of Mother Moriarty, and her coming home from the fair-day, and by cripes, that same takes some doing and her with the drink then.

'Well now, I'll be telling you that it got so bad that the dad creeps up to me and says: 'Himself will be after having a sthroke.'

But at that moment the ould earl opens his fly-book and, with a grand curse, hurls that and the rod both togither into the water.

'Isn't it ivery dom fly in the book I've tried ye with,' he bawls. 'Here, take the whole bloody lot and choose fer yerselves.' And he stamps away up the bank, cursing and swearing like the Ould Wan himself.

'Do ye fly down the river, Paddy, and cotch that book before it be schwept away entirely,' says the dad to me. 'And I'll be trying for the rod with the shrimp tackle.' And away I belts and sees it floating there in the flat below 'Parker's Gut,' and says a prayer that himself above on the bank won't see me schwimming out after it. And faith when I gets back, wasn't the dad up to his neck in the water after that same rod, and when he came out with it, an the two of us stood there with the water running out of our boots, wasn't it dhrowned entirely we were.

'While we were up at the farm changing, in stamps the earl. 'Holy murther, Sean,' he says to dad. 'I've thrown me book and me rod into the river.'

'And why wouldn't ye?' says me father, peaceable like, and he not knowing how the old gintleman's temper was.

'And I after wanting to be fishing again this afternoon.'

'Sure now and we have the both saved on you,' says me dad.

'God be good to ye, but that's grand hearing. It's a trifle annoyed I must have been to be doing the like.'

'By the holy cripes, if it's only a trifle annoyed ye were, may I be out o'hearing when it's real angry ye are.'

'Off with ye now, Paddy,' says the earl, 'and be bringing the

25

waders. Haven't I fished this river for years from top to bottom, and don't I know every stone of it from Coolcour Bridge to Cork, and haven't I fished the whole countryside all me life, day and night, even to standing in the water after dark under the walls of Carrigadroghid Castle, and me wondering all the time when the 'Pookha' would be catching me. And at my time o'life I'm not going to be beaten by these dom salmon, even if they do be making me lose me temper. Sean, I'll be fishing the 'Wood Hole,' and do ye be fishing the 'Island Stream' and the 'Orchard Turn' with that dom shrimp ye're always advisin.'

'I will so,' says me father. 'But it's heedful ye'll need to be of the 'Wood Hole' with the water there is in it. The rain was black in the hills, and the Sullane and the Dripsey may be roaring down.'

'But divil a thing would he hear, and off he goes to the river, lickity split.

'I see him start in at the top end of the 'Wood Hole,' and it's wading down the bank side he was when I goes upstream to the dad, and him bawling for the shpinning rod. In thim days they did not have the road cut under the bank, that ye can fish the stream so, and that without wading. I was only with the dad a tin minutes or so, and wasn't I kaping an eye cocked that himself did not meet with a fish the whilst I was helping to whip on a shrimp, when suddenly we hears a terrible wallop in the water below.

'My cripes!' says dad. 'And that's the biggest fish that ever lepped in the Lee.' And we looked down to see if himself had met with the salmon.

'Well now, I'm telling you, all we could see was a pother in the water, and two brogues sticking up above the surface.

'Tis himself is drowned entirely,' bawls me father. 'Do ye be runnin' to the turn beyant, and shtick the gaff in him and he passin' ye in the shtream, and I'll be thowin' the shrimp to him, the way it'll be catching the waders.' And we both fled down the bank.

'But it was the ould earl himself that did all the saving, didn't he throw himself on his back and paddle himself ashore in the shallows below there as handy as a duck.

'Sean,' sez he, and him lying on his back the way the water

would be draining out of him, 'it's a judgment on me, it is, for losing me temper, but it's you and Paddy will be getting drowned saving the rod for me. It's there it is at the bottom of the river. I'm off to the farm to be drying meself.

'And with that I pulls the waders off him, and away he tramps up the hill with the water running off him fast enough to be giving a duck the toothache.

'We gets the boat down from the flat above, and the divil and all of a time we has in getting it over the shallows and houlding it in the stream while I dives below for the rod. It's an hour and more we were before we gets the boat back above, the where himself would be wanting it to cross over home for the night, and just as we were walking down the bank, soaked to the bones of us, the earl comes down the hill as dry and jaunty as ye please, but looking odd about the legs and arms of him.

'Me father has one look at him as he comes up. 'Houly murther,' sez he, 'it's me best suit ye have, taken off me. How will I be getting to mass at all, and me with nothing to wear but me bare skin?'

'Sure, it's all right, Sean,' says the earl. 'Wasn't it herself above there at the farm who'd be giving it to me, to save me catching me death of could, she said. I'll be sending it back to-night, so as ye'll not be going naked to mass on the Lord's Day; and by the same token, I'll be paying for a new suit for you and Paddy there for the wettings the two of ye have had the day.'

W. Durand, *Wanderings with a Fly-rod*

Two Shillings a Day

Your Irish attendant is a man *sui generis*; at least, there is nothing like him in our own land. Compare him with an English gamekeeper – be that functionary land rat or water rat – Pat is as much like him in body and mind as he is in dress, and in this particular there is no great degree of comparison. Our well-fed friend in neat velveteen, gaiters, and botts, stalks solemnly after you, as though he had reluctantly made up his mind to do a disagreeable duty. He shows not the smallest interest or pleasure in the business – neither exults at your success nor commiserates your failure, and pockets his half guinea with a silent touch of his hat and an aspect of being the most ill-used man in Christendom.

Now look on this picture of rags, hearty interest, indefatigable zeal, and active good humour, all for two shillings a day. If he cannot show you sport (and you may take your corporal oath he has done his best), he will tell you what might, could, would, should, or ought to be done – some of it truth, more, probably truth embellished. But with all his failings – and poor Pat is only a man after all – he is the best and pleasantest attendant, through heat or cold, hunger or thirst, in good fortune or evil fortune, that can be found out of his own tight little island.

With your florin in his hand, he bids 'yer honor the best of sleap,' says something hopeful about tomorrow, and with his duddeen in his mouth, and very little under his waistcoat, talks by his bit of smouldering turf for the hour together of what you did, he did, and they did.

W. Peard, *A Year of Liberty*

No Fish for Frank

I have often noticed that a good gillie will always carry your fish and never attempt to hide it in case a dog or human being might be on the prowl. This particular day my brother decided to fish up river and we were to fish down to the Junction Pool, a long walk. We had only started when I beached a nice fish. I suggested to Frank to put him in the drain and cover him with sods. He very reluctantly agreed. We had only fished a short distance downstream when we grassed another two fish and I had no trouble getting Frank to hide them in a drain running from the bog and covering them with sods.

We fished down to the Junction and there called it a day, knowing we had three fish to collect on our way back. When we came to the first hide the fish was gone, likewise the other two. Frank was full of temper. 'I told you the locals had eyes like hawks,' he said. I went into the sitting-room to find my brother happier and contented having a large Paddy.

'I only fished for half an hour and got three lovely fish. How did you do?' he asked.

'I killed three fish in the morning and when we came back to collect them they had disappeared.' (We always had a pound bet on who would have the largest bag.)

'Here, give me my pound,' he called. I parted with it reluctantly and went to the fish house where there were three fish on the slab. Frank came in and looked at the fish.

'They are mighty like our fish,' he said turning them over and over. 'Master Eric, I know how I gaffed your fish as sure as I'm McManoman. These are your fish.'

I went to my brother and told him what Frank had said. But no. He had killed one in Kane's Pool, one in Walsh's and the last fish by the lodge. I had no redress on my pound. My brother had a marvellous little bitch called Pip which always landed his trout and salmon. After an hour's fishing he had decided to give up and walk down to meet us. He had only gone a short distance down the river when the bitch set. Thinking it was a badger he armed himself with stones and put Pip up the drain. She returned with a salmon in her mouth and then the other two fish. She had a marvellous nose and a mouth like velvet. I would never have had my pound returned only my brother was so anxious to let us know how good his little bitch Pip was. From that day to this Frank saw that each salmon was put into the fish bag and stayed there.

That was many years ago but I'm pleased to say that I still get much pleasure from the river, and much of it is thanks to Frank who taught me, my brothers and all our children to fish.

Eric Craigie, *Irish Sporting Sketches*

Patsey

At the time I first met him Patsey was somewhere about fifty years of age. Fully six feet in height, had he taken full advantage of his inches, he was broad of shoulder, but lean of figure. He looked like a man of great endurance rather than one of great strength. Patsey was a tireless oarsman, but a deceptive walker. If I would have his company on the road, I had constantly to slow down, and even then he would somehow get a step to the rear. But let him get you on to the crags, and you would find the relation reversed. Hour and hour over those broken, treacherous rocks, gun and game-bag weighing him down, he would go on and on until his companion, bathed in perspiration, was forced to beg for a rest.

His complexion had been ruddy, but exposure to sun and wind and rain had permanently browned it; when he removed his hat the broad expanse of exceeding whiteness came as a surprise. His hair, inordinately thick and already grizzled, he wore cut close to a well-shaped head. Originally it had been sandy, like his eyebrows and heavy, drooping moustache. His eyes were light blue and regarded one steadily as he spoke – kindly eyes, though lacking the humourous twinkle one finds so often in the eyes of his countrymen. What they lacked in humour they made up in steadfastness. Taken altogether his expression was gentle, but the long stubborn chin told its own story.

He spoke in a low, well-modulated voice, his words were well chosen, and I have never known him to utter a word of slang. Patsey was almost always serious, even when narrating events that convulsed his hearers with laughter; it may be that no small part of his success as a story-teller rested upon that sustained solemnity. 'I'll tell you a tale, sir,' meant that Patsey would soon have us all in good humour, whatever had happened to put us out of it.

'The Pipe' was a great factor in Patsey's life. I learned to discover his humour from the way he filled it. When things were going well he was most deliberate in his preparations. The plug was first looked at; then the 'old knife' had a rub up on the gunwale of the boat. The cutting proceeded slowly, each fragment put carefully as it was cut into the hollow of his left hand, where in due time it was rubbed into consumable condition between his palms, while the 'old knife' was still retained between thumb and finger. Next the pipe was cleared and the dry crumbs placed on the new charge to facilitate ignition. Even then Patsey would dally with his gratification; survey his position, and pull a stroke or two before taking a match from his trouser pocket. The match might be struck on the oar or the thwart, but the favourite method was twice or thrice on the rough edge of the metal pipe-cover, so rapidly that the match crackled.

When less tranquil than usual he would be less deliberate and burn more matches before the blue cloud arose and betokened that all was well. There followed a still more characteristic action with the pipe – to ease the draw he would hold the bowl inverted and strike it on the hard palm of his left hand with just two strokes – never more and never less – 'plunk plunk.' If there was a woman in the boat Patsey would go the livelong day without the solace of his pipe, until postively bidden to smoke.

Though an experienced fisher himself and quick to see an error, he was never over-free with advice. When he did venture to advise it was with great tact, and his suggestions were always worth consideration. How any one could resent his kindly advice I cannot imagine; yet one man did, and, as you might suppose, he was not a good fisherman. Patsey said no more – he devoted himself to pulling the boat and thinking – the gentleman fished in his own fashion and there were few trout in the boat that evening.

F.D. Barker, *An Angler's Paradise*

Whiskey Galore

To the salmon angler a gillie is indispensable. The trout fisherman enjoys an independence which his brother in quest of larger game must forgo. The former, wandering along the banks of an unknown river, cannot well mistake the likely spots where trout lie, but a strange salmon river has few landmarks to indicate the habitat of Salmo salar. Besides, the impedimenta of gear and tackle require an attendant, and the gillie – patient beast of burden that he is – will shoulder everything in this way, and make light of it.

Every Irish gillie worthy of the name is an enthusiastic sportsman; he will drop the last or the plane for the sake of the sport which is the breath of his nostrils, and if he is attached to a reasonably-minded master will serve him with unflagging fidelity. He knows every stone in the river, has a keen eye for the conditions that make pools fishable, and will cast a fly with unerring accuracy to within an inch of the spot where a fish lies. Salmon-angling is hard work, but the gillie is never tired, and is always ready to mitigate the toil by taking a hand at the rod. He has a perfect talent for misleading his compatriot gillies when there is a rush for pools, and will tell Tim Sullivan that his governor is to be on the spot at 6am., two hours later than the time arranged.

His poaching proclivities make him an early riser, and one must not complain if he is awakened at three o'clock instead of four by a shower of pebbles hurled at his dormitory window. To know that he has been a poacher is a commendable grace. It is generally alluded to as one of the cardinal virtues.

On one occasion, in summing up the merits of a new gillie, I was informed that he was the biggest poacher on the river, and with an air that showed that the vice was counted to him for righteousness. The accomplishment, however, has its drawbacks, and the poaching fever in the blood on occasion shows itself in ugly spots. Once I had arranged to fish a pool on Monday morning, which was full of salmon. The nets had been off from six o'clock on Saturday morning, and on Sunday afternoon the salmon were freely showing in the pool. At four o'clock the gillie was to call me. I awoke with a start at six, and, thinking that my attendant had overslept, I set out for the river. On calling at his house I was informed that he had started at daybreak, and was supposed to have gone in quest of me. I proceeded to the pool, and on reaching it found the gillie fishing with all his might!

But the principal vice is whiskey. This is even worse than the weakness for poaching. The free use of the flask on the part of English anglers robs many a fisherman of a valuable servant. The taste of liquor to these hot-headed Celts is like blood to the tiger. They will have more of it. One of the finest gillies I have known – a splendid fly-tyer and out-and-out enthusiast – was lost to me for a week through lending him for a day to a brother angler. When he turned up again, full of apologies and regrets, I ventured to lecture him, and, with the best intentions of appealing to his better nature, asked, 'Why do you touch it at all? You know the very taste of it means a week's drinking.' But he was equal to the occasion, and replied, 'Arrah, sir, it was a mistake altogether; I thought it was a bottle of Kops the gintleman offered me.' Anglers, if they are to retain their men, must avoid offering them whiskey. Years ago a novel method of securing the gillie's sobriety is said to have been adopted on the Galway River. At the close of a day's fishing, the moment the gillie left the fishery he usually disappeared for two or three days for an obvious reason. The police-station was close to the river, and a constable was bribed to arrest the gillie the moment he passed through the gates. He was straightway taken to the guardroom and provided a bed for the night. Thus his sobriety was assured.

When the gillie fails to turn up, drink, as a rule, is the explanation. His friends will assign plausible and even virtuous reasons for his disappearance. One, who was a carpenter by trade and an angler by profession, was missing one morning. The run of the grilse was at its height, and the prospects of a day's angling were unusually promising. I determined to hunt him up, and called at the house where he lived. His father opened the door, and when I inquired for Dan – which was not his name – I was informed that he was in bed. 'Drinking again!' I ejaculated. 'No, indeed sir,' came the reply, in a half-indignant tone, 'the drink had nothing to do with it; he was up all night making a coffin.' I hastily apologized and withdrew, meditating on the virtues of the man whom I had been mentally maligning. I had not gone far before I encountered the virtuous Dan emerging from a public house in an advanced stage of intoxication. Evidently he had been up all night making his own coffin.

It is advisable to study this phase of the gillie's character to prevent being victimized by it. He is conscious of it himself, and by no means indisposed to enter into your plans for insuring sobriety. If one is fishing for three or four weeks a gillie's payment will amount to a considerable figure, and he will be ready to agree that payment should be deferred to the end of the engagement. Tips after a successful day's angling are dangerous. The attendant regards it in the light of an extra to be spent in a jubilant fashion. An angler will sometimes say, 'Now, Dan, half a crown extra for every salmon we catch today.' A crown may be due at the end of it, but no gillie will turn up next morning in all probability. It is far wiser to add all extras to the sum total at the end of the visit. I have known gillies who feared the danger of handling money during their engagement so much as to ask a local tradesman to be treasurer for them.

The optimism of the gillie is unbounded. The graphic description of the prospects, when one feels disposed to 'chuck' sport after a series of bad days, is stimulating. 'Where's the use,' you exclaim, 'in going on thrashing the river? The water is too low for a run of fish, and there is nothing in the pools but old stagers.' 'No run of fish! It's entirely mistaken you are, sir. Sure, when they want to come up the river it isn't the height they'd be mindin'. They'd travel if the river was dry when they set their mind to it; and, sure the pool by the wood is teemin' wid fish. I went down late last night, and they were so thick that you could walk across the river on their backs without wettin' your boots!' Then would come a touching appeal at the possible consequences of wandering about the town and the temptations of the public-house.

'It's yerself that's kept me sober for the last month, and the divil a ha'penny o' pay I'll take today if don't give ye a tight line.' Who could resist this? And the gillie will have his way in the end.

After a blank couple of hours you feel disposed to comment on the obdurateness of the fish. 'They don't seem to be stirring, Dan.' 'No, sir; there's thunder in air, and when it's like that it's hard to move them; but it'll clear presently, and the rise will come on at such a rate that if ye throw a copogue – Anglice, dock leaf – to them they'd take it.'

But, with all his faults, something like a genuine affection springs up between master and man. There is no use in setting up a high standard of consistency and expecting these gillies to conform to it. To be a little blind to their follies is a wise course. The chances are, from an angler's point of view, that the balance is in favour of redeeming qualities. There is no prouder man than the gillie when he leads the way to the hotel with a brace of fish slung by the gills. He receives the tidings of your leaving with a look of genuine regret, and, as he puts it, 'will be counting the days till yer honour returns. Sure, the sport ye've had is nothing to what it'll be then, for this was the worst season ever known on the river.' He will be down in the morning to take the rods to the station – 'it isn't himself that'll be trusting to them divils of jarvies.'

So he hovers round you to the end, insists on shaking hands for the second time, and, as the train steams out of the station, the last pathetic object standing on the platform and waving his adieu is the person of the faithful gillie.

Joseph Adams, *Salmon and Trout Angling*

Dapper Danny

To the dapper a Danny is absolutely indispensable. The success or failure of your operations, the pleasure or otherwise of your experiences, depend mainly upon him. Your Danny is a good fairy in homespun. He does everything or thereabouts. He takes charge of you, protects you, teaches you, cheers you up, rejoices with you appropriately when the occasion arises, catches flies for you, puts up your rod, mends it when necessary, directs you as to the number of flies to mount, puts them on for you when you fumble with them, decides as to the weight of line to use, navigates your boat, hooks your fish sometimes; and, if you are wise, invariably lands them; lights your fire, boils your kettle, saves you from a watery death now and then, and generally does all things needful. And what your Danny does not know about the etiquette of dapping, of winds and waters, of where to go for trout, and what to do when you hook them, you certainly don't know, whoever else may.

On Lough Derg all the best people have Dannies. There are Dannies and Dannies, of course; but in my experience there is no

Danny like my Danny. Year after year we have dapped almost unbro-
kenly, since we were boys together. We have had red-letter days of
glorious sport. We have had many a bad day as well. But when the
May-fly appears on Lough Derg we are inseparable; and when one
season ends we look forward to the next; and we are both inclined to
think that when our course is run, and the kindly Irish earth covers
us over, we won't be completely happy, in that place to which all
good fishermen go, if we can't still go dapping together.

Sir Thomas Grattan Esmonde, Hunting Memories

Pulling a Stroke

Jamesie was willing to be helpful, even forthcoming, in a discussion
on flies, but when it came to the business of catching fish, he was a
different man. He liked fishing, liked better to catch fish, but best of
all he liked to show his superiority over rival boatmen. This was a
necessity for his complete happiness. He would rather bring back a
mediocre catch which was larger than that of any other boat, than a
really good bag which only took second place. So far so good.
Anyone fishing with Jamesie could be certain that he would leave
nothing undone to get fish. But it did not end there. He craved also
the personal triumph of beating the other rod in his own boat, and to
make sure of this he was willing to use devious methods. He did
draw a line. I have heard him refer with disapproval to leaving his
companion's fly-box behind or weakening his gut by the touch of a
cigarette. Physical interference was a foul, but when it came to a
contest of wits anything was permissible.

It took me a couple of days to smell mischief. Most boatmen are
only too glad to set the boat on a long straight drift and leave it so.
Not Jamesie. From the bow came a continual murmur of directions
to Jimmy. 'Pull a stroke now' – 'Back her a couple' – 'Pull easy,
easy' – 'Back half a stroke' – and so on. This called for no particular
comment. I knew that Jamesie had fished the lake for fifty years, and
had an eye on him like a travelling rat. All parts of the shallow
sliding past under the keel might look equally enticing to me, one

part of the bay as good as another, but to his observation, backed by experience and a most remarkable memory, there might be a significant difference. He was always recalling past victories. 'Twenty throut did I get to my own rod on the shore of that island in an easht wind and a shining sun, and all of them on a Grey Monkey. It was the September of the year that the ould Queen died and maybe the throut were still in half mournin'. With such a precedent, the wind east and the sun bright, what was I to do but put on a Grey Monkey and let Jamesie control the drift? And sure enough the trout took it, even though no royalty had lately deceased.

I began to work out the effect of his orders. 'Pull easy' and 'Back easy' kept the boat working diagonally to left or right across the natural line of drift, and were explicable on the assumption that there was an underwater bank running obliquely to that line. 'Pull a stroke' and 'Back a stroke' or 'Pull two' and 'Back two' shifted the boat two or four lengths to right or left of the line she was on and set a new drift parallel to, but some distance from, the old. Each of these manoeuvres gave both rods fresh water; no doubt, in Jamesie's judgment, better water.

But what about 'Back half a stroke' or 'Pull half a stroke?' The result of the first was to allow Jamesie to fish the line I had been fishing, and of the second to put me on Jamesie's line and give him new water. I became suspicious that Jamesie would not take my line,

or give me his, unless he thought the change was to his advantage.

On the morning of the third day a trout took a daddy directly down wind of me and about forty yards away. If the boat were left to her natural drift I was bound to fish the spot where the trout had risen; but when we had gone about twenty yards there came the order for which I was waiting. 'Back half a stroke.' It was time for me to act. 'Do no such thing, Jimmy,' I said, 'If anyone is going to fish that trout it will be me and not Jamesie.'

The effect of my remark on Jimmy was startling. For two days he had been following directions, comprehending perfectly that Jamesie was trying to get the better of me, amused and yet a little disapproving, for he was naturally loyal to his employer. Still, it was none of his business to interfere. Let me find out for myself if I was able. Now that I had found out he was free to enjoy the biting of the biter. He shipped both oars carefully, put his two hands on his knees, and laughed out to the heavens. 'Begob, Jamesie, you're losht. The gentleman has ye discovered.' Jamesie looked at us both with dignity, and then delivered a rebuke addressed to Jimmy but aimed at me. 'Ye should know by this, Jimmy McDonagh, that that was a thravellin' throut and wherever he is now he is not where he rose lasht.'

Jamesie had saved his face but he had been warned. 'Pull half a stroke' and 'Back her half' ceased to figure in his instructions. He still held the trumps. He knew the lake and I did not. If he said 'Pull two strokes,' or gave any command which gave both rods a new line, I was helpless. Automatically to halve his order might do us both harm, and anyhow Jamesie would have been quick enough to counter by directing the boat to be moved twice the distance he wanted. I felt sure I was being foxed and could not prove it. I tried bluff. 'Look here, Jamesie, either you play fair or there will be only one rod fishing in this boat.' Jamesie looked at me. His moustache moved. His eyes creased. Then he in his turn broke into laughter. He had had his fun, and it was time to stop. 'Very well, Sir. I'll play fair.' And play fair – or very nearly fair – he did from that on.

T.H. Kingsmill Moore, *A Man May Fish*

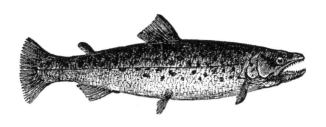

Two of a kind

Mr Pat. Lysaght, a tolerable angler, and a sporting character named Luke Morony, were fishing Tedane before dinner, and each had killed a very large trout. The two fish were so nearly equal in length and breadth, that the most practised eye could scarcely perceive a difference. A bet of a crown or two dozen of flies was made as to which was the heavier. On coming to dinner they were weighed; when, to the astonishment of Mr Lysaght and all beholders, Luke's trout weighed a half-pound more than Mr Lysaght's.

'Why,' exclaimed he, ejaculating a round oath, 'is not this most extraordinary? Surely no one could suppose that there could be more than an ounce or so between them at most; yet see here!' Taking his trout by the tail, and shaking him – when lo, a large stable key protruded from his mouth! At this, as may be supposed, there was a general laugh.

'Be not surprised, sir,' quoth Luke, also taking his trout in the same way, and shaking him well; when there issued, one by one, from his gullet, thirteen large bullets! – Luke had been shooting seals on the sea-coast. The laugh was now universal, and the bystanders adjudged that the bet was fairly won by Luke, and it was accordingly paid. How Izaac Walton would have been startled by an occurrence of this kind!

O'Gorman, *The Practice of Angling*

The Hare and Salmon

'Hear the major,' says the priest; 'he'll tell the story.'

'By the sowl of me, and I'll tell it any how.'

'Tell it right, major.'

'Is there a man would say that to me but your own good-looking self, now, Father?'

I begged to hear the story.

'You must believe it,' said the priest.

'And who doesn't?' said the major, gulping down his third tumbler of punch, and slamming the glass on the table. Then, turning to me – 'Sir, everybody knows the fact – I caught a hare and salmon at one cast of the fly!'

'Oh, Benedicite,' says the priest.

'None of your holy bother, now, Father. I'm after relating to the gentleman this remarkable adventure. Give me the materials.'

The needful was soon prepared; and the major, directing his conversation exclusively to me, proceeded to say that, while fishing in the Lee, not far from Macroom, he saw a fine fish rise under the opposite bank. He immediately drew out his line, so as to enable him by a cast to reach the exact spot. He had previously put on two large flies, such as are commonly used for salmon in high water. He drew back the line which would extend thirty or forty yards behind him. On endeavouring to make the cast, he found he had, as fishermen call it, 'hitched behind.'

At this moment the salmon rose again in the same spot, and, in his eagerness to cover him, he gave a strenuous jerk, with the intent of breaking one fly, and covering the salmon with the other. Splash into the river went something heavy, which immediately took to swimming towards the opposite bank, close to the spot where the salmon had risen. The action of the animal so effectually played the other fly before the salmon, that he forthwith seized it, and both were well hooked. The major continued to relate that hereupon commenced a hard struggle; sometimes the salmon was on the surface, and sometimes the other was drawn under water, till, by judicious management, both were safety landed, and proved to be a fine hare, hooked by the leg, and a salmon of twenty pounds weight!

R. Allen, *The Sportsman in Ireland*

The Biter Bit

As an example of the daring determination of the poachers of this out-of-the-way district, it may be related that some years ago, when the tacksman, who since the opening of that particular season had hardly had a fish in his nets, happened to be at the mouth of the Bunown on one Sunday morning, and, seeing a few fish splashing in the sea, he persuaded his men to shoot the net, which when brought to the shore, to his great joy, held more than one hundred splendid silvery fellows. Thinking that he had done sufficient law-breaking for one day, and delighted with the result, he had the nets hung up to dry, while resolving to be hard at work again early the next day.

On coming to the river on Monday morning he found that his nets had vanished during the night, while, maddening to behold, the fish were pushing their way up the river in hundreds. Now, the poachers of the district had heard of the Sunday great haul, so, fearing that the tacksman would get every fish, they stole his nets, which as long as the run lasted they kept possession of, while poaching the river every night and making large takes. As soon as the run was over the missing property was returned to the poles it had been removed from! In this case, perhaps, the tacksman was as bad as the poachers; nevertheless, our sympathies have always been with him, although probably enlisted on his side by hearing a friend relate the story in the terse, strong language in which it was told to him by the unfortunate victim.

Augustus Grimble, *The Salmon Rivers of Ireland*

The Monster

'Hould on,' cried Owen, in the midst of our apostrophes; 'he's here, your honour.' He had hooked a fine fish on the flat.

'Faith and there's corn still in Egypt,' exclaimed the major, 'Where the deuce is my fly-book?'

He was soon prepared, and as soon rose a salmon – another – he is hooked.

'The landing-net,' cried Owen.

'The landing-net,' cried the major.

I stood between the two combatants, knowing not which to assist.

'The gaff,' cries the major; 'let the spalpeen hould on.'

At that moment a magnificent fish leapt from the water – down went the major's rod – 'and that's a fair one, anyway,' said the major; 'he'll give us a run, yet. A hand for the saints!'

I assisted him to disencumber himself of his coat and hat. 'Now we start fair' – but the fish was lodged. It was the largest salmon I had seen, and I confess I shared all the sportsman's anxiety with the major. 'Off again' – he was off, indeed; and it was impossible to follow, so ludicrous a figure did the major present, puffing down the stream, utterly unable to guide his steps, his whole attention being on the reel which was running at a fearful rate, notwithstanding his own exertions to follow the fish.

'Gone, by St Patrick!' exclaimed the major, dashing the rod into the stream, and falling squat into a bog on his face. I hastened to his assistance; and Owen, having landed his fish, was before me. We raised the major in anxiety – he scraped the mud from his eyes and mouth, and, as quickly as he could, exclaimed, 'Never mind me; follow the fish – I'm done' and, in a pathetic but earnest manner, made out in signs what the masses of mud in his mouth would by no means allow him to utter.

We were both sportsmen too well seasoned to hesitate, but the rod was gone, and a long run we had to overtake it. There it was, in the middle of the stream – nothing but the top to be seen, the weight of the reel sinking the but; and, to our mortification, a slack line.

'That's a misfortune, anyway,' said Owen; 'the fish is gone.'

'Gone!' cried the major, who now came up, and who had by this time so well effected the process of cleansing by his pocket hand-kerchief, that he had succeeded in well covering every part of his face, hair, hands, and clothes, with the brown bog mud – he looked like an animated masterpiece of Vandyke.

'Give me your rod' – with a dexterous cast he covered the top, and caught the line with the flies of Owen's apparatus – 'gently, and don't disturb him if he's there.' It was a moment of real suspense – the rod was recovered – the line reeled in, which had at least one hundred yards out. It was now found to have taken a different course, and the fish had again turned up the stream – the line was fixed.

'He's here,' cried the major.

'Huzza!' exclaimed Owen, in extreme delight; 'this is a fishing!'

'Now, major, for your skill – if you lose that fish -'

'Be aisy,' said the major, 'the time's against me – he has not been idle all this time – he has been busy enough grubbing at the bottom, to get the hook out of his mouth – faith and he'll give us another leap yet.'

As he approached the spot where the fish was sulkily ensconced, I could perceive the paleness of the cheek – the quivering of the lip – both so indicative of extreme excitement, that I began to question my own nerve. I was not much more calm – this was a prize. The major did not venture to hint at the weight, but it was obvious that he felt he an an enemy worthy of his utmost skill.

The fish now gradually and gently moved up the stream; a steady but tight strain was kept on the line, which the reel gradually received, giving token of an approach to the surface. He came, like a log of wood, to the top. A fish, indeed – for one minute I had a perfect view of him as he broke the water with an enormous tail.

The major grew still more nervous; yet the steadiness with which he held the rod was admirable. 'Beware now,' says he. Up went the fish, at least five yards into the air! – the rod was again down, and recovered at the moment of the splash occasioned by his fall. 'He's safe,' whispered the veteran – 'that last spring has tired him.' He struggled with some violence for some minutes – I was ready with the gaff – he came gently to the shore, turned two or three times on his stomach, and I plunged the hook into his side.

It was well that I did so at that moment – the fly had worn out of his mouth, and he was free from the line.

'Huzza!' cried Owen and the major, in which I heartily joined – up went our hats, in token of our triumph – the monster floundered on the shore.

'Salmon,' cries the major – 'the devil a salmon at all!'

It was, indeed, no salmon but one of the great Lake trout, the largest that had been seen for many years, even from the broad waters of Lough Corrib. Its weight exceeded thirty-three pounds. The memory of this fish has not passed away – it may still be heard of among the cottagers, many of whom saw it.

R. Allen, *The Sportsman in Ireland*

Feathered Friends

'I remember now wan of the strangest flies I ever tied to be catching a fish with; and it did so, though by the same token I niver did be tying it all, at all, except to me hook. I was only a ladeen at the time and was doing gillie to the ould earl. Herself was wanting a salmon for the gintry at dinner that night, and himself was away at the Parliament House in England, and that at the start of the fishing season! So I took me rod down to the river, and well I remember I was fishing downstream for three hours without meeting with a fish.

'Well, now, I knew that Mary, the cook above there at the castle, would be roarin' and bawlin' if so be I was late with the fish, and it's worried I was getting that I could not meet with one. I was wading in the shallows at the head of the 'Blue Hole' when I saw a fish boil at the tail of it, just where the water breaks, and where the branch of a tree leans over the water, and at the same time a pair of blackbirds starts yellin' and shriekin' like Bridie Malone, and her with the high strikes.

'Phwat the divil's all that?' sez I, and I goes down there to see. 'Well now, I'll be telling you, wasn't there a bird's nest right out on the end of that branch, and weren't the young birds crawling and squaking on the edge of it, and thim with just a fluffeen of feathers to their backs, and the ould birds swooping down to the water and bawling blue murther. 'Hah,' sez I, 'hasn't one of thim wans fallen in and pike had him cot at once, it was never a salmon I saw at all.'

'But as I was standing there, didn't a salmon, as big as a calf, roll over in the water just below me.'

'Well,' sez I, 'if it's young birds ye be wanting, don't I know of a frosted nest of dead wans ye can have with all the joy in the world.' And I drops me rod and goes tearing back to the garden as fast as the Divil himself, and I comes back with two three dead birds in me hat, and whips one of thim same on to me hook before you could be shpitting in the water.

'Now, me foine lad,' sez I, 'let's be seeing if it's still hungry ye are.' And with that I flops the young bird on the water where the stream will just be catching it.

'Up that fish comes with a 'Wumph' and I drives the hook home in him, me roarin' and bawlin' so Dan Meggarty above there on the road would be hearing, and him the darlin' man with the gaff. Dan comes rowling down the hill, spachless with the haste of him, thinking maybe that it's drownding in the river I was.

'Have ye hoult of the Ould Wan himself?' sez he.

'I have so,' sez I, and with that the scamer leps six feet clear of the water and starts for the sea with his back fin out.

'Hould him tight,' sez Dan, running down the bank after me.

'And how would I be houlding him tighter,' sez I, 'and him tearing the line out, and me lepping like a goat to be kaping with him at all.'

'Well now, he turns at Sir George's rock, and it's more than an hour it's fighting him I was before Dan can get the hook in him.'

'And that's the biggest fish that ever came out of the Lee,' sez Dan, and him sthruggling up the bank with it.

'It is so,' sez I.

'And phwat fly did ye have him cot with at all?' sez Dan.

'Oh, just wan of me own tying,' sez I, hoping Dan would not be looking too close; but with that he opens the fish's mouth, and belave me or belave me not, there was the hook, fast in his jaw, as bare as the back of your hand.

'Well now,' sez he, 'and that's the strange sort of fly to be using at all.'

'Ah,' sez I, 'he has the feathers ate off it, and him leppin' and kickin' like Mother Moriarty's ass.' And I turns over me hat with a skelp of me fut so Dan would not be seeing thim other young birdeens.

'It's a poor fly ye'll be tying that has the feathers ate off it so soon.'

'Maybe so but it has the fish cot that herself does be wanting above there in the castle.' And with that I humps it on my back and starts out for the kitchen, and when Mary comes to be cleaning that wan, divil the sign of a bird was there in its stomach. Will ye be telling me now, why was that fish taking thim two birds and not to be swallerin' thim at all? It has me bate entirely.'

W. Durand, *Wanderings with a Fly-rod*

Stones of Fish

One more tale and I must say farewell to the Liffey. Another officer, also a rival, had agreed with me that a day's trouting near the famous bridge was desirable from every point of view. But at the last moment I was delayed by some wretched orderly-corporal or something, and he went on ahead. I fished after him to the lodge gates, but caught nothing. Going inside to leave my rod, I saw his bag, a peep into which revealed five brace of most excellent trout. To transfer them to my own and fill his up with stones delayed me but a few minutes more, and very soon I reached the house, where they were all going into lunch. Her Ladyship asked after my sport, and I begged her acceptance of my catch, which I proudly turned out on the lawn. 'Oh! how splendid!' said her eldest daughter. 'What a fisherman you are.' I glanced at my rival. 'Indeed,' said he, 'I have just as many down at the lodge. I hope you will accept mine too.' But this they said they could not consent to, and as we biked back in the cool of the evening my comrade complained bitterly of the weight in his bag. Next morning he told his servant to have a trout done for my break-fast and one for his own, and he'd find them in his bag in the next room. 'Will ye have them broiled or fired, sorr?' asked his man a minute later, producing a handful of stones to his astonished gaze. Oh! Bard of Athy! You are not often sold, but you were done very brown that time, my boy, and you know it, though you did try so manfully to brazen it out. Very pleasant were those days beside the beautiful Liffey, albeit the fish were few and far between, and most of us suffered dreadfully from midge bites.

A. Mainwaring, *Fishing and Philandering*

A Salmon's Taste

Colonel Cane, who was a keen fisherman and an artist with the prawn, told me a salmon story which I should not have believed from anyone else. He said that one day when the water was low he was sitting above the fall and saw two fish lying below him. He threw his prawn above them and beside them, time after time, and they paid no attention. Finally he put it in front of one of the fish and let it lie there. Then the salmon slowly approached it, lifted it with the edge of its lips, swam with it to an adjacent flat rock just covered with water, left it there, and swam back to its original position. Colonel

Cane's theory was that it was just bored with the perpetual reappearance of the prawn, and wished to remove the annoyance as soon as it could be done without danger. I wonder.

Maurice Headlam, *Irish Reminiscences*

Rod at the Double

Then the Chairman intervened and called on me to continue, which I did more or less as follows:

'I also have had one curious experience,' I said, 'Only the other day, when salmon fishing with a friend in Ireland, we saw a nice fish rising in an easy flowing flat. My friend hooked this fish at his first cast and eventually brought him into the bank for me to gaff. This I duly did. 'All right: I've got him,' I said 'but the fly is out of his mouth.' 'No you haven't,' he cried, and looking up I saw that his rod was still bent in a curve. The salmon I had gaffed, was, as they sometimes do, one which had followed his hooked companion to see what was going on. We got them both.'

G.D. Luard, *Fishing Fact or Fantasy*

To Catch a Goose

I will relate a curious adventure which took place on the river Donbeg or Cooraclare, an excellent salmon river, but very foul and full of stumps. I had lost so many flies and salmon by these stumps that I determined on cross fishing it, and I got a tolerable angler in my neighbourhood to accompany me.

We have a strong five-fly cross line, with silk line droppers, and our flies on all good three-gut; and came on an excellent reach, with a fine breeze against the current, which was slight. We had only just commenced, when a large flock of tame geese flew very swiftly over the river, and in a direct line with our cross line. We most unfortunately raised our hands, and instantly had three of them firm.

It is almost impossible to describe the scene – splashing, swimming,

48

flying, running up and down the river for nearly an hour; and, to complete our confusion, at my companion's side, a set of outrageous women, hearing the noise and outcry, came down, and if they could have got stones, would have annihilated him, charging him as the cause of the state their geese were in.

At length he was forced to run for his life, having cut the line and the concern at one. At length (but not until the geese were nearly dead) I contrived to land the line, and with great difficulty extracted the flies. The reach was destroyed, my companion had fled, the wind fell away, and I walked disconsolately to the village of Cooraclare, about a mile distant, where I was glad to take some rest after the great fatigue and vexation I had undergone.

O'Gorman, *The Practice of Angling*

Riding a Salmon

'Extent! is it extent you mane? Look ye, sir – I am a Major in his Majesty's army, and am paid by a rascally government: and, sir, I have never lost my character for veracity. Extent! – by the honour of the commission I hold, I once rode a salmon astride out of the stream, and spurred him ashore!'

A burst of surprise and admiration, from those least acquainted with the major, followed this assertion.

'Rode a salmon ashore? Impossible!' says the priest.

'Verum quia impossibile, I presume you mean,' said I; 'the major will explain.'

'Troth and I will, and the devil help the spalpeen that is not satisfied with it. I repeat again, I rode a salmon astride, and spurred him ashore. – Father, you know the shallows leading to the mill of Ballyvourneen.'

'A good spot for salmon,' says the priest, 'but bad for riding him.'

'You shall hear – I had been to Ballyvourneen, and was returning to Macroom, on horseback, in the evening. I had had a long ride. Where the road passes by the side of the river, and along the shallow which falls into the good people's hole, whom should I see, hard at work with a salmon, but Phelim, the piper. Hold on there, says I - and, booted and spurred as I was, I dashed into the stream, and seized the rod from the piper, who never had a steady hand, and was timid. The salmon was in the hole, above which I stood in the shallows, and about mid-stream. The moment the fish moved, I knew his weight to be above forty pounds, for it's meself can tell to an ounce the weight of a fish at the first plunge. Away went the salmon, and away went the reel. I held on firmly and tightly till the line was nearly out; when, all at once, the fresh run fish dashed up the stream. I reeled away as quick as lightning, lest I should lose my hold; and, as the stream was strong, I bent my knees in the water to get a firmer hold on my legs, and to give me the power of winding quick. Suddenly I felt myself lifted off my legs! Oh, Bubbaboo, says I – it was but an instant – Is an Irishman ever at a loss? – I caught hold of the line for a bridle, stuck my spurs into the side of the fish, which I now found closely stuck between my legs, and with one bound we were both in the high shallows, where I safely landed the monster, to the immortal honour of fishing and the excellent dinner of Lord V, who swore if any other man had said he had caught him in the same way, he would not have believed him.'

R. Allen, *The Sportsman in Ireland*

'Tis a Bad Place

Nevertheless, fond of it as I am, this fishing alone at night can be an eerie business, and inured as I am to it, there have been occasions when I should have found it pleasanter – I might even say reassuring – to have had a companion.

One such I remember years ago, when I was about seventeen. I had set out alone to fish the Grove, a gloomy length of the Little River, a long way below the house, where the trout are big and there are many trees.

The trout were inclined to take, but it was exceptionally dark, trees and bushes took on strange shapes in the obscurity, and gradually a sense of uneasiness began to steal over me.

I did my best to throw it off – told myself it was nonsense. But it was no use – the feeling only intensified.

It was extraordinarily still. I began to listen, a fatal thing to do, but all I could hear was the tinkling of the nearby river, and the surreptitious rustlings of small creatures in the grass.

The atmosphere was definitely evil, and suddenly my childish nightmare days seemed to grip me and I began to feel that at any moment I might be confronted with some amorphous horror. Then my nerve gave way and I fled, as if the devil was after me, as perhaps he was. Roots tripped me and brambles tore my clothes as I hurried home through the pitchy blackness. How my rod escaped damage I do not know, but not until I had entered the big sleeping house and turned on the lights did ease of mind return. I have experienced other eerie moments, as most sensitive people have, but never with such intensity or with such a sense of surrounding malignity. Possibly if I had had the sagacious Jock as my companion, I should not have felt so alone and helpless.

Next morning I met Tom Lonergan scuffling the drive and laughingly told him of my experience. He took it perfectly seriously. After ruminating a moment with his eyes on the ground – he looked up and said, ''Tis a bad place altogether; ten thousand asses wouldn't drag me there at night for all the fish in Ireland.' He then told me the following tale, which I reproduce as nearly in his style as I can remember.

'It's a long time now there was an old woman lived in Grove House.' This the farm just outside the front gates of Ballyhimmock, and a little above the spot where I had been fishing the night before. 'It was she was a queer one. Wasn't it unnatural the way she lived to herself entirely and hardly crossed her own doorsteps, and she with plenty to live on and nothing to show for it all.

'Well, in the end she died – a great age she was – and what did she leave? Only an ass as old as herself and a few pounds tied up in a dirty handkerchief. That couldn't be all there was anyway – an old miser, that's what she was of course, and somewhere or other in the house she had her treasure hid, and little good it had done the old witch – God rest her!

'That was what the village said. Be damn, there was treasure too – and as the place was empty the half of the men would going there one time and another to look for the treasure – in the day I mean, for not one of them would venture there in the dark, and I wouldn't blame them. They searched the house from the roof to the cellar, and from cellar to roof; they dug up the potato patch and garden – divil a one of them had ever worked so hard in their lives.

'Twas all one, not a penny did they find, and the end of it was they got tired and gave it up.

'But there was one young fellow – and a bad one at that – he was not so young either – and he had an idea where the treasure might be.

'He was a mean sort of a man, the kind that wouldn't share a crust with his own mother. Well, one night off he goes to the house in the dead of the dark to search, and I wouldn't say but what he had drink taken to keep up his courage. It would be about midnight two young men at the top of the village saw him pass running like mad and he panting, 'The old woman's after me – old woman's after me' – and with that he dashed in at his own door, which was near, and fell down dead. Faith, there's some says the old woman walks yet.'

Tom Lonergan shifted the weight of his lean body on the handle of the scuffle and a fleeting smile passed over his face and disappeared as he added: 'I wouldn't say but what he had drink taken – but anyway 'tis a bad place.'

Superstition dies hard in Ireland, and in these days of over-rationalization – horrible word – when the masses with their misapplied smattering of science believe that the only miracles are in the hands of man – perhaps it is no bad thing.

G.D. Luard, *Fishing Fortunes and Misfortunes*

The Tinker

'The best practical lesson I ever got originated in the following accidental occurrence. Some years ago I received private information, that a travelling tinker, who occasionally visited these mountains to make and repair the tin stills used by the peasantry in illicit distillation, was in the constant habit of destroying fish, and he was represented as being a most successful poacher. I was returning down the river after an unfavourable day, a wearied and a disappointed fisherman, and observed, at a short distance, a man chased across the bogs by several others, and eventually overtaken and secured. It was the unfortunate tinker, surprised by the keepers in the very act of landing a splendid salmon; two, recently killed, were discovered in his wallet, and yet that blessed day I could not hook a fish! He was forthwith brought in durance before my honour, to undergo the pains and penalties of his crime. He was a strange, raw-boned, wild-looking animal, and I half suspect Sir Walter Scott had seen him before he sketched Watt Tinlin in the 'Lay.' He was a convicted felon – he had no plea to offer, for he was taken in the very act. But he made two propositions wherewithal to obtain his liberty – 'He would never sin again – or he would fight any two of the captors.' My heart yearned towards him – he was after all a brother – and admitting that rod and coat were not worth threepence, still he was an adept in the 'gentle art,' although the most ragged disciple that ever Walton boasted. I forgave him, dismissed the captors, and ordered him to the Lodge for refreshment. 'My honour had no sport,' and he looked carelessly at my flies. 'Would I condescend to try one of his?' and he put a strange-looking combination of wool and feathers on the casting-line. There was a fine pool near us – I tried it, and at the second cast I was fast in a twelve-pound salmon! My ragged friend remained with me some days; and in his sober intervals, 'few and far between,' gave me lessons in the art, that have been more serviceable than any I had hitherto acquired.

'Two years after, I was obliged to attend the winter fair of Ball to purchase cattle. It was twilight when I left it, and I had proceeded only a few miles towards a gentleman's house, where I was to dine and sleep, when my horse cast a shoe, and forced me to leave him at a smith's shop, which was fortunately at hand. The evening was chilly, and I determined to proceed on foot, directing my servant to follow. I passed a lonely poteen-house – several ruffian-looking fellows were on the road beside it. They were half-drunk and insolent –

I was rash – words borrowed blows, and I soon discovered that I should have the worst of the battle and was tolerably certain of a sound drubbing. Suddenly, an unexpected ally came to my assistance; he dropped the most formidable of the assailants as if he had been struck down by a sledge-hammer. A few blows settled the content; and I turned round to recognise and thank my deliverer. 'Pon my sowl, you're might handy, Master Julius; it's a murder that ye don't practise oftener!' The speaker was my gifted friend – the tinker.'

W. H. Maxwell, *Wild Sports of the West*

Lost and Found

I was fishing from a boat on the Upper Reservoir at Bohernabreena, a few miles from Dublin, with my friend, Mr Bindon Scott, a solicitor, now with God. In those days the Rathmines Town Council was in being, and controlled the fishing and performed the functions that now come under the Dublin Corporation. I had three small flies on my cast – my pet Red Spinner on the bob, a Silver Priest on the tail, and what the middle dropper was I forget, and it is of no account. There was no nylon then; we fished gut and nothing but gut. Gut in some respects, not all, was better than nylon; but gut needed soaking, and if worked or knotted dry, it would crack or draw and weaken; in consequence breaks occurred often. Moreover the trout were gut-shy, and we fished fine. I was casting from the stern of the boat; my Red Spinner was bobbing attractively in the surface ruffle; a fish rose; there was a short, sharp jerk, and nothing more happened. It was a break. Most anglers have known that anguish. The fish had broken the fly from the cast. Presumably he broke it with his mouth; but sometimes they lash out at the fly with fin or tail. In such cases the fly is usually left sticking in the fish, and he goes off to the rubbing stump, or engages the help of the tench, reputed the doctor-fish.

Nothing like that occurred in this case. That trout broke my Red Spinner somehow from the cast; but he did not go off with it in mouth or fin or tail. Neither I nor (so far as I know) any other angler met that trout again; yet the fly he broke off is back in my fly-box. That clever trout somehow managed to break my Red Spinner from its gut-point, and spit it out or otherwise get rid of it instantaneously. How he did so I cannot imagine; but he did so; it was a strange happening.

A stranger happening was to follow. I recovered my fly against all the chances in a scarcely credible way. I tell it in the words I wrote in the correspondence columns of *The Irish Angler*, Summer Number, 1939:

'We were in deep water; by all the chances that fly, falling from the fish's mouth, should have sunk to rest and rust at the bottom of the lake. But no; fate and the long arm of coincidence willed otherwise; for as I, slowly and sadly, drew the cast back into the boat for repairs, first the bob-point, flyless, then the middle dropper, and the Priest on the tail – when the silver tail-fly came up over the edge of the boat, to my amazement there, caught and safely held, hook in hook, was my lost Red Spinner.'

A.A. Luce, *Fishing and Thinking*

The General

From the first there was friendly rivalry between us. The General, as the doyen of the party, had many interesting experiences to tell to anyone with time to listen to them. The trouble was to get him to stop. 'Luck be d.........d,' he would say, 'catching fish is a matter of skill and skill is the outcome of experience. What the younger generation is suffering from is too much luxury. Damme, sir, they want to be bottle-fed. Now you,' he would continue, looking at me, 'may make a fisherman in time. You're young yet.'

Unquestionably he was a very fine fisherman, but constant bragging frays the stoutest nerves and soon in matters piscatorial I began to hate the General as cordially as I liked him in the ordinary way.

It was after he had caught a lovely fish of 14lbs, and we were treated from soup to savoury with a recapitulation of the life history of the salmon, the fly that caught it, and the skill of the master hand that tied the fly, that my patience snapped. When he revived the topic before breakfast the next morning I fled incontinently lest I should forget my manners.

For a whole fortnight I longed for nothing so much as a chance to kill a fish an ounce or two beyond the specimen. Then came the eagerly awaited day, on which the General had business in Galway City, and I had the river to myself. Bright and early I reached the hotel beat to find, instead of my usual gillie, one Larry Hogan. He seemed a genial and knowledgeable bird, but neither his obvious acquaintance with the best lies nor my own unflagging industry could stir a fish, and we sat down to our sandwiches at mid-day with a solitary sea trout of about ½lb to show for the labour of the morning.

This was scarcely good enough, and Larry scratched his head. 'I'm thinkin' ye cud do better at the Wall Pool,' said he, 'seein' the day that's in it, and the water the colour that it is.' And he pointed to a bend in the river half a mile downstream. 'But see here, your honour,' Larry said, 'ye'll never take them in that water with these flies. A shrimp is what ye'll need,' and from a capacious pocket he produced a stock of prawns, and bade me carry on.

Well, believe it or not, in less than five minutes I was into a tidy fish. I will not labour the ups and downs of the encounter, suffice it to say that after as bonny a tussle as one could wish, Larry gaffed a salmon that turned the balance over 16lb. Then I sank into the heather positively gloating over the General's discomfiture anon.

And if one salmon, why not another? So I started to work the pool again with the faithful Larry at my elbow, when a light laugh broke the silence of the afternoon, and turning I saw a girl contemplating the scene with some amusement. 'Well, Larry,' the damsel enquired sweetly, 'up to your old tricks again?' and then she turned to me and asked, with a suspicion of a twinkle in her eye, if I knew I was trespassing. 'But of course you don't,' she went on, 'though you have succeeded in annexing the biggest poacher in the country as your gillie.'

'Sure now, Miss Nora,' began Larry, 'this was the way of it......'

But she cut him short. 'You can save your breath,' she said, 'for you couldn't tell the truth, even by accident!'

By this time I was feeling thoroughly uncomfortable, and probably looked it, for the lady began to take pity on my misery. 'I suppose you are staying at the hotel,' she said, 'but this beat is the next one to their water, and well that oldblackguard knows it. Oh! it's not the first time by a long chalk that he has persuaded a stranger to use a shrimp in this pool. No one knows better than himself that only fly fishing is allowed. But of course you aren't to blame.'

Well! There was only one kind of restitution and apology I could make, and that was to render forthwith to Caesar what was most distinctly Caesar's. Besides, it struck me forcibly that even were I to return with such a handsome fish, I should be required to give chapter and verse of the exact spot and method of its capture. Then how should I get over that illicit prawn, explaining why my colleagues might not follow my example?

But at first the maid was adamant. She would not take the salmon under any consideration. She repeated that I was not a poacher by intent, that there were plenty more where it came from, and that she was sick of salmon anyway, and it was only when I hinted that my honour as a sportsman was involved that she laughed and said that in that case we might make a compromise.

'I'll tell you what,' she said, 'my old nurse, who lives in the cottage over yonder, has been ill, and I was going to take her some delicacies this afternoon, so I will put in the salmon as a makeweight, and if you come to tea tomorrow, my father will surely give you a day or two on the river, when, let us hope, you will get an even bigger fish!'

So with nothing but my little sea trout in the bag, I trudged slowly home. Too slowly, as it happened, to avoid a rencontre with the General, who having returned from Galway rather ahead of expectation, had strolled out to see how I was getting on. 'Any luck?' he asked. 'Not much,' I answered.

'Ah, my boy,' he said, 'what you want is more patience. You youngsters do no good because you don't know where to look for salmon in the first place, nor how to fish for them in the second.' (I nearly hit him). 'Why, I've just passed one of the prettiest girls I ever saw with a salmon nearly as good as the one I got the other day. Girl after my heart, damme; rare fisherwoman she must be. Could give you some lessons, my lad.'

'But,' I began, now thoroughly exasperated, 'that salmon was ....' and then I shut my mouth again. After all, what could I say? What could anyone have said? I could not even tell him it topped his own rotten fish by a good 2lbs. Inwardly raging, I turned and walked beside him sadly and in silence.

J.B. Drought, *A Sportsman Looks at Eire*

Stoning the Otter

I chummed up with a very nice English fellow called John Burberry who knew how to fish and loved the Butler Pool. The night before he was due to leave he had a small farewell party which went on into the small hours of the morning. I was about to go to bed when I was accosted by his wife saying that John was missing. She asked me to take a car down to the Butler Pool to see if he was there. They were due to take the 8am train from Cahirciveen and it was now almost 7am.

I left the car on the bridge and strolled down to find John literally bent into a salmon.

'Eric. You'd hardly believe it. With my first cast I hooked him and I'm in him for the past hour.'

'I would think, John, he's foul hooked.'

'He's snagged under the far bank and I just can't get a move out of him,' he went on.

I would not be swayed and after watching the procedure for ten minutes I told him his wife was becoming very anxious as the train was leaving at 8am. However, this conveyed nothing to him so I suggested getting a couple of rocks and dropping them down beside the fish. John flew at me.

'After an hour you want me to lose the biggest fish I've ever taken from the Butler Pool?' I left him alone, the train had gone. Then, really annoyed, I went to him.

'If you really want that fish let me throw a couple of bricks at him to liven him up.' By this time his arms were giving out.

'Here. You take the rod,' he said.

'No. Certainly not.' I pulled a couple of rocks from an old wall and landed them about three feet above the cast. The fish came like a tornado across the river never breaking the water and went under the near bank. A worse position than ever. By this time I had taken charge of things and I said to him, 'If you want the fish there is only one remedy. Stone him.' I brought half the wall over to the bank and slung in brick after brick. The fish took off down stream and headed for a small path on the opposite bank. Up the bank, under the wire fence and the last thing I heard was the snap of the line and the backing gone. It was the largest otter I've ever seen. I'll never forget the look on John Burberry's face. It was queer. His hands and arms were numb. All I could do was to step behind what was left of the wall and break my heart with laughter. The one that got away!

Eric Craigie, *Irish Sporting Sketches*

The High Jump

It was now Delaney's turn.

'Well now,' he began. 'I have nothing to disbelieve in what we have heard today. It's queer things happen to us all.

'I remember once I was salmon fishing in Ireland. There were four of us on the different beats. There was a grand run of fish too, but divil a one of us could catch anything though they were jumping everywhere. Now it's a biggish river and I and my gillie were using the boat. The cream of the fishing was just below a mill, and here they were as thick as sardines, all pushing one another and leaping at the weir. We pulled the boat up to the very top, and I had just started to fish from the tail end of it when there was a thump on the boards behind me. At the same moment the boat began to drift swiftly down stream.

'What the divil are ye doing Pat?' I called – and looking round there was Pat, who had shipped his pole, grovelling on the bottom of the boat after a nice fish of 12 lbs, which had jumped clean into the boat and was now kicking about all over the place. 'By damn,' said he, as he got a grip on the fish's gills, 'here's one anyway that prefers dry land and I wouldn't disappoint him,' and he cracked him over the head with the 'priest.'

'Then he picked up the pole again as if nothing had happened and pushed us back to the top again.

'I hadn't been fishing more than five minutes when 'bump,' another fish of 15lbs. landed in the boat and was quickly disposed of in the same way. Would you believe it? Before we had finished, three more from 10 to 18lbs. did exactly the same thing. You can imagine the faces of my friends when I got back to the Inn that evening with five fine salmon. They hadn't touched a fish. I may say I had taken the pains to put a hole in each of their mouths the way my friends wouldn't suspect foul play. Naturally Pat said nothing. Extraordinary that five fish should have committed suicide in this way, but Pat certainly pushed the boat up as near as he safely could to where an extraordinary number were jumping at the weir. The old villain!'

There was a groan from assembled company and not little laughter for here was a story it would be hard to beat.

G. D. Luard, *Fishing Fact or Fantasy*

Having a Stroke

I always had a liking for Waterville, Co. Kerry. In 1928 I started to go down there twice a year with my brother Jack, once for the woodcock shooting and again for a week's fishing on Lake Currane and the Inny river. Currane is one of the prettiest lakes in Ireland; it is set at the base of the Macgillycuddy Reek mountains and joins Ballinskelligs Bay at the famous Butler Pool. Regrettably, it is too far from Dublin. We always stayed in the Butler Arms Hotel in the village, which was packed with British officers who, it appeared to me, let the gillies do the fishing and only took the rod when a fish had been hooked! In those days fishing stopped at 7pm and one could not get a boat or a gillie after that hour. Thirty-five years went by before I felt I would like to take my family down there for a holiday. To my amazement I was welcomed with open arms by the staff and I was pleased to see my old boatman still hale and hearty.

At lunch one day Canon Scanlon from Dunshaughlin, Co. Meath, came to our table and asked me if I would take his son John out in the boat after dinner as he was bored stiff sitting around the hotel. Needless to say I was delighted to oblige and we arranged to meet on the pier at 7.30pm. I asked John if he had ever rowed or if he had any interest in fishing. His answer to the latter was a very definite no. So taking up the oars I showed him how to feather them and after a quarter of an hour's instruction John could whip the boat round onto a fish better than I have seen many an expert. We finished up by landing six brace of lovely trout. I took the leading oarsman back to the hotel with no need to further instruction and was highly delighted with our night's entertainment. I told John I had never seen a person get into the swing of using an oar as he had done.

'Well,' he said, 'you are a good instructor but, as a matter of fact,

I'm stroke for the Trinity Eight.' I nearly fell off the chair. The amateur instructing the professional how to use his oars! He was quite modest. He had never sat on a fixed seat or rowed with rollocks. We had many happy days together and I often wonder what became of him.

Eric Craigie, *Irish Sporting Sketches*

Treble-Hooked

The mention of S. reminds me of one of those odd events which enable fishermen to gratify their taste for narrative without transgressing the bounds of truth. One evening, S. being with me in the boat, Patsey was regaling us from his inexhaustible store of stories as he pulled leisurely toward the house. Sport had been dull and I fancy our tactful boatman was endeavouring to lead our thoughts from disappointments to higher things. His conversation was directed over his left shoulder to S., who was in the bow, and I was often called to witness to the accuracy of his reminiscences. After many remarkable yarns Patsey began to speak of my exploits. 'Did you ever see, sir, a double-tailed fish?' 'No, Patsey.' 'Well, 'tis himself netted one there in the very bay that's before you.' 'Did you ever hear, sir, of taking three sorts of fish in the one cast?' S. had not heard of it. ''Tis himself did the same. Now, sir, did ever you know of a trout jumping into the boat to you?' S. again pleaded ignorance, and began to express a certain scepticism. Patsey, always hurt by doubt, again declared that it had happened to 'himself' (that is, to me), and said no more, though everything had happened exactly as he had stated.

The next day we fished Bally Moher. The trout were in excellent humour and Patsey was kept busy with the net – first one and then the other calling for his services – sometimes both together. I was busy with two fish, when S. called for assistance. 'Lift your hand, sir, and hold him; I'll be with you in a minute.' S. did as he was told, and a bit more; the trout made a jump, and not only came into the boat but into S.'s lap. He unhooked the fish and cast again while Patsey and I were still struggling with my brace. Immediately he had a rise at which he struck, but the playing of that fish was uncommonly heavy. It was a long time before anything was seen. Then he cried out, 'Why, I've got three!' He had, and the three were a big perch, a trout, and a lump of a roach.

After that he was gracious enough to promise that never again would he question a statement of Patsey's.

F. D. Barker. *An Angler's Paradise*

The Yellow Dog

'Did I ever tell ye the story of the trick me father once played on Major Geoghan? Twas many years ago now, and I was only a lad at the time.

'The Major had the little white house near the river. A great sportsman he was too, and a keen one to hunt, for all his bad sight, but 'twas the fishing he loved best.

'A queer affliction of the eyes he had, for one day he would see a fair half mile in the open and the next not more than half a yard, or a few yards at the best.

'Well, he and my father were out salmon fishing. It was one of the Major's bad days too, and well my father knew it.

'There was the Major casting away for all he was worth, and little enough did he know where his fly landed, or what became of it after.

'Now just below where he was fishing was a big lump of rocks, sticking out into the river, and 'twas in the curl behind it that the salmon lay.

'It was early spring and the river very high and strong, so me father went down below the rocks, to see if the curl was fit at all for fishing.

'Just then, what should come swirling round the corner but an old swollen corpse of a big terrier dog. Ye see it was near the time of the licence and I suppose the owner would not be inclined to pay it. One yellow ear he had, and a yellow spot on his side, and his teeth grinning the way a drowned dog's do.

'Then it was he saw the Major's fly curling about in the eddy. Now my father was fond of a joke and that gave him an idea. He gaffed the old corpse and though it wasn't nice to handle he soon had the fly fixed in its scruff, the way it would swim nicely, and pushed it out into the stream. As soon as he felt the pull, 'I'm in him!' shouts the major from above, which was just what my father was waiting for.

'Hould him, sorr – hould him!' he shouted back, 'or he'll be away in the next pool and have you destroyed.'

'I can't make him out at all,' shouts the Major again. 'He's as heavy as lead and not a stir out of him.'

'Bring him up to you,' my father answers him, 'or ye'll lose him. I know the tackle is strong.'

'So the Major reels in with all his strength, and it was no light matter with the stream running, and the old dog rolling round and round and all.

'It's the queerest fish I ever struck!' cries the Major.

'That may well be,' me father says to himself; then loud enough to be heard above the water, 'Can you see him yet?'

'See, is it?' bellows the Major. 'Come on you and see for yourself. He has a tail as yellow as mustard' (that was his ear) 'and rows of teeth like a shark.'

'By that he had brought the dog to the bank, and was peering at it in the short-sighted way he had, poor man. 'Curse ye, ye damned auld divil,' he yelled, turning to my father, who had come up behind him, 'I've a mind to give ye the sack.'

'And with that he grinned, and the two of them set roaring with laughter.'

G.D. Luard, *Fishing Fortunes and Misfortunes*

Breaking a Record

'You get grand trout on the wet fly from the end of March all round here,' said John Lydon, *a propos* of nothing except the sight of water, which always seems to make him think about fish and fishing. 'Round this island and over beyond near Oughterard the catches are heavy, though I think my own favourite spot would be in Salthouse Bay or maybe Ballynalty Bay.'

'And what about Golden Bay,' said I. 'Is that only golden to look at and not fish?'

'Indeed no,' said Tom, 'Golden Bay isn't a bad place for the trout at all, nor Carrig Bay either, nor Annaghkeen itself behind there.'

As we made our way back to the east side of Inchagoill, where our boat was tied up at the pier, the angler's talk ranged here and there and many a story Tom had to tell.

'The best fun of all,' said he, 'was the jokes they used to play on poor old Mr Brackenbury. He was often a guest of Mr Guinness at Ashford, and a great fisherman altogether, with nothing in his head most of the time but ways and means of catching bigger fish than anybody else had ever caught. I could laugh yet when I think of the jokes Lord Oranmore and Browne, Mr Guinness's son-in-law, used to play on the old man, and the way every time Mr Brackenbury made a record his young Lordship would find some way of breaking it on him. When you go back to Ashford to lunch let you look into the Fish Room at the stuffed trout there in the glass case. You'll see a label on the one I mean and it will tell you that the fish weighed fifteen-and-a-half pounds and was caught by Lord Oranmore and Browne in April of 1932. There's a bit of a joke in that, I tell you.'

'I think I've seen that fish already,' I said, 'but I don't see where the joke comes in.'

'Then you couldn't have been examining it very closely,' said Tom, 'and that's a fact. For the fish isn't a trout at all but a spent salmon his Lordship sent up to Dublin to be stuffed, aye and painted too, the way you'd think it was a trout. And what do you think of that for a joke? Poor old Mr Brackenbury, I can see him yet. He'd just broken the record and Ashford full of his pride and big words about it, when what does he see in front of him but this bigger fish killed only a few days afterwards. And I don't think he ever knew anything about the joke at all. I'm thinking 'twas kind of a broken heart he had as well as a broken record.'

Richard Hayward, *The Corrib Country*

An Earful of Angler

'Tell Mr Trotter about Jack and the big minnow, Patsey.' I heard Pat chuckle. 'Sure you didn't know Jackie, sir,' he said to Bob. 'He was a terrible man for turning everything into a joke, and he wasn't particular about his jokes either. Well, sir, he had a great minnow, 'twas a desperate bait. 'Twould frighten a fish entirely, the length of it. 'Twas a cold day in the month of February and he had been pike-fishing in the river below Lough Daun. 'Twas too cold for him and he came home and laid the rod on a couple of nails on the wall with the minnow hanging – he was that way, sir, with everything. Some of the lads came in and were sitting down – Jackie was after entertaining them – when one feller, Pat Keiff it was, roaring with laughter, leaned back in his chair and drove a hook of the tail triangle through the ear of him. The devil such a roar as he let out. What does Jack do but take the rod and play him above to the Doctor, the two of them roaring through the street. Sure a very careless man was Jackie.'

F.D. Barker, *An Angler's Paradise*

Four in a Row

My water on the Slaney ran through a valley reputed to be peopled by fairies and my best pool was named the Fairy Seat. A high diagonal weir keyed on a boulder (which was probably the Seat) sent the stream slanting across to hit against the far bank and run parallel with it over a nest of rocks which gave ideal lies. Standing on one identical spot I once hooked and landed in rapid succession four spring fish with not more than three or four casts intervening between landing one and hooking the next. My upstream neighbour, who was not devoid of jealousy, was watching through field glasses and her remarks were retailed gleefully to me next day by her companion. 'Good, Kingie is in a fish.' 'My god, the judge has got another.' 'The bloody fellow has hooked a third.' 'This is too much, the bastard has a fourth.'

T.H. Kingsmill Moore, A Man May Fish

Denny Power's Fish

One day when the river was high and coloured Tom and I were sitting by The Pool on a grassy bank watching Dick at work. He was casting an exceptionally heavy minnow, and the sight of it must have touched some chord in Tom's memory. He looked up at me sideways, from beneath the peak of his old tweed cap, and I knew a story was coming.

'That's a great lump of a bait the master's fishing with. Och, I'm not saying at all it's too big for the way the river is this day,' he added, ''tis only it chanst to put me in mind of Denny Power.

'You'll have seen Denny Power, him that keeps the public-house at the corner of the village. He's an old man now, but you can tell from the big frame of him what he must have been. Red hair, he used to have, and big hairy wrists. He was terrible strong and the wildest lad I ever saw when he had a drop of drink taken.

'He was a grand fisherman too, and could sling a heavy salmon-bait across the Big River, fair-and-square on to the far bank, any wide place you'd care to name.

'I'll say, too, he wasn't always caring greatly whose water the salmon he caught came from, and he caught a fair share of them.

'Now there's a deep hole above the bridge, below the village. Yourself must know it well, of course. I wouldn't say it was free water, but 'tis rarely fished by them that has the rights, for except when the water's very high, and clear as well, 'tis useless to fish it. The fish are there all the same, and big ones at that. Often's the times I've seen them rolling there like a lot of hogs.

'This was Denny's favourite spot, and right or wrong, when the water was in order, many's the salmon he had out of it.

'One year an Englishman had the fishing of it, a small dark mean-eyed little man that expected thirty shillings' worth for every pound he spent, as well I know, having been employed by him for a season, and jealous as hell of anyone else's luck. Now walking down the bank one day, Denny had seen a monster of a fish disporting himself in the pool, and had made up his mind, by hook or crook, to have him out of it. One afternoon a day or two later, he had just returned from a fair and had some drink taken, the amount of drink that only sharpened his wits and didn't affect his legs at all, when a gossoon comes running up the hill to him on his doorstep shouting, 'The Englishman have a great fish hooked in the big hole above; he's as big as an ass – he threw a lep and I saw him.'

'Hell,' roars Denny. 'The bloody thief – 'tis my fish, he have!' and with that he dives into his house, and in two-three minutes out he comes with his bait rod and gaff. 'Twas the stoutest rod I ever saw (he kept it always mounted to save time), and dangling from the end of it a spoon bait as big as your hand fixed straight on to the line without any trace, and a mass of lead strung above it.

'We'll bloody soon see whose fish it it,' he stormed, and pushing through the crowd of us at the bar entry he hurried down to the bridge.

'We could not think what he had in mind at all, but well we knew that Denny was sure to provide sport.

'In two minutes we were on the bridge and there sure enough was the Englishman, his rod bent double and the big fish ploughing about somewhere in the depths of the hole.

'And there on the opposite bank was Denny Power, slinging out his great spoon for all he was worth, and it making slaps like a plate when it hit the water – and he all the while cursing and swearing at the Englishman on the other side.

'At last he made an extra long cast right in behind where the Englishman's line cut the water. Of course the two lines soon crossed, and the hooks of the spoon caught firm in the dropper which the little Englishman had on.

68

'I'm in him,' yells Denny in triumph, and started to reel in as hard as he could. Nothing could stand against that rod and line.

'There was the three of them all pulling different ways. The little man didn't know what to do. First he held hard till we thought his rod would break. Then whether he gave up, for a minute, or his hand slipped, I couldn't say.

'Anyway there was an awful screech from his reel, and as Denny reeled in harder than ever, the Englishman's line came streeling out, and gradually, for all its struggling and splashings, the fish was drawn in, gaffed, and thrown on the grass.

'Whose fish is it now?' Denny bellowed. Then he carefully cut off the little man's cast with his knife and let the line go.

'The Englishman, dancing with rage, swearing he'd have the law on Denny – but all Denny did was smile and take off his hat.

'We carried the salmon up to the village, and weighed it at the butcher's. Thirty-six pounds he weighed and he as bright as a new shilling.

'Then what must Denny do, but pack up the great fish in a bass and send it back to the Englishman, cast and all attached, with a polite note by the hands of that same gossoon that brought him the news.'

G.D. Luard, *Fishing Fortunes and Misfortunes*

In the Bush

I remember another day of foul weather when Patsey and I were driven off Inchicrag to take refuge on the river. To be honest, nothing of interest happened on this day; I only mention it because it reminds me of Jackie and some of his stories. We had not fished the first pool when we were compelled to take shelter under an overhanging crag from the driving rain. Patsey had no more than got his pipe into action when we heard the crashing of brambles, and a prolonged r...r....ip followed by an inelegant remark, addressed to no one in particular. The next moment Jackie, Patsey's eldest brother, stumbled into our retreat. Half the skirt of his rain-coat was flapping round his feet, but he was, as usual, cheerful. Nothing was ever able to damp Jackie's spirits.

At this time he was fully engaged in mothering two inexperienced sportsmen from Lancashire and, for want of something better to do had taken them into the bogs to shoot. While I was pinning up his coat – which he was all for cutting off – I asked if he had been having any sport. 'Sport, is it!' he returned, in his rapid jerky manner of speech; 'devil a better, sir. Sure the young one was twice in bog-holes yesterday, below at Bally Portree. 'Twas twenty minutes we were scraping him. Sure one suit of his clothes is that shrunk 'twouldn't hold Mickey Ryan, that's but a slip of a lad.' 'Yes, but did you get any birds?' 'Don't mention, sir! Birds? devil a feather but one did we knock at all – an old coot that Father Haley was after crippling last Sunday.' 'I heard you shooting.' 'Why wouldn't you? Never fear but there was shooting and plenty. The devil as much powder was burnt since the last Boer War!' 'Where are they now, Jack?' 'Begor, I dunno. They were worm-fishing below in the big hole. Have ye a fill of the pipe, Patsey?'

One of the Lancastrians could cast a fly and, given a chance, would have taken a share of the trout, but he of the shrunken suit could not put his cast within yards of the wished-for spot. What time Jack was not picking the flies out of the fisher's coat he was disengaging them from his own clothing and flesh. One evening, just as it was getting dark, Patsey and I were at the river's mouth when we were joined by Jack and his party. The man who could fish was in the bow of the boat, the other was under Jackie's immediate eye. The evening's amusement must have been planned in advance. For a fourth fly had been added to the pupil's cast, and Patsey (evidently in the know) observed quietly to me, 'We'll be after a diversion, sir.'

At the point opposite the heap of stones was a large waterlogged thorn-bush – left there by the last flood – scarcely to be seen in the dim light. Getting the boat where he wanted it, Jack, in a low excited voice, called to his pupil, 'Cast there, sir, there, into that dark spot, there's a whacker! Again, sir, again! cast over him, sir!' A pause – then 'Raise your hand, sir; raise your hand, sir!' At the same time he gave the boat a sly pull with the oars and away went the reel as merrily as you could wish. 'He has him in the bush,' Patsey whispered. It was exceedingly well done; the bush gave and sprang, the reel ran and the fisher wound; Jackie gave directions and enlarged encouragingly upon the size of the fish. Meanwhile we escaped to a distance where our laughter could not be heard.

F. D. Barker, *An Angler's Paradise*

A Purist's Misadventures

It will take years to efface the clinging memories of my first adventure with a dry fly. When I went forth equipped with all the latest scientific implements to perform, preening myself that I, and I alone, amongst my many angling acquaintances, was IT – the immaculate Purist. The angels must have been watching and smiling. Heaven must have rung with their mirth before the day was ended, for, I suppose, like mortals here below, they derive a lot of amusement out of a poor devil's discomfiture.

It was on a Monday morning. I got up early intending to go to work. I had to search for a pen-knife that I had mislaid, and found it in the drawer in which I kept my tackle. In a weak moment I picked up an aluminium box containing dry flies, with glass lids covering the various compartments; I sat down, wrapt in admiration, as I gazed on the lovely little creations. Then by some process of reasoning I concluded that I would be many a day in the grave pushing up the daisies, when one day stolen for sport wouldn't make much difference one way or the other. If my enthusiasm hadn't been overproof I would have taken warning at the omens of misfortune that crossed my path before I got clear of the street I live in. When I opened the door the first person I saw was a woman pushing a handcart full of apples; her hair was as russet as the bloom on some of the fruit in the cart. In the casual glance I got of her I noticed a shade over one of her eyes. I would never have thought again of the incident had she not in passing wished me luck.

Halfway down the street I noticed a gentleman knocking at a door on the opposite side. It was with a twinge of regret that I noticed he was a clergyman. Though I give first to no one in my respect for the cloth, I would sooner have met him when I was returning than when just setting out for the day on my maiden trip as an exponent of a new cult.

Far be it from me to suggest that meeting the reverend gentleman would bring me bad luck, but my father often said that the day you are sure to have Will-o'-the-Wisp's blessing (that is, an empty bag and a wet foot), it is part of the ritual that you meet his reverence before the pipe you lit at your own door is empty.

The journey seemed very long; the old steam engine hissed and coughed up the tiresome climb from Tallaght to Brittas. The sharp walk of a mile from Blessington brought on a happy frame of mind. Just as I sighted the scene of my objective, I was thrown into a fit of depression by the sight of a chattering pin-feathered magpie.

It was then it dawned on me that the appointed day in my career had arrived, when I was to be the laughing stock of the devil and all his imps.

Short was my shadow on Burgidge Bridge where the Liffey and King's River meet when I put the rod together. An up stream breeze was faintly rippling a good depth of water in the pool below. Fish were rising freely near both banks. The fly on the water I never thought of, but choosing my quarry, a quick riser at the near bank, I put a match to the briar as I waded in to fight the fates arrayed against me, shouting 'muck for luck,' as I mounted a cow dung fly. After a few unsuccessful attempts I got it up to him at last. In his innocence he sucked it down. Did I strike? No. My surprise was so great that my arm remained like unto the right one on Grattan's Statue outside Trinity College, Dublin. Back came my fly to the surface, and with it a tiny bubble to mock me for the idiot that I was.

I fished another rise, determined to correct the non-striking habit if I got a chance, which I truly did. I got a side view of him as he took the fly. With the left hand I pulled in the slack and with the other I struck with all the speed I was master of. He was for making a fight, but I wasn't in the humour of indulging in any of the finer tactics of the game – giving him line or playing. I yanked him out with a jerk, swinging him high in the air against the parapet of the bridge twenty feet above me. The resounding thud re-echoed from the wall. Then I marvelled at the nerve I showed in defying convention. My ecstasy had a short life.

Walking along the bank a few minutes after this success, carrying the rod in the left hand, I fell into a deep, disused rabbit burrow. The top of the rod caught in a wire fence that ran between me and the water. I broke it clean across above the second ferrule. I wedged it in and lashed it on as best I could, determined to carry on, though well I knew the witch's brew was simmering. Inside the next hour I tore the back out of a new mackintosh on a barbed wire fence, and punctured my right rubber thigh boot on a sharp branch in the bank. I did not know until I waded in to cast a fly over to the far side, when I felt the shock of the cold water pouring in on my foot. I am not going to record the many times my fly was hung up in obstructions that at other times in wet fly fishing I would have missed, or will I tell of the many breakages of casts or loss of flies. Needless to relate my stock of both was sadly depleted after all I went through. I have faithfully noted my misfortunes in the order they occurred, so I suppose that it was fitting that the climax of my blunders – if blunders you can call them – should be reached just after I gave up in dismay, and plodded my way across the fields to catch the steam tram for home and comfort.

To apprise the extent of my final catastrophe it is necessary that I describe an instrument that I had some time previously constructed. The reason it was ever fashioned was to do away with a cumbersome landing net which caused me endless worry by catching in briars, shrubs and fences.

Once when looking at a very large triple pike hook I conceived the idea of inserting the shank of it into a piece of light cane one yard and a half long. I lashed it with wax end to secure it firmly. Next I bored a hole in a cork bung, and passed it through from the other end of the cane, embedding it firmly in the barbs of the hooks as a protection.

This substitute for a net I called a lifter or trout gaff. When I first removed the rod from its cover I laced the cane handle into one of the compartments and secured it to the left lapel of my mack, and also below the bottom button with two safety pins. I was quite proud of the idea. Little did I think that I had forged another link in the chain of mistakes that eventually went so near to encompass my destruction. When crossing an earthen ditch on top of which was placed a lot of freshly cut whitethorn bushes, all the butts pointing in the same direction and firmly sodded in, I slipped and fell across it. The cover caught in the bushes, and when I strove to rise the barb of the hook came through my cheek and got securely fastened in my upper lip.

The bung got knocked off the barbs when I fell. I gave another frantic plunge to try and rise, which only drove the hook further in till it grated on my poor teeth. Imagine my horror when I found that I couldn't get up or slide back. I prayed with devotion that was both earnest and fervent for deliverance from my crucifixion.

As I lay there the thought crossed my mind: was this to be my miserable ending, to be found dead on top of a ditch in the wilds of Baltyboys?

Then I remembered having a knife and luckily I found it in my right hand coat pocket. I opened it as I lay there and severed the cover and cane. I struggled to my feet a free man once more with a foot of cane hanging to my upper lip. I went down on my knees and offered a prayer of thanksgiving for the freedom I had regained.

I made my way to the nearest farmhouse. When I appeared in the doorway the sole occupant, an elderly man, roared out some words in Irish and bolted into the bedroom with fright when he saw the streams of blood and the pendulum swinging from my upper lip. I borrowed his mirror off the wall, and brought it out into the sunlight. Then I cut the lashing at the end of the cane and inserted the blade of the knife and released it, leaving the pike hook for the doctor in Blessington to remove.

A car passed along the road, and the occupants observing my predicament, gave me a lift to the doctor in Blessington to be operated on. The local MD was away on holidays when I arrived there. A lady doctor was deputising for him, and to her lot fell the task of freeing me.

She tried to cut the hook with pliers and pull the broken part through, but couldn't manage it. She had to dig through the sinews of the lip eventually, and the lance she used was as blunt as a table knife. After untold agonies the hole was large enough for me to push the hook upward and release it. She persuaded me to take a restorative like a seidlitz powder from a long glass phial. I must have drank it too quickly, for the breath left me and I remembered no more.

After coming to I suffered from a headache and had to rush away to catch the steam tram poorer by half a guinea.

The foregoing incidents happened a few years ago, and lately I flattered myself that I had lived down the idle rumours that were floating about after the occurrence.

But I got a rude shock when passing through Blessington recently, when I heard someone shouting 'There's the fellow who gaffed himself.'

Laurie Gaffey, *A Freelance Angler in Ireland*

Your Lordship

Fishing was reserved for the holidays when, a suitable rod having at last been acquired, I roamed the countryside on a bicycle, stopping at any bridge over a likely stream and casting my fly where I fancied. Only once was I questioned. I had unlimbered to fish a deep pool in Donegal where first a white trout of a pound, and then one of over two pounds, came to me. As I was landing the second fish a bailiff approached and asked me for my licence. Of course I had not got one, and I said quite truthfully that I had come to fish for brown trout. He smiled. He had heard that one before. But all he said was 'There's another good pool round the corner' and left. Forty years later he gave evidence before me in a fishery case. I had no recollection of him and asked if there was a good run of white trout in a certain river. 'Faith and there is, and your lordship wouldn't be long in whipping them out' was his disconcerting answer. He had recognised the poacher turned gamekeeper. He did not omit to tell counsel, nor have counsel allowed me to forget.

T.H. Kingsmill Moore, *A Man May Fish*

CHAPTER FOUR: WIND AND WATER

A Rough Sail

During a certain September there were two whole days of heavy rain with a gale from the south-west. As a consequence the river was over its banks in many places. Though the rain had ceased twenty-four hours before, the gale was still with us. Patsey remembers that day vividly – he tells of it to each newcomer – it was the day when I won his confidence in boatmanship.

In the hall of the Grey House we held consultation, and decided on the river. 'Sure the lake is covered with waterspouts' was Pat's report; we could see them from the study window chasing each other past the end of Wood Island. As we came out of the door Patsey started off up the avenue. 'Where are you going, Patsey?' 'To the river, sir; where else would I go?' 'Yes, but I'm not walking.' 'How will you be going, sir?' 'In the boat.'

'The boat, sir! Sure the boat wouldn't stop on the lake; it wouldn't float ten minutes.' However, I insisted, and very unwillingly he went with me to the bank above the boat-house. It was certainly rough. The little whirlwinds were spinning and dancing until they broke on the far shore. The air was thick with a mist, the waves were up amongst the trees of the island, and the spray was everywhere drifting in light clouds. But I had no fancy for the long walk. With a little care I thought that I could make a fair wind of it if I could but get a little to the east for a start. 'Patsey man, can you take the boat as far as the point of the island?' 'I can, sir; but what will you do then? Sure it's not the island at all you'll be wanting.' 'No, Patsey, it's the river, and we'll not be long getting there either.'

For the first bit we had the shelter of the land, but even there a sea was running and the wind came in heavy blasts. Patsey kept on gamely, glancing at me over his shoulder from time to time, his white head bare, 'the hat' on the floor of the boat, safely under one foot. When there was room enough I told him to raise the oars clear of the water, and upon no account to let them down. All we had to do then was to go before the wind fast enough to get away from the following seas. So I stood up at my steering oar and squared away for the river, opening my oilskin coat whenever there was need for a little more speed. Certain it is that Pat's boat had never travelled so fast before. I kept so close to the point, west of the castle, as to scrape the end of the starboard oar – which was a further shock to my crew – but I wanted all the room there was.

I don't think Pat knew when we entered the river, for his eyes were fixed on me all the time. 'Faith, the first thing I knew was a bump, and we were above in the big hole, the bow of her in the bank, as nice as you please, beside a little quay of turf, and what to do but step out of her? 'Twas forty miles an hour we went – faith, a steam-boat wouldn't go faster.' Before he got up, however, he said to me: 'After that, sir, I'll go with you where you like, devil a fear but I will. I went because you would go, but I never thought 'twas to the river we'd get at all, but to the bottom entirely. I'm your man, sir.'

F.D. Baker, *An Angler's Paradise*

Boat Lore

And now a word about engine-craft and boat-craft; for there is more to learn about the western lakes than the art of catching fish in them. When running the engine between the drifts in a moderate wave, drive straight into the wave, as far as possible; it is safest and driest, and keeps the boat steady in its whole length, and there is little or no splash. If the wave is heavy, slow down. Driven fast against a high wave, the boat rears up like a mettled horse, and the bow comes crashing down, shivering the timbers and opening the seams, and the bow thwart will break if a heavy weight is on it. Run slow, but not too slow, lest the engine stall. A following wind is heady, like champagne, and, like it, calls for care. The boat is soon running at twenty miles per hour, and when the wave gets long and steep, the boat may side-slip on the crest and slither down the slope. Slow down at once. Side winds are a special study. Usually one can drive with safety down the long furrow with a wall of water on either side; but watch the crest of the wave, and if it looks like breaking, take no chance; go slow. A side wave can sometimes be negotiated in corkscrew fashion, like a crab. There is a big wave a-beam that looks threatening; sidestep into it; the boat will rise to it; then straighten out again into the long furrow, till the next big one comes along; then repeat the manoeuvre. The ancient Greeks thought that every third wave was the big one, and they gave it a name; on the western lakes the rhythm of the big wave is nearer one in seven than one in three.

Head wind, side wind and following wind – each one has its thrills and its dangers. Experience soon teaches how to deal with them. Boats are built to float, and provided your boat is seaworthy, broad in the beam, with a good deep keel, and provided the helmsman keeps cool and the children do not stand up or panic, all will be well. The worst situation to meet is the huddle of waters; you meet it rounding a point on a gusty day; wind and wave come at you on both sides all at once; and you have hardly time to think or take your bearings; in such a cast shut off the engine at once, and leave it to the gillie. Boats are made to float, and they do float; they right themselves in a wonderful way, provided they are given time, and are not forced at speed.

And now for boat-craft. Boat-craft proper is much more than pulling an oar or a pair of oars; it is managing the boat like an artist or craftsman; it involves a certain oneness between boat and boatman; for he must express himself, his intentions and purpose, in the movements of his boat. King Solomon found three things too wonderful for him, yea four which he knew not – and one of the four was the way of a ship in the midst of the sea. Watch the bow of the violin in the hand of the maestro, or the fingers of the organist on the keys of the cathedral organ, and watch the oars in Michael's hands. King Solomon had seen his proud ship of Tarshish in full sail with its cargo of ivory, of apes and peacocks; and a gallant sight it was. Michael's way with his boat on a drift on Lough Conn is a thing of wonder, too.

Gillies do not pull a very strong oar, as a rule; they eat so little meat, and their technique in pulling is not what it might be. The College student in his old school tie or boatclub tie, down for the fishing, will beat the gillie in the boat race at the local regatta; but the gillie has what the student cannot have, boat-craft. The gillie is one with his boat; he is born to it; in action his two oars are extensions of his two arms; to see what should be done, and to do it, with him are one and the same thing. In the tricky launching or landing, when strong winds are blowing athwart, he seems to feel the boat as a whole; he knows the exact position and angle of bow and stern and centre; he reckons sub-consciously with currents and sideblast; he feels in his bones the amount of freeboard, and the strike of the wind on bow and stern; he is one with his boat; if he shifts his seat, or bids you do so, that is the reason why.

On the drift his craft rises to the level of an art, and anglers often owe fish to the gillie's art as well as to their own. Seated towards the stern on the last thwart but one, the gillie angles the boat to the breeze, bow-in for an in-shore breeze, bow-out for an off-shore breeze. With one oar or scull out behind he is in full control; with one push in she goes; with one pull out she comes, no matter how high the wave. If you want fish on the western lakes, you must cast near the rocks, and the gillie has one eye on the look-out for the yellow gleam of wrecking rock. In a very light breeze he works sideways, like a crab; he makes the most of every flurry of air; and often it is his oar that imparts to your fly the twist or turn that gives you a trout.

A.A. Luce, *Fishing and Thinking*

Caught in a Storm

Let me round off the picture of my friend with a true story of a storm on the lake. This is an aspect of a gillie's life that fair-weather anglers and river anglers do not see. We learn to appreciate our gillies, when we realise that their job has its dangers that form character, and display it.

Few gillies can swim, and on the whole it is better so; the non-swimmer will not let himself be caught, if he can help it, in a situation that calls for swimming; he will not expose himself or you to danger; he trusts his boat, and he means to stay in it till he reaches land. Water is his friend and ally, not an enemy; when he is water-borne, he is in his element; he has been at the job since boyhood; it is second nature to him to do the right thing in a crisis; he understands wind and wave, and the way of a small boat in a big storm; he would not be there with you if there were any real danger. Given a good boat, two pairs of strong oars, resolute arms, stout hearts and cool heads, anglers on the western lakes will make shelter, even if they cannot reach all at once 'The haven where they would be.'

Courage and coolness are great qualities in a gillie, and you do not really know your man till you have been with him in a storm. Nothing tests a man like danger to life. I knew a boatman on Lough Mask who went as white as a sheet when a stiff nor-wester blew down Mountrasna Bay, and the waves were topped with white. It was no place for him, and he was not typical. Most gillies have cool heads and hearts of oak. They must have these qualities; to be cool and courageous is part of their job. Anglers want fish, and are often willing to take a chance. Whatever precautions are taken, you may be caught at a disadvantage. Storms arise suddenly; winds swing round, and plans 'go all a'gley.' When that happens, the courage required is not the active heroism of the soldier in action; but it is resolution, the ability to be calm and cool and collected.

On a stormy lake there is little one can do; man cannot pit his puny strength against wind and wave; he cannot fight the forces of nature, he must use them; and that means keeping calm and cool, and doing the right thing at the right time.

Michael and I have shared not a few anxious moments – moments that to me were anxious; but I never once saw him flustered, much less frightened; in a tight corner he always seems to have something in reserve. His worst day on the lake is worth describing. He has often told me about it in general terms, such as, 'The lake went up in smoke that day, Sir.' The angler who was with him in the adventure wrote an account of it at the time, and he has shown me the record, and it is frightening still.

It was the day of an angling competition in April, 1943. The rendezvous was Coryosla Bay at the Pontoon end of Lough Conn, some eight miles by water from Cloghans, where Michael lives. It was wartime, and there was no petrol for outboard engines or for driving round by road. After breakfast Frank, a young engineer, and Michael set off in their good, solid nineteen-foot boat; it was a calm morning, and Brendan, Michael's son, decided to go, too, in Michael's dinghy on the chance of a job as gillie. The dinghy was little more than a canoe, about twelve feet long, as light as a cork, with an up-turned prow at either end, like a Viking ship; it was meant for coasting about in sheltered bays in fair weather. They reached Coryosla without incident in a couple of hours; but clouds were piling up in the south; the wind was freshening; and the men knew that they were in for it.

The competition gun was fired, and the anglers started work; but almost immediately the storm broke, and very soon fishing was out of the question. Lashed by wind and rain the boats ran for the nearest shelter, and tied up; anglers and gillies took refuge in hospitable cottages, where they found a welcome, warmth and tea. All the afternoon the storm raged, but lulled off about 6pm. Then Frank, Michael and Brendan forgathered at Coryosla and held a council of war.

The issue was simple – eight easy-looking miles by water, or a trudge of twice that distance on a rough and stony road, with the prospect of returning on the morrow for boats and gear. The wind was still strong, but southerly; it should be with them all the way; rowing would be easy, and if all went well, they would be safe and sound at home within an hour and a half. That is better than a four hours' trudge, it is not? The ayes have it. They decided that all three should go in the big boat, and take the dinghy in tow.

For a while they were in sheltered water, and all went well; but as they drew out into the open lake, the wave was longer, and the dinghy began to misbehave. Towing is never easy in a wave; in a high and following wave it is almost impossible. Now the light dinghy would overrun and bump; now it would act as a sail and confuse the steering. To weight it and control it Michael volunteered to enter the towed dinghy and guide it with an oar. He did so, and found that he could guide it up to a point, but not control it; for as the wave grew steeper, the dinghy would poise like a surf-board on the white crest of a breaking wave, and then come sliding down the forward slope and crash against the boat.

It was a terrible position for them all. Frank and Brendan shouted to Michael to come back into the comparative safety of the boat and cut the dinghy adrift. He would not hear of it; he stayed in the dinghy, cut the tow rope, and pulled clear. It was a high act of cool and calculated courage. The two men were in a solid boat with a good keel and considerable freeboard, and if they shipped a sea, the one could bale, while the other rowed; but Michael was alone in a cockle-shell, alone in the middle of an angry lake; his craft had little or no freeboard; it could spin round at a touch, and if it met a breaker broadside on, it would swamp instantaneously. But Michael never relaxed for a moment; he kept his head, and, watching every wave like a lynx, by sheer boatcraft he remained in full control of his frail barque.

An hour passed, and now in the gathering gloom the following wind had brought boat and dinghy to a point within half a mile of Rinmore Point, and if they could round that headland, there lay safety and a lee shore. Suddenly the wind failed them, and veered; the south wind that had blown all day dropped, and there was a for a few moments an oily calm, an ominous calm, more fearsome than the storm; away to the west, high up in the sky over the shoulder of Mount Nephin, appeared the lurid red glow that told of a change of wind and of a hurricane on the way. They pulled frantically; for they were abreast the long, pitiless Brackwanshag Reef. The last few yards made all the difference. They had just cleared the reef, and had entered Storm Bay, when they heard a rumble; and with a roar like an express train a tornado from the west struck the lake. Then (in the words of Frank's record) 'The squall hit us in a cloud of spray. It enveloped us completely and sent us hurtling towards the shore. All I could do was to keep our stern square to the wind. I kicked my rubber boots off. Soon the boat was travelling at such speed that I feared she would split in two when the crash came. A thole-pin broke, and I lost the last vestige of control. Suddenly Brendan started; he saw the line of white breakers ahead. I felt the keel grating on the rocks. Then a great wave took us up and hurled us broadside-on right over the rocks and into the sandy pool beyond. Twenty yards away we could dimly see Michael calmly tying up his tiny dinghy.'

A.A. Luce, *Fishing and Thinking*

A Connemara Twilight

As I got out of the boat, the sun was nearly down, a little west of the Twelve Pins. They stood out now, absolutely clear cut, a jagged solid mass, purple as a plum. To my right, the moor, a huge expanse, was ringed about by hills, olive-brown as the bog grass; the western horizon was luminous and golden. But it was one of the moments when colour shifts as you watch it; I walked towards the sun; it had sunk before I reached the lake, but there was still a golden ray on the water. Far from me, I could distinguish on that lucent sheen the broken line where the stream entered, and I pushed down the boat and pulled towards it. Everything was extraordinarily still and tranquil: even a leaping fish broke the silence, and my oars seemed to make absolute tumult. I landed, and my fishing was over in five minutes: it had given me only the pleasure which every angler knows of straightening a line over a swift run of water; but it had, as so often happens with fishing, made an errand which led me into the heart of beauty.

As I paddled back, I saw the sky changed: radiations like an aurora shot up through the ruddy gold. The little lake on which I was led by a narrow cut into a larger one, and along that whole vista of water the sky's colours were reflected, under the sombre purple of heathy banks. I stowed the boat safe and took the footpath home across that solitude – leagues of it on every side, where 'Only God exults in silence over fields no man may reap.'

So the poet had written for my reading of that afternoon, and though it is only now I think of his line, perhaps he had affected my mood. To the south-west was a planet, glorious and golden; to the north-east, over the hills that run down from Joyce Country towards

Screeb and Costello, another star answered it. A grouse crew in the heather to my right. I had been walking southward, but as I started to pull back I faced north, and saw again the sunset glory. It spread beyond the Twelve Pins; and just where the Joyce Country mountains over Maam joined in to them was a region of half-light, delicate and wonderful; a glimmer rather than a glow. These mountains were not solid and purple, as were the Pins; they had a colour ill-defined and tremulous that was neither green nor grey nor brown, yet had something of them all; and it passed imperceptibly into the long range of unlighted slopes and skyline. I pulled fast across, rounded the points as neatly as I could, and made for the quay; but as I slackened to enter, the beauty I looked at held me. I could not go in, but paddled out again and lay on my oars. It was dark now; the island mass with its trees seemed inky blackness; yet as one looked one saw it was all green – water, ilex-trees, mountains beyond, and sky. Overhead, stars grew thick; the grouse's call came again across the water, and a mallard quacked. From the upper island a heron flapped out squawking; and behind all these was the steady roar of a distant waterfall. I stayed there in a sort of dream, half anxious to go before the spell had ceased to hold me, yet unwilling to shorten such an hour. Water has for me at least an odd magic: it affects my whole consciousness with a pleasure that is not exclusive, for other things can enhance it, but that nothing can replace. The sea is different: it heightens one's sense of vitality; it has its own joy; but its strong breath does not blend so subtly with a mood as do the exhalations of clean unspoilt lake or river – above all, when the scent of turf is in the air. Never had I felt more strongly than this day the influence which tranquillises rather than stimulates, and makes the mind extraordinarily receptive of beauty. Probably if we could read our own impulses it is this emanating charm which accounts for the wise folly of fishermen. I was glad to have caught a salmon again after a long spell of lost opportunities; the sea-trout one has taken are a gracious dish for dinner; but what turned my day into something happy and memorable was my wild-goose chase across the moor, and my solitary paddling in that dewy twilight.

Stephen Gwynn, *Duffer's Luck*

The Streams of the Bog

The other rivers in Ireland that we fished with the dry-fly were like nothing that I have seen in England. They had a character of their own, 'eigenartich' as the Germans say, something peculiar to themselves – the Brosna, the Silver River, the upper Suck, the bog-stream at Kildangan, the Dee of the County Louth. The Brosna held fine trout and some peal (as they call grilse in Ireland). But it was thoroughly poached and it was rather too big to be an ideal dry-fly river, so, attractive though it was, we did not go there much after we discovered the Silver River.

It should rather have been called the Golden River, for its water was the real deep brown of the true bogland and showed clear gold, when the sun shone, over the white sand of the shallows. No doubt that sand, exposed and white and gleaming when the river shrank in high summer, gave it the name of Silver – every little seaside place in Ireland has its Silver Strand. But it is always associated in my mind with the dark brown of the deep stretches where the big trout lay, rather than with silver; with absolute solitude – only twice did I meet human beings on its banks in many visits; with vast miles of heather stretching level to a blue hill on the horizon; and with the most poisonous midges and horse-flies in Ireland.

Unlike many Irish bogs, it was not dotted with cottages. There was one farm-house on the banks of the stream to which certain annoying ducks belonged, but I never saw a human soul either inside or out. And there must have been cattle above, for sometimes the river came down muddy when they had been standing and champing in the water to get away from the flies and the heat. Once a local angler arrived, and was much annoyed to find us. But we had leave to fish from the owner (as was not always the case), and he could say nothing. He went away after telling us that the fish in this river always stopped rising at ten minutes past nine every night and I always regret that we never noticed what they did when summer time came in: did they keep 'God's time or Protestant time' – which was the Irish antithesis? I shall never know.

Another time, when the water was muddied by the cattle and we had gone upstream, away from the best places – many miles, it seemed in the heat – and were resting under one of the rare thorn bushes, but still below the polluting cattle, we were surprised by an elegant apparition in white kid gloves, attended by a man carrying his expensive rod, and landing net, and large lunch. We were so indignant at the completeness of this angler, at his cool appearance, at the unfair protection of his hands from horse-flies, that we, selfishly enough, let him go past us away from the water which we knew to be good for three-pounders. After all, there might be as good places above – let us hope he found it so: at any rate, we never saw him again, and we were never bothered again by fishermen, natives or visitors. Probably the little river was too far away for the natives. It was a long journey, when the motor was not so easily available, and they probably did not think it worth while to go so far, especially as the Brosna, a bigger river open to everyone, as is usual in Ireland, was at the doors of the village.

So we used to start out alone in the morning from our unpretentious little inn, through the wide, dirty, village street, with its asscarts and pigs and potato sacks: the straw and the dust blowing in our faces or behind us, for it is rarely windless in Ireland. Beyond the bridges over the big river and the railway, the roads bends to the right round the 'demesne,' the trees of which, neglected and covered with moss and lichen, lean through the broken fence over the road. Then the corner is turned, and, after the canal, there is nothing but flat bog as far as the eye can see.

Mile after mile the bicycles bump over the uneven road. Very occasionally one meets an ass-cart going to the village: sometimes one sees a few grouse taking their diet of stones off the road. Not many, though this is one of the few places where they drove grouse regularly in Ireland – the owner used to have 100-brace days before the war, and one can see the line of butts. It seems impossible that the shooting can be other than dull in such a dead flat, or that one can find running water. But we come to a stunted plantation, the roads bends at right-angles to the left, turns again, and, just beyond the wood, there is the low grey bridge and the sparkling river deep in its high banks.

These high banks were one of the features, and the hazards of our bog-stream. At long intervals it was cleared out by the Board of Works – deepened and straightened to prevent floods. After each clearance the banks became higher and on the sides the grass and nettles and thistles, protected from the wind, grew high. So that, as one had to climb down the bank to get a proper approach to one's fish, there was great danger of disturbing them – and often, at the critical moment, one's fly got caught up in the high vegetation behind. The water was so dark that one could never see one's fish – one had to judge whether the rise was a four-pounder or a half-pounder. But whatever the size, each fish required a careful stalk and a lot of catching, for, apart from other dangers, the river became a mass of weeds as the summer went on, and these were of course never cut.

Needless to say, the percentage of losses was high. Once I hooked a great fish which took me into the weeds, at a place where the water was shallower, and one could see the sandy bottom. Hand lining was tried in vain, but the fish was still on and seemed firmly hooked. I put the rod down, took off all my clothes, and waded in, holding the rod in one hand and the line in the other, till I reached the fish. He seemed to me enormous, and he had twisted the cast round a branch stuck in the weeds. Reaching my hand down I broke the branch and he was free but still hooked. And still full of life, for he darted down-stream again, and I was left to get ashore and pursue him.

Then might have been seen – if there had been any to see – the spectacle of a middle-aged gentleman, stark-naked, struggling through nettles and thistles, and over rocks and stubs, on a slippery bank with rod held high, shouting and roaring for help which never came from his companion deeply engaged far away. The fish went faster than the fisherman, got into the weeds again, and broke me. He won the battle as he deserved to do. More than ever did I rejoice, as I dried myself in the sun, in the solitude of the Silver River.

Maurice Headlam, *A Holiday Fisherman*

Tons of Fish

When we were clear of the little bay but still in shallow water, I asked where I was to begin fishing. Patsey's answer is among our classics. It came as a matter of course – 'Where you are, sir; fish away, there's tons of them below you.' I laughed and repeated the phrase in mocking disbelief. 'There's tons of them below you!' My scepticism hurt Patsey, but he bided his time. Two years later he took his kindly revenge. Again it was May, but later in the month. It was a warm and balmy evening with scarcely a breath of wind. Patsey had gone home, as I thought, and we were just finishing dinner when the maid came to me and whispered that Patsey was in the hall and wished to speak with me. When I joined him he was a trifle excited. 'Put on your coat, sir, and come in the boat; I have something to show you.' I protested that a dinner-jacket was hardly the costume for a fishing excursion, but as there was to be no fishing I put on the coat and went with him. It was a perfect spring night; the lake was a polished mirror reflecting the light of the moon, almost at the full. He pulled swiftly to the southern shore and paused. 'Listen, sir!' All about us were feeding fish – one circle flowing into the next; their 'chopping' could be heard distinctly and among them were some very heavy fish. They were feeding along the shore up to the very edge of the grass. Then away he pulled to one of the islands, halting in the shadow of the overhanging trees; chop, chop, chop; everywhere it was the same – under the overhanging bushes, at the ends of the oars, out in the deep as far as we could see. Then he carried me off to a shallow, rocky bay, and there it seemed as if all the trout in the lake were congregated – it was unbelievable! As we crossed the lake on the way home he paused again, in the deepest part, and as far as one could see there were feeding trout. Then he spoke and his voice was very serious. 'Do you remember, sir, the first day you were here? You were after asking me where you should fish, and I told you – 'Where you are, there's tons of them below you' – you laughed at me, sir, and thought I was telling what wasn't true. Well, sir,' – and here he spoke with a new firmness – 'was I right?' Then I made the best apology I was able. He had been right, perfectly right. He had not overstated the facts by so much as a pound. When I had made my apology he merely said, 'Very good, sir' – and the boat sped back where the lights shone out from unshaded windows and the sound of the piano came sweetly across the stillness. I have believed all Patsey's stories from that moment.

F. D. Barker, *An Angler's Paradise*

By Boyne Banks

Among the many scenes of beauty and of interest with which this fair islands abounds, we know of none which combines such variety of the former or so many objects of the latter as the Pleasant Boyne. And although this river does not burst upon us amidst the wild and stern grandeur of the mountains, with dashing torrent o'erleaping in its rapid course all the barriers of nature, or making its echoes heard among the deep hollows of darkwooded dells, but pursues the quiet, even tenor of its way, through a flat but rich and fertile country, winding by 'its own sweet will' through broad savannahs and by green inches, where the calm ripple of its placid waters disturbs not the song of the mavis; still it possesses charms and beauties, and that, too, without a rival in this or perhaps any other country. Slow, calm, and tranquil in its early course, the mower wets his scythe in the deep meadows by its brink, and the reaper gathers the corn from the very margin of its waters; the swift and martin skim over its clear surface, and the robin sings in the ancient thorn that rises out of the adjoining hedge-row. The very may-fly, as it lights upon it, breaks the mirror of its surface. The wide-spreading circles which mark the springing of the trout, or the timid breathing of the roach, are all, save the flapping of the water-hen, or the easy paddle of the baldcoot, that disturb its placid bosom.

In this gentle stream there is no inequality – no roar of waters nor spray of cataract; it is not boisterous nor yet sluggish; neither broken by the sudden rapid, nor calmed by spreading into the broad lake;

but, pure and undefiled, its source sanctified by religious veneration, and commemorated in legend and in song; serene and peaceful, like a true philosopher, it glides noiselessly on, in deep but calm repose bestowing the blessings of fertility on the counties through which it flows; bearing on its bosom the inter-course which socializes man; enriching, beautifying, and civilizing, it receives in return the homage of its tributaries, and finally mingles with that eternity of waters, the sea.

Sir William Wilde, *The Beauties of the Boyne and Blackwater*

Trout

Hangs, a fat gun-barrel,
deep under arched bridges
or slips like butter down
the throat of the river.

From depths smooth-skinned as plums
his muzzle gets bull's eye;
picks off grass-seed and moths
that vanish, torpedoed.

Where the water unravels
over gravel-beds he
is fired from the shallows
white belly reporting

flat; darts like a tracer-
bullet back between stones
and is never burnt out.
A volley of cold blood
ramrodding the current.

Seamus Heaney, *Death of a Naturalist*

Sunset on Lough Derg

We wait and watch the sunset. These Lough Derg sunsets are indescribably glorious. The sun hangs low in the west – a great crimson ball swinging in ultra-marine deepening to darkest sapphire. He drops lower and lower, and his reflection streams across the black water – a broad pillar of fire. A cloud swims in front of him and the whole western sky is red, and the waters turn blood-colour, reminding us of the legend from which Lough Derg derives its name. And the mountains to the west stand out black as ebony, with a fringe of fire, and the eastern hills light up in the after-glow; and then the gorgeous spectacle fades away, and Danny shivers and says: 'It's time to go home, sir!' So we go home; and no sound breaks the stillness of the night save the creaking of the thole-pins, and the gurgle of the yielding water at the bow, or the far-off lowing of the cattle on the Galway shore.

And then the grey seabirds come. They come from the east, and they go to the west. Why? No man knows. But they come, and float over us, following some inscrutable law of their own. They come from the east, they vanish in the west like wraiths; without a sound, without a trace – they are gone.

I think of them as the spirits of the many races that have lived and loved and warred and passed away over this mystic land. Fomorians, Milesians, Celts, Danes, Normans and Saxons – they have all left their traces here for those with eyes to see. We carry on our dapping – and this to me is almost its greatest attraction – in a region inconceivably rich in legendary lore: of Maeve, and Finn, and Oisin; of Bryan of Kincora, when he crushed the hosts of Asmond, and the Leinster men broke before the Dalcassian battle-axes. Of the wars of the Geraldines and the Butlers, of Confederates and Covenanters; and even still in the homes of the people they tell of Sarsfield and his irresistible dragoons. And so my story ends.

Next morning Danny and I exchange regretful but not hopeless farewells.

'Ye'll be back for the dapping next year, sir?'

'Please God, Danny. Good-bye.'

He returns to his fruit trees and his flowers – and I to noise and smoke and civilisation!

Sir Thomas Grattan Esmonde, *Hunting Memories*

Cloon Lake

Cloon Lake lies high up in the mountains, yet not so high but that farther still from the sea is the Red Lake, above whose shore a steep cliff rises where the golden eagles had till some few years back their last breeding-place in Kerry. I have been there in my time, and have caught from the bank trout very unworthy of such impressive surroundings; but this year Cloon Lake was far enough and good enough for me. Ten miles from the little hotel, it is twenty from the nearest railway-station: and thank heaven, the road to it leads across a ford which effectually shuts out the motor-driving tourist.

There were four of us, two ladies and a tall lad who, despite much patient endeavour in English waters, had never compassed the capture of even a herring-sized trout. I passed my word that in Kerry he should catch more than we could eat; and on this day a gridiron was brought along with us, though the ladies were most doubtful of its finding use.

We had got the rods ready, one with a spoon bait up to troll for salmon, and before we launched the boat, 'Patsy,' I said, 'did you put in the life-belts?' Patsy grinned at me reproachfully with his one front tooth. Last autumn I had made an earlier fishing raid to Cloon, and as we drifted down the lake shore, cheerfully employed in hooking and landing a succession of small trout, it became fairly evident that the boat was leaking. However that is nothing unusual on Irish lakes; but the breeze freshened and as we turned to row back from the end of the drift, she met the wave, and every dip of the oars drove her deeper into it and streams poured in from all the upper seams. I sat in the bow and bailed, while Patsy and Patsy's father,

Micky, rowed; but the bailing did not lower the water in her, and my friend in the stern, W.S. Green, who knew as much about boats as any man living, called out that she was sinking. Neither the boatmen could swim, and I thought myself very unlikely to reach the shore in boots; there were some very uncomfortable minutes while the oars tugged at the water-logged craft and I bailed frantically. But she kept afloat till just before we reached the bank, and as we scrambled on to an outlying rock, Micky observed very placidly; 'You were right enough, sir, she was sinking.'

'And what would you do if she sunk sooner, Micky?' I asked. 'Walk out, sure,' said Micky, 'Sure I knew with the last five minutes there wasn't five foot of water in it.' Patsy turned to his father in a rage. 'You knew that. And me tearing the inside out of me rowing!'

That mishap had put the fear of God into Patsy, and he had the boat staunch enough this year; and as we began to troll, one of the ladies screamed out that 'her rod was jumping.' There was much exhortation and advice before the line could be reeled in, and when the cast came in view, not one trout but two were on it, and we landed them, set the flies fishing once more, and in a couple of minutes the rod 'jumped' again, and again she had caught a couple. So it went on for the whole drift, and we had fully a dozen landed before an hour's fishing was over and it was time to think of luncheon on the island.

As we paddled up, there was a great turmoil in the trees and a grey crow flew off sullenly; a flutter of wide wings showed where a heron had been hunting the robber from her nest. But she left it with a croak and much flapping as we landed and made our way through the hollies with which the island is chiefly wooded: I climbed up and there were the two eggs, blue like a duck's, and about the same size. We ought to have found a duck's nest too, for one rose almost at our feet out of a tangle of undergrowth: but it was too cleverly hidden and we gave up the search to superintend Patsy's cooking.

He had lighted a fire by this time, an easy matter that dry day, and he was busy cleaning the trout with the help of my pocket-knife. But it would be unjust to Patsy if I left it to be supposed that he needed all conditions so favourable. There came another day when he and the schoolboy were out on another lake, with nothing but bread and trout for luncheon, and the rain came down in torrents. Patsy had only two matches, and no knife; but he had also the stump of a candle and a safety pin, and with these aids he prepared the trout and got a fire to cook them by. You never can tell what will come in useful on a day's fishing.

But at this first venture all was plain sailing, and soon the grid-iron was laid on the glowing cinders and we all sat with our eyes centred on the trout that curled up as they grilled first on one side then on the other. On that day we affected to be civilized and ate them with pointed sticks of holly. Later, we dispensed with the sticks; but whether with fingers or with forks we found trout so cooked and so eaten delicious beyond expression – and a welcome change from the inevitable sandwich.

Finally, when we had well eaten, the boy went off with Patsy to renew the slaughter of trout, and the rest of us were content to be idle under shade of holly and arbutus, where a mossy rock sloped into the lake: and as we sat there quiet, the noises of the island life began to be heard about us, all the talk of birds. It soon revealed the presence of a second heron's nest with young birds in it, clamourous to be fed. They were the oddest pair that I saw when I scrambled up, three-parts fledged, beak complete of course, and menacing, in front of the bright yellow-ringed eye: the wing coverts were fairly furnished, and as I saw them at first crouching into a confused heap into the saucer of loose-piled sticks which is their nest, they seemed very tolerably plumaged. But presently when I moved nearer, both got awkwardly on to tall tottering legs and revealed the most indecorous lack of feathers about the rump. They staggered uneasily out to the extremest rim of the nest, and in terror that they would fling them-selves out, I climbed down. But when I reported my find, needs must the birds be looked at; and having made arrangements to catch them if they jumped, I went up with a landing-net and got it over their heads. One I left, the other came down in the net's bag, quaintly entangled, and very droll when we got him out. That heron will never know how near he came to taking the journey to London in a railway-carriage; but a heron's personal habits are untidy and I pointed at the state of the branches about the nest and that decided it

– that and some uncertainty if the creature would live. I carried him back again and left for a peace-offering two trout in the nest, which may also have served to confirm to the old bird the young one's story.

After that, we had decided to climb one of the surrounding mountains, and there was great cutting of hollysticks; but our way from the shore led past a cottage, and trusting to the traditions of the country, I went in and begged that tea might be ready for us when we came down. Thoughts of that tea acted perhaps as a drag, for the climb did not reach beyond the lower slopes: and lovely as the view was, the tea was lovelier. I never saw whiter linen than was spread for us, with good scones, with butter that had been in churning when we passed up, and creamy milk and eggs enough to feed a regiment. We were glad to have a score or more of trout to leave in return for that cordial hospitality, and on our way down the lake we picked up perhaps another dozen to bring home.

It was late when we left, and passing almost into twilight from the golden close of day. She for whom chiefly I had planned the excursion turned round on the car as the horse started for his long trot down the narrow alarming little mountain road. 'Oh, Cloon Lake' she cried back to the water, 'you've been very good to us.'

And that is the best of all the memories in this book of mine.

Stephen Gwynn, *Duffer's Luck*

Mayfly Time

It's a grand time in the Corrib country when the Mayfly starts to rise. From all over Ireland the anglers come in their hundreds, and from most parts of England too in the days of peace and sense and decent travel. Accommodation anywhere within sight of the lakes is at a premium and most of the fishermen have their rooms booked at Ashford and other hotels year after year, and are ready packed and waiting at home for the telegram that will be sent to them to say that the first Mayfly have taken to the air. You'll see hundreds of boats on Corrib at this season of the year, and hundreds of men, women and children all round the lake shores, armed with butterfly nets and ventilated collecting-boxes, chasing after the elusive Green-drake Mayfly which is considered best for dapping. The hatch usually rises at about eleven o'clock in the morning, and as soon as possible after that you'll see the flycatchers gathered on the lawns of Ashford and elsewhere, offering their fragile winged stock-in-trade to the impatient anglers, who are not at all particular what they pay so long as they are not delayed in their eager rush to the boats nor kept too long from their all-absorbing sport. For time is not to be wasted – the rise only lasts three weeks at most, and but ten short days of the period can be counted on for the real rigour of the game. It is a light sou'-westerly breeze they look for, these disciples of Walton, and given that, and a spot of luck, a pair of them will come in with thirty good trout between them against a day of excitement and hope and tantalising encounter. Fish that would never rise for an imitation fly, big wily experienced fellows up to fourteen pounds in weight, will cast caution and discretion to the four corners of the lake and take greedily the greenish-yellow lure that is dangled above them on the roof of their home. For, as Izaak Walton said: 'They love the Mayfly, which is bred of the cod-worm or caddis.'

And what a strange breeding it is to be sure. Hatched from eggs laid in the water, the larvae, predacious, hungry, and armed with formidable jaws, spend a long worm-like existence of twelve months in the lake, fighting for food, growing, changing, and casting the while maybe twenty coats or skins on the long road to perfection. And always striving towards that exciting exhilarating day when they may thrust up towards the light and the air and the sun, and burst their water-bound strait-jackets to take to the air on fragile wings, light as gossamer, the perfect imago at last. No thought of food then – no need for food – no means of eating it – for the Mayfly has no jaws and but the veriest rudiments of a mouth. Such mundane things were cast aside with those other vulgar trappings of a half-lit wormy world. What need of food anyway when the imago has but a few short hours to live – and less than that if the fly-catchers are about. Up, up, up into the sunlight, sick and crazy with love, up in that mad delirious nuptial flight, guerdon of their long dark months of striving.

And with their mating done, and future generations assured, their new-found winged life so madly begun comes to a quick and sober end. But the eggs are already being laid and soon more larvae will commence their strange slow pilgrimage towards the light and the few intoxicating hours of life and love and air-borne frenzy.

A light bamboo rod is used for this Mayfly dapping, from fourteen to sixteen feet long according to fancy, and the special dapping hook is attached to this by means of a thin silk blow-line. Two Mayflies go to each hook, neatly impaled through their bodies at the wing junctions, and the secret of the art is to work with a touch as light as the bait itself – lightly – lightly – and never drenching your fly nor giving way to coarse handling when your victim takes. Easy does it now – easy and lightly. There he goes – and a big fellow too. Yerra man, don't strike yet or you'll lose him. Count one – two – three – and strike now. You have him, begob, and a fine bucko too. Ten pounds or I'm a Dutchman. Good man, me da! It's a great game, and whilst it lasts the excitement is intense. The whole countryside is transformed into one vast paradise of anglers, and you'll hear nothing else but talk of fish and breeze and light and water. And it's not only trout that are killed but many a good bottle of the wine of the country too, and that's no word of a lie. For it's a thirsty pastime this same dapping, and sure what's drink for anyway.

It all starts towards the end of the third week of May, and by the middle of June you wouldn't see a dapper in the world. But the grilse have come into the lake before then and sure they take the loneliness of it. And there's always August ahead, but it's Daddylonglegs and Grasshoppers we'll be dapping with then, and the fish rising for them nearly as eager as they were for the Mayfly itself.

Richard Hayward, *The Corrib Country*

CHAPTER SIX: BIG FISH

A Great Silvered Shape

Evening sedging has given me some great fish and fishing. My biggest trout, which as I write stands nobly mounted in a case on my study wall, as stately and plump as any Buck Mulligan, was taken in total darkness on a mid-September evening on a small limestone lake. A day of wild wind and rain had been succeeded by a like evening. As darkness came, my companion Morrough (most aptly-named) and I were fishless. Then the wind dropped with the coming of night and I took a poorly-conditioned rainbow of some two pounds. It seemed our one and only fish of a dreadful day.

We were fishing out a last drift towards a shoreline guarded by dense reed-beds when ahead of us in the blackness I heard a trout feeding. Several times, casting with mechanical care, did I put my Green Peter where I thought the sound came from. No rise could be seen – it was impossible to see the other end of the boat even. So I twitched the fly gently towards me.

On the third or fourth cast there came a resistance, slight, then immovable. I tightened, whereupon it became movable, sheering off to the left from where I sat in the bow. I knew the fish was big. The very power of her run (for it proved to be a hen) thrummed solidly up the line to my fingers – I play fish with the hand rather than the reel. I could not see where she ran; only by bending low and sighting against the faintest of afterglows could I tell from my bending rod where the fight was taking place.

Try as I might, I could not persuade her upwind. In front of us lay the reed-beds. I lived in mortal fear lest she would run herself deep into their comforting shelter and send my cast twanging back. In the stern Morrough coped with and cursed a tangled cast.

101

I was aware suddenly that the boat was moving, slowly but enough to send a ripple spreading from the bow. I could not see it but I heard clearly the water parting on the stern. The trout was pulling the boat along. How big was this fish?

By now the battle had fallen into a pattern. The fish cruised back and forth in front of the bow some ten or twelve yards away. I could not gain more line nor could she. Now and then she varied this procedure with a spurt – although her stately power could not fairly or with dignity be called such – straight ahead, pulling the boat with her. Such control as I had was minimal. I kept the line tight, gave her some when she wanted it, though with reluctance, and took it back when she wasn't looking.

Looking back on it all, I had throughout the battle a clear head. My fears were many but at least I could reason with them. I must not let her get her head into the reeds. I must play her right. But my point was a bare three pounds and by this time my fly must be a sad sight indeed. Would it hold? Or – horror of horrors – would she straighten it?

I had reached that stage where I must see the fish.

'Morrough – shine the torch.'

Cursing me, the fish, the night and his tangle, Morrough fumbled forward and the beam of his torch lit the water. The bottom sprang up as though looked at through the bottom of a glass. We were in no more than a foot of water and almost aground. Then there swam deliberately into the circle of bright light a great silvered shape, the eyes bright as diamonds. In the calm water and the torch's sharp light, I could see the slender hold of the fly. My heart failed me.

It must be now. Or not at all. I put side pressure on the fish and she moved reluctantly to the side of the boat. Morrough put the net under her in the torch light and lifted her great bulk inboard. As he did so the net bent and the fly fell out. But she was landed. And my old Hardy scale, as accurate as any computer, put at her six pounds and eight ounces. My biggest then and still.

Niall Fallon, *Fly-fishing for Irish Trout*

Cruisers of the Dee

The most extravagant cruisers I ever met were on a river in Co. Louth, Ireland. In mayfly time the big fish – and they had been killed up to six pounds – would traverse regularly a beat which might be a hundred yards long. Invisible, a heavy trout would sail up and down this in sedate and leisurely fashion, devouring the mayflies he met on his road. Now such a world-traveller was in a different category from the stroller of the Test, whom you can reach without changing your place, merely by lengthening or shortening line. The Irish fish soon passed out of range; if you ran after him, you either found that you were usefully showing your fly to his tail, or else you put him down. The better plan, the one I was advised to adopt, was to choose some place about the middle of his beat, where there were no obstructions and the regular flow of the stream allowed your fly to float long without a drag. Once there, you noted the path through the stretch which he took on his journey up and down, a path which varied little, and you selected a spot where you could cast straight across to him. Then you knelt down when you saw his rises getting nearer and nearer, you waited till he was ten to fifteen yards off, then you cast, kept your fly floating to the last second, and then immediately cast again, so that your fly was on the water without an interval.

There are many exciting incidents in angling; a big fish splashing at sedge in the still dusk; a salmon of thirty pounds boiling at your fly; the last stage of the fight with a three-pounder on 4x gut, but I have rarely been more shaken than by one of these cruisers, whom I verily believe to have been five pounds. I had chosen my station cautiously and prudently; I studied his paths to an inch; I knew him to be sixty yards below me; then suddenly there he was, taking a mayfly, forty yards off. I waited what seemed an endless time. Had he passed me? The mayflies were drifting down in a string and I watched them idly. They were fifteen yards below – and he took all three, one above the other.

Quickly I cast; my fly floated two yards, I whipped it off before it dragged, and instantly put it on the water again, beautifully cocked.

103

It had hardly sailed two inches when he had it; he had it with a gulp, but with my usual fatuity I missed him. I hit him hard, there was a boil like a submarine mine, and that five-pounder was seen no more.

J.W. Hills, *A Summer on the Test*

Castle Connell

When the captain saw my flies, he offered to back the black and orange, and the orange fly, half-a-crown each, against the yellow heckle fly. I took him up on each. Kean whispered to me, 'Sir, there is no click to your new wheel, and it runs smooth and silent, so let out a little more line, that your fly may be a little below the other.' I did as directed, and caught two more large fish. We had now ten; when it was proposed to fish the next stream, a very rapid one, called Poul a Herra. Here I was obliged to take the second oar, but keeping my yellow heckle fly still near me.

We had made several turns, and could scarcely keep the boat against the stream, when my rod had a tremendous pull. I instantly shipped my oar, and found, from the weight and strength of the fish that he must be very large. We, as usual, went to shore, at the Clare side of the Shannon, and, after about twenty minutes' hard and fatiguing play, he showed enormous: he was a new run fish, not long in the river. I brought him within reach of the gaff, when Kean made an attempt at him, and only scraped his back; away he went, then across. We were again obliged to take to the cot, and follow him to the other side, and bring him back again, the banks at the Limerick side being high, and it being highly dangerous to attempt to gaff him into the cot in deep water. We at length killed him. He weighed forty-eight and a half pounds, and was the largest salmon I ever killed, though I have hooked much larger. Captain Cotter, in the month of May following, killed, with a fly on three-twist gut, on the stream of Donass, a salmon fifty-nine pounds weight: he was turning a little brown, but he was a splendid fish.

O'Gorman, *The Practice of Angling*

Sixty Pounds

I think it must have been the next year that I went over to stay with Dick for Whitsuntide. We fished hard and did fairly well everywhere, except in Cummeragh stream, which always looked perfection, but was in fact extremely dour.

Then, one day something stirred up the fish and we got three in it all within an hour, and I rose what appeared to be a very big one. The river was not high, but there was a good flow, and after fishing Cummeragh all down with a prawn, Dick decided to try for the big one with a worm.

The moment he reached the spot where the fish had risen the line checked, and then began to run out with those surreptitious jerks which are so exciting and make self-control and patience so difficult. Dick gave him due time and the fish was fast. Obviously it was no small one, for with astounding ease he ran right up and stayed for some minutes in the neck of the stream where in those days thousands of gallons of water came shooting down from the pool above in a long smooth and glassy glide, while the line hummed with the vibration.

Then he turned heavily and slid swiftly into the stream, and, swimming deep, passed the slip of shingle on which we were standing. After taking a short turn round the eddy opposite, he ran down some eighty yards, this time more quickly, towards the very end of the stream. There, still unseen, he turned head up and remained stationary. We therefore waded down and out as far as we could to try to get some control by having the rod as much over the fish as possible. But at the first increase of pressure he began to drop down tail first towards the rougher water. This was most dangerous, for the rapids ended in a violent stream, known as the 'Whirls,' where many a good fish has been lost. I waded out as deep as I dared below the fish and threw stones to prevent him going down, but without any effect. Very slowly he dropped down and down. The water was shallower; a quarter of the trace was showing. We were almost in the rapids now. Then he stopped again and remained stationary. He was not more than five yards away, but still invisible, and for five minutes nothing would move him up or down. Dick put on all the strain he could. Even the leads were now visible, twisting and trembling with the strain. I half thought of trying to gaff him where he lay. I think it might have been done, though the wading was very deep and rough, and the stream strong. Even today it gives me a twinge of regret that I did not – for suddenly his tail just showed for a moment above the surface – an immense tail, and incredibly far from the trace. He must have been well over four feet long, a super-fish! Then, with one rush of a hundred yards, he was off into the 'whirlpool.' The line gave a twang and came flying back minus leads and hook – clean cut through. 'Gone!' ejaculated Dick with a gasp, 'and on a worm too,' and he slowly wound in the line.

That was, I am convinced, an unusually large fish, sixty pounds weight at least, judged by its length.

G.D. Luard, *Fishing Fortunes and Misfortunes*

A Question of Scale

I have been, once at least, in touch with a really big trout, and this is how it happened. There is a small lake that lies deep-set among steep, low hills, some two miles and more from the Grey House. It is a lonely spot, not an inhabited house within sight. At the lower end of the lake is a rugged crag from the summit of which rises an ancient tower, now a roofless ruin, heavily hung with ivy, the tenement of countless jackdaws. Another ruin – that of an ancient church with a crowded and disordered burial-ground about it – crowns one of the hills. A tiny beck winds down a grassy valley and enters the lake at the end opposite the tower.

In this dark and sombre lake there are trout in plenty and perch, but never a pike. Originally the trout were brought from Inchicrag, some seventy or eighty years ago, and have prospered. Plentiful though they are, to take them is no easy matter; indeed, there are days, and many of them as I know to my cost, when to fish here is as useless as to cast on the lawn. There is an exasperating unanimity about these fish. When the mood for fly possesses one the multitude is possessed; then, without rhyme or reason, down go the lot, and that's the end.

One bright sunny afternoon in May we walked across to see what an evening might afford us in the way of sport. We were early and we sat in the shade of the tower and talked fish until the sun dipped behind the hill. Even then we did not go out, but watched the fish feeding close in to the banks. It was getting pretty dark when at length we took to the boat. There was not enough breeze to move the light boat, and I was paddled along within easy casting of the shore. So many fish were feeding that it was puzzling to decide over which to cast; but we did very well and picked up nine nice fish of over a pound each. Here again I found the trout not in the least shy of the boat or of my casting – repeatedly they rose within a yard of the boat.

Then came a great excitement. Somewhere out in the deep and the dark was a 'gobble' that made us both cry out. 'A whacker!' said Patsey. I fervently agreed. We went in search of that fish and, through the noise he made, were able roughly to locate him. He appeared to be moving about, working toward the middle of the lake, and apparently taking everything that came his way. Then began, I am ashamed to admit, some pretty hasty and bad casting. He was here, there and everywhere, except where my flies happened to be; but even my thrashing failed to frighten him. On he went, sucking in the flies with a noise that could be heard across the lake. I was at such a tension that when the 'knock' came, as it did, I struck 'fit to lift him,' as Patsey said, with the inevitable result – away went the Monster, taking my upper bobber with him, and with him went the chance of a lifetime. Oh! the misery of that moment.

Patsey did his best to console me. 'Faith, it might happen to any one, sir, waiting so long. Many a time I did it myself, gave a welt and left the casting-line and all in a feller. 'Tis a pity, sir, a great pity, but it can't be helped.'

'Ah, Patsey, if only we didn't do stupid things! It was a big trout.'

'It was, sir, a very large trout; devil such a trout did I think was in the lake at all.'

We were still lamenting, when a fog came down suddenly and put an end to our fishing.

The next morning I took down my cast to repair the damage and found, sticking on the point of the middle fly, the scale of a trout. When I so madly struck that big fish the upper fly came away and the middle one tore across his back. How big the trout was you may say for yourself, you who have caught trout, when I tell you that the scale would cover the butt-end of an ordinary lead-pencil. Patsey says fifteen pounds; his brother, an experienced fisher and not my boatman, declares that no fifteen-pounder ever wore a scale of that size.

F.D. Barker, *An Angler's Paradise*

The Sway of Corrib

We are all of us anxious for the credit of our counties, but it has to be allowed that trout-fishing in Donegal means catching herring-sized fish. Ever since I began to use a rod, I have been seeing brown trout caught there, and till I was forty I could count on the fingers of my hands all the fish among them that turned a pound. But also, ever since I began to hear fishing stories (and to tell them), I had been hearing of the Big Trout – three pounds, five pounds, and so on up to any reasonable figure – hearing but not seeing; he was still 'a hope, a joy, still longed for, never seen.' Literally, until I began to fish Sessiagh lake in 1904, I had never set eyes on a brown trout of even two pounds. There, however, I met them, and then, I saw and (through sheer stupidity) lost a really big trout.

One thing, however, had resulted. The Big Trout of fiction had ceased to be mythical for me, and had become an object of pursuit. But, however ardently I hunted him in Donegal, with spinning-bait and with fly, I never approached the one I had lost, never could even pass the four-pound limit.

Perhaps providence thought of my disappointment and my perse-verance; perhaps, as an Irish proverb says, 'A fool does be lucky.'

Certainly I felt fool enough for anything when, in the end of August 1906, I unpacked my rod-case at Cong, preparing for my first day on Lough Corrib. A hurried journey to Galway had suggested the possibility of this fishing, and I came away with no time to examine gear, and by consequence was confronted with the fact that all my spinning-tackle was forgotten. I had nothing to show to my boatman, Lydon, except a green and silver wagtail minnow which his namesake, the tackle-maker in Galway, had persuaded me to buy – may providence reward him! For a companion bait, a spinner for the natural minnow was soon rigged, roughly but effectively; a couple of swivels which I chanced to have were let into a strong casting-line; and then, by Lydon's advice, we repaired to the local draper's shop, where it appeared other swivels could be got. They had no detached swivels, but offered me a very light spinning-trace, which after some discussion we decided to fish with as it was; and so equipped we started.

Even on that bleak ugly day of northerly wind and colourless skies the upper end of Corrib showed a fair challenge to Killarney. Thickly strewn with wooded islands, it is backed by ranges of bold mountain; but its chief charm lies in the romantic suggestion of the pass towards Maam, where its winding water, lost to sight between the cliff-like hills, tempts one to row continually onwards and explore what recesses may be enfolded among the gaunt crags that guard the entrance to the Joyces' country. This day, however, we were due to lunch near Lord Ardilaun's fine house and famous woodcock covers, and so we dodged and wheeled about round rocks and islands, aiming at the points where deep water fringes a shallow, and the big trout and pike cruise about looking for incautious fry.

Meanwhile, naturally, we talked about big trout; and it appeared that Tom Lydon had captured the show fish of the hotel, which, glossy in its glass case, had impressed me solemnly while I breakfasted. It weighed twelve pounds, he told me; and after it was sent to be stuffed he caught another half as big again. This fish, eighteen pounds, took a bait attached to a hand-line, and, as Lydon said, you could do nothing but throw the reel at him. It, being wooden, floated, of course, and the fish was eventually landed.

I listened as to a chapter of mythology, and in the meantime nothing happened. At last we turned homewards to lunch, and shortly after there was a pull at the rod from which the wagtail was fishing; but this first fish proved to be only an inconsiderable pike. It broke the ice, though: five minutes later there came a savage pluck at the same line, and the moment I had the rod in hand I knew we were into something heavy. Probably another pike, I thought, and sighed for waters where a big fish can be relied on to be a good fish. But at the next instant the unknown quantity made a short run – luckily cross-wise, for his first race had nearly stripped my reel – and then floundered head and tail up. At all events, here was no pike; the sickly yellow gleam did not show itself. I set him down for a salmon long up and discoloured, and the boatmen found confirmation in the fact that he was now moving constantly up-wind. We got the boat parallel with him, and I shortened line as quickly as I could, while Lydon exhorted me to handle him gently, for he was on the light trace. We are accustomed to fish very light in the north of Ireland and the mere thinness of the gut would not have terrified me; but when I thought of the local draper's shop, grave doubts – which I retract and apologise for – rose up in my mind.

Then suddenly, perhaps thirty yards off, the fish rose so high in the water that we could see him plainly; and his broad golden side was covered with huge black spots. Young Lydon shouted: 'It's no salmon; it's a splendid great trout!' But his father was more eloquent. Dropping his oar, he shifted his place to the bow. 'Maybe you'd better take the gaff,' he said to the son. I felt then that this was indeed a great occasion, when this hardy veteran would admit the advantage of youth; and, Heavens above! how I wished that we had put our swivels into gut which commanded my confidence.

There are few incidents in the business of wearing down a heavy fish in a lake with light rod and tackle, but the strain on one's nerves is considerable when the prize is so uncommon as we knew this fish to be. Somewhere about ten pounds, I guessed him – at any rate, a bigger brown trout than my wildest ambitions had ever aspired to; and, contrary to all precedent, the nearer he came, the bigger he looked.

'He's fourteen pounds!' Johnny Lydon cried, when a great back

110

showed for a moment above the water. Inwardly I set this down for exaggeration, but it added to my excitement that I had never seen experienced boatmen so eager and anxious. There was a continual fire of snapping injunctions from one to the other – generally speaking, instructions to do the thing which the man instructed had already begun to do. The boat in reality, and not I, was playing the fish; my part was only to keep an equable strain and watch that the reel kept absolutely clear.

We had come about half a mile with the fish, humouring him away from all dangerous possibilities of weed or rocky shallow; and another boat near by had stopped fishing and pulled over to watch the event. We were all anxious; but luckily the old grilse-rod's top was very limber, and I could be tolerably secure that no sudden plunge would meet with too much resistance. With an ordinary spinning-rod and that trace the odds would have been on the fish; and as it was, the tackle was wholly too light to lift his head. Gradually, however, and most skillfully, the boat was sidled down.

I had learnt enough not to try to drag or force the fish, but rather to go to him. Still he kept sheering off from the side of the boat; and suddenly Johnny Lydon passed me and took up his position in the stern. It was an awful moment, for as he leant over he hid the line from me, and every angler knows that the eye, quicker even than the hand, tells when to ease off the strain and stop a heavy fish from floundering on the top of the water. But right or wrong, I left Lydon his way, and kept up the strain through seconds that were like minutes, while he shouted his directions and the boat was backed quietly down.

One felt rather than saw when he actually struck; and he had reached out so far that he paused for an instant to recover, while the trout hung over the water on the gaff. Another lift, and it was in the boat at last. Lydon held it between his knees while he lifted an iron thole-pin for a 'priest,' gave a couple of decisive taps, and then laid it on the boards of the boat. If he was big in the water, he looked bigger now, for all of us gasped. 'Fifteen pounds,' I said. But the other boat drew over now and hailed us, and we did not venture to commit ourselves beyond thirteen or fourteen. This angler had scales, and lent them; and the pointer hung somewhere between sixteen and eighteen, as nearly as possible midway. It was a great moment. I never saw another fish weigh so much heavier than he was guessed at. The exact figure when we got him on the kitchen scales was 16¾ lb – and I quoted it to some one the same evening. But Johnny Lydon looked at me with pained eyes. 'Sir, for the love of God, say seventeen pound.' And for the love at all events of Johnny Lydon, I have always used the nearest round figure to the truth. How many anglers can say as much?

This was my first trout on Corrib. Lydon of Galway told me he had seen one killed a pound heavier, and my boatman, as I have said, also had an eighteen-pounder to his credit; but these things happened a good while ago, and my piece of luck was portentous. There is, of course, no question of skill in trailing a line behind a boat; and if it is true that in playing a salmon from the bank much depends on the gaffer, the same is far more emphatically to be said in the case of lake-angling. This fish, as we happened to be able to determine, took from fifteen to twenty minutes to kill, and he was gaffed before I ever got him on his side at all. With a less competent boatman I have been kept nearly an hour in killing a ten-pound salmon on tackle very little lighter. Consequently, it seems that we all had good reason to be pleased with one another, and certainly we were.

The rest of my day's fishing is of no interest. I killed altogether six fish – three trout (making twenty pounds), two small pike, and a large cannibal perch which took the minnow. But the history of the big fish has ramifications. It was decided that he should be stuffed, and accordingly, when we went in to lunch at my friend's house on the lake, careful preparations were made to send him off, and the fish reached Cong that afternoon in a well-secured box. We arrived not long after from the lake, and young Lydon announced the capture to the factotum of the hotel. He smiled pleasantly, and said, 'May be!' Lydon grew eloquent and indignant, but I suggested that the hotel-keeper should go down to the post-office and heft the box. The proposal was scouted; of course he believed me implicitly. I went upstairs to my room, and approached the window in time to see this convinced person hot-foot to the post-office. He came back in a wholly altered frame of mind, eager now for measurements. I gave them him: length, thirty-three and half inches, by nineteen and a half inches girth, and the girth almost uniform over the whole body of the fish, which was extraordinarily deep behind the dorsal fin. But if I had been wise, or he had been wise, he would have had the box opened, had had a public display in the street of Cong. For on the next day we were on Lough Mask and told there, only to be treated with the bare civility that is accorded to extravagant liars; and we returned to find word had reached the fourteen anglers fishing near by from Clonbur, and that all fourteen had refused to believe because none of their informants had seen the fish.

On the day following I departed, but a month later again passed through Cong. My carman met me some miles out, and at once launched out in copious Gaelic. 'There was not the like of such talk in Ireland as was on your trout. Arrah, why did you bring him to Cong in a box? – and me getting my head broke over all the country!' Last Wednesday, he went on to explain, he had been in Ballinrobe, 'and says one of the boatmen to me, 'No such a trout was ever caught in Corrib.' 'Your're a liar!' says I to him; 'I seen it.' An' with that he struck me. An' sure, sir, I never seen it at all; only, what was I to say?'

He quoted to me also the opinion of a certain captain. 'Where is the man you say caught him?' says the Captain to me. 'Gone,' says I. 'And it was Saturday you say he caught him, and this is Thursday. Don't tell me,' says he. 'A man that caught a fish like that would fish a month for the comrade.'

So it is to be feared that my fish, although quite authentic, is somehow clouded in myth at the place of his capture. Moreover, desire for the Big Trout is now extinct in me, since there is no reasonable probability of my catching one bigger; and, given my choice between the fly on a free-rising stream or lake, and the chance of heavy fish to be got by trolling, I shall henceforth always make for the place where there is less glory perhaps but more fun going. I trolled a blank day at my last visit to Cong, and it left me very disconsolate. But at my departure the carman consoled me with a magnificent phrase: 'No matter, sir; you have the sway of Corrib!'

That is the advantage of driving with a man who translates his thought from Gaelic. The phrase rose up in my mind when I walked one day this year into the shop where my fish was stuffed, and found two men in natural exultation over a twelve-pounder from the same lake. The stuffer turned to me: 'It's a poor fish beside the one you got,' he said. I felt for the man who suffered by the odious comparison, but it was something to be reminded that I had still 'the sway of Corrib.'

Stephen Gwynn, *Duffer's Luck*

Fish at Finlough

Finlough gave me my best sea trout, a fish of rather over six pounds, firmly hooked at the base of the dorsal fin. Over a fish so hooked there is little control. He is not in the least incommoded and there is no bit in his mouth with which to steer him. The moment after he was hooked he made upwind on a forty yard dash. Sea trout, unlike salmon, do not allow you a few seconds to collect your wits and a big sea trout runs faster than any salmon. Having finished his burst he turned broadside on and rested. A trout rod or even a salmon rod cannot drag a large fish, hooked halfway between head and tail, broadside through the water. The correct tactics are to row up wind of the fish and drift down, taking in line as you go. That fish would have no such nonsense. Every time the boat drew level with him he was off in another up-wind dash, again to rest broadside on. As he tired from running the spurts grew shorter, but he was still able to put himself up-wind and lie there recuperating. It became clear that he would have to be netted from his down-wind side. At last it was done.

The boatman stole the boat up to him while Noll* crouched in the extreme bow. There he was, still broadside on, about a foot under water. I held as hard as I dared. The boatman ceased rowing and Noll standing up and stretching out till he looked bound to fall in, slipped the long handled net under him, drew him nearer and lifted him in.

That was the toughest fight I had with any fish, trout or salmon. No doubt a purist would have put that fish back, for he was foul hooked. I did not.

T. H. Kingsmill Moore, *A Man May Fish*

* The 'Noll' who landed the trout was Oliver Gogarty, son of the noted Irish man of letters, Oliver St John Gogarty.

A Floor of Fish

On my first visit to Antrim, I had a very natural wish to see what the lake produced, and called on a professional for information, who promised to gratify my curiosity as soon as he could. Late one evening he came – it was after dinner, and a pullan had formed part of it, which fish you should know bears a very drowsy reputation. Now whether it was that fresh-water herring or a twenty-mile walk, I cannot undertake to determine, but certainly no young gentleman was ever more awfully sleepy. Hardly awake when we reached the cottage, I yawned out 'Where is the trout?'

'Your honour is standing on the same.' The floor was thickly covered with flags and rushes, which, when partially removed, showed a sight that made me broad awake in a moment. There were fish of 4lb, 8lb, 12lb, 15lb in dozens and dozens. That night my nervous system received a shock so severe, that I did not get over it for a week. How plainly that night comes back to me now! A thin stripling – the farthing candle – my poor comrade – the wretched hut – the flags and rushes – the dead bodies laid out in decent order, like heroes after a 'stricken field' – you must admit the sight was very touching.

Not being anxious to gain a reputation for 'tall talking,' it is right to say that at this time I was not a very correct judge of weight; besides, my head was off, and the light bad. Nevertheless, I remember perfectly my companion telling me that in the previous season a trout weighing 31lb had been sent as an offering to Shunes Castle. It is hardly necessary to say this nice little lot had been netted for the Belfast market.

W Peard, *A Year of Liberty*

Last Chance on Ennell

It was my last chance, and I determined to make the most of it. My boat-boy had an awful cold, but I dug him out of his bed, and finding him fairly well I kept him at it from eleven till ten without a break! It was lovely on the water, with a warm breeze from the south, so it did him no harm. Yet though all looked favourable, it was a disappointing day, only a moderate fish or two, and but few rises to the dap. As the day advanced the breeze fell more and more and with its fall my hopes rose. It turned out a lovely evening, and by 7.30 practically a dead calm, so we made our way to the spot where we had seen the fish previously. Sure enough they began to rise, and earlier than usual, and they were big fish too.

The first I spotted was greedily taking spent gnats in a small circle about fifty yards away. My dry-fly rod was all ready, line greased, and spent gnat oiled.

The boy, who had become much more skilful, backed the boat towards him. Fifteen yards away, I made him stop the boat; the fish had ceased rising and I was afraid we should run over him. No, there he was again, poking up his big nose and gulping flies as fast as he could. Four times I covered what I expected to be the spot where he would rise next, without success. The fifth time I anticipated his movements aright, and after my fly had sat on the water for a few moments, during which my heart beat fast, there was a sploshing heave, the fly disappeared. I struck – no contact – fish put down. Damn!

By this time a good number of fish were rising in the rosy opalescent calm, but they were far more restless than the first. Several we hunted for two hundred yards or more without any success. Then one rose fairly near the boat. Three times he rose – three times I cast and three times he changed direction; but the fourth time up he came and missed the fly altogether – another damn! The tension of this trout-hunting is so thrilling as to be almost intolerable.

Two or three more we pursued unavailingly and then another big fish took the fly beautifully – I have him – no! gone! Damn! too slow. Why did I forget to re-grease my line? Then two big fish began to rise steadily about thirty yards away, on each side of the boat. These were travelling more slowly than the others and moving definitely in the direction of a large island. They obviously meant business. I elected to pursue the left-hand one while keeping an eye on the other. He, or rather she, rose about every ten yards, and I covered her several times, but to no purpose.

At last my quarry reached the island shallows, with us some fifteen yards away, and turning along right-handed, proceeded to suck in flies at yard intervals. Over and over again I cast, but there were so many spent gnats that mine went unobserved. Then she turned back upon the same course, and seeing a spot where but few flies were collected, I put my fly on to it. Two more naturals she took in leisurely fashion, then strolled up and sucked mine in.

There was no mistake this time. I knew it was a good fish, and the weight and strength on my little rod were unmistakable.

Twice she circled the boat, and then realising the situation, set off towards deeper water with us following, which suited me better owing to the danger of the sharp edges of submerged limestone rocks.

A good fighter, she kept deep, any pressure on my part being answered by deep runs, and several times there was an unpleasant twang from the fish's tail, and once a dangerous scraping sensation, obviously a rock deep down.

At last, however, after some twenty minutes, by which time my arm was getting quite tired, the fish began to weary, and her tail showed several times above the surface. Nearer and nearer I brought her, the boy carefully put out the net, the fish saw it and made a deep dive. I was astonished at her strength and resistance. I could see her far down standing on her head, and the effort to bring her up again was far greater than I expected. Up she came at last, however, and this time too weary to resist further. The boy gently put the net under her. For a moment her great length was balanced precariously, then she slipped in and was safely brought aboard. The boy was astonished at her size. I saw at once that it was female fish. She was beautifully shaped, thick and short with a small head and big shoulders; of a lovely steel and blue shade and with quantities of rich black spots. I estimated the weight at something over five pounds, and eventually she proved to weigh 5 lb 7 oz. The biggest trout I had yet caught.

It was now getting dark, the second fish had ceased to rise, and we made our way home, thankful that my last day had been kind and that I should return home with a real West Meath trout and sufficient of those feelings of triumph and unreasoning pride that always form such a satisfactory conclusion of an angler's holiday.

G. D. Luard, *Fishing Fortunes and Misfortunes*

CHAPTER SEVEN: TRIUMPHS AND DISASTERS

Getting it Right

Evening fishing is very much a question of getting things absolutely right. If you know your river and its moods, you will know those particular stretches where the blue-winged olive hatches regularly. Be there – and do not move. Do not above all be tempted by rising trout far above you or immediately below you; concentrate on your stretch and fish the rise when it comes.

When I first fished my favourite local river, I was aware that drainage had wrecked it and that while the trout were back, I did not know how many there were. On a July evening of calm sunset I found out. There was a perfect frenzy as they fought to gulp down the blue-winged olives – oddly enough a splendid hatch whose density I have not seen repeated. Their frenzy transmitted itself to me; I miscast, got tangled, caught myself and my rod in the reeds and rushes, fell down the banks, was eaten by midges, put fish down one after the other, pulled the hook out of others and reached that stage of incoherent anger where I would willingly have cried with rage. And not a fish landed.

Contrast this with an evening a season or two ago. I had marked down a rising fish in a narrow run between two banks of tall flags. To reach him, I had to cast my fly some fifteen yards upstream; he lay in about two feet or so of swift water with no more than eighteen inches between the banks of flags. There would be one cast – and it would have to be not just right, but utterly, totally, absolutely right.

It was. The blue-winged olive landed two feet above his nose. The fight was predictable; I bustled him down stream and held him tight in a deep hole at my feet and within a couple of minutes his two-pound weight was in my net. He had not been so much as caught as ambushed.

I find a wonderful satisfaction in such catches, where the set of angling circumstances is largely against the angler. Oddly enough the next outing after that one had a similar result. I decided to fish a stretch of slow running water which was full of pike and perch but which I reasoned must hold a trout or two worth the catching. I walked upstream for two miles or more, over barbed wire fences, through draining ditches, fields of cabbages and corn and saw not a rise. Then, a hundred yards upstream, I saw a fish feeding steadily and intently.

I reconnoitred with great care. He lay in the middle of a wide, smooth stretch of river, just above a dip where the current buckled smoothly over a limestone ledge underwater. So eager was his feeding that his back was frequently out of the water – and what a back! But this was a fiendish cast; I could not wade this deep water and so must put a fly again about fifteen yards up and across into smooth water. My line and part of the leader would fall in faster water and within a yard of landing the fly would drag.

Distance and placing were vital. I lengthened line across the river and put the fly a foot above his head and about six inches to one side. He took with instant confidence and surged right across the river to my bank with tremendous power. But the odds were against him; there was water to spare and I had him on the bank within five minutes. Three pounds two ounces – my best fish from that river. And he was the only fish I saw the entire evening.

I instance these two fish and how they were caught because they are a reflection of how I fish the evening rise today. I mark my fish down and pursue them to the exclusion of others.

Let me tell you another story – against myself. I had marked down two good feeding fish in a little pool and for many evenings had tried to catch them. Such were the vagaries of current that to avoid drag was next to impossible. The technical questions set by the water, the strained way in which I had to stand to cast, and the feeding patterns of the trout themselves made an overall problem of impressive difficulty. And it found me wanting.

And yet this is the sort of problem I most enjoy. I determined to get a least one of these fish. They would feed on the surface for three or four minutes, one three yards behind the other, and then go down. Instantly a trail of bubbles would come to the surface. They were grubbing for shrimps or nymphs in the weeds about three feet down. This would go on for three or four minutes and then they would re-surface to feed on floating fly or nymphal life which they had disturbed underwater. The pattern was always the same, evening after evening.

I was not without some success. Several evenings I pricked one or other of them. The disturbance they made then showed me how big they were. I tried to catch the lower one, figuring that this would not alarm the upper one who must be the bigger by all the standards of trout behaviour. But this lower one lay in such a way that no cast could prevent drag.

The solution I found was to wait until the trout were rising vigor-ously and then by casting short and often, keep the fly on the water even for a foot or two before it dragged. Several times the lower fish rose and missed; and then he came at it determinedly and I had him. He rushed upstream with great strength; but there was in his pulling something which forewarned me. Sure enough he had been hooked in the dorsal fin and at about half a pound, was most assuredly not one of the big fish which had occupied so many of my evenings. And of course the pool was disturbed.

I did, weeks later, catch the upper one who weighed just over two and a half pounds. In the end, a Coachman put on his nose fatally tempted him. But I will long remember the extreme problems both trout set for me.

Niall Fallon, *Fly-fishing for Irish Trout*

A Narrow Shave

Of all the narrow squeaks that ever befell me in angling, about the worst was one which happened yesterday. I had been fishing our big river that was running two feet above its ordinary height, and the water was somewhat too dark for fly, except upon the shallows, where a big Jock Scot or a black and gold of the largest size sometimes scored. Truth to tell, we had several days previously been reduced to the use of big spoons and silver Devon minnows in the bog-coloured water, and had met with but little success.

On the morning of which I am now writing I found myself some half-dozen miles down stream, below my quarters, paddling upwards a small canoe against a powerful current, and trailing a gold spoon from a short salmon-rod, in the wake of the boat. Now I am by no means an expert canoeist, and it soon became apparent to me that I had quite as much as I could do to get the crazy little craft along, without the dead pull of that long line and big spoon over the stern. Just as I was on the point of banking her, to wind up the tackle, there was a tremendous pull on the bait, and the winch flew round at a wild rate. The nose of the canoe was at once grounded, the paddle dropped, and the rod got into fighting position; but the fish had, meantime, shot across to the opposite side of the river, with a hundred yards of line out. Pressing him all that one could safely, some of the bellied line was recovered, and then it became apparent that the fish had found shelter in a leaf-covered branch, about six feet long, that had come down with the flood and got stranded. What was I to do? You cannot paddle a canoe and handle a salmon-rod at one and the same time; and after debating the 'pros' and 'cons' for some minutes, I decided to push off the little canoe and wind her across stream by the salmon-winch. It appeared feasible to me at the time, because the line was firmly fixed on the opposite side, and my utmost strength failed to move the branch to which it was fast. Of course I assumed that the salmon was gone, and that the big spoon had got securely anchored. But my plan did not work out satisfactorily, for no sooner was the boat in the swift current, than she was swept down stream, the strain on the line dragged the branch afloat, and away the whole lot went towards the weir, barely two hundred yards below us! The next few seconds were about as exciting as could well be imagined; for the rod had gone overboard, and was hanging over the side, attached by a lanyard round my waist, and I was paddling frantically for the bank. The nose of the little craft grounded not twenty yards short of the dreaded weir. In less time than it takes to write this description I was on 'terra firma,' with the rod up, and rushing round below the fall to see what had become of that wretched branch. There was the horrid thing, bobbing about close up to the wall of the weir, at times floating out two or three yards, and then being drawn back by the under suction of that seething water. Winding in the line, every inch of which had been run off my reel, I put a steady strain on the offending bough, and eventually got it away down stream. In a shallow shelving bay the bough was stranded, and then, to my great astonishment, I discovered that the salmon was still on! He had got two turns of the treble spinning-trace round a springy branch, which had yielded to his struggles and prevented him getting a direct pull. The salmon was quite dead, and he proved to be a nice bright fish of fifteen pounds, with the sea lice on him. As I had done quite enough boating for one morning, the canoe was hauled up, I tramped home, carrying the rod and fish and all the way it kept running through my head that something very like a fluke had saved me from losing the number of my mess.

C. W. Gedney, *Fishing Holidays*

The Pig

As soon as we heard that the Mayfly was up, those of us who knew left our proper occupations and made for Brophy's Hotel, where Willie, the best of the local fishermen, generally met us to tell us of the big fish. 'I seen the Whale, sorr, him below the Thorn tree, and thim ye call Jones Major and Jones Minor along the straight, and the Pig and all. Tis a grand lot of fly we have this year,' and so on: all the fish had names given by us and Willie adopted them. What is more, he seemed to be able to catch more than we did. He said he only used the artificial fly, like us, and perhaps he spoke the truth. Willie was a sportsman himself and may have resisted the temptation to use the deadly cross line with droppers carrying natural Mayflies, which was the local way of fishing. And, as he was the leading Sinn Feiner (in those days Sinn Fein was not taken seriously), perhaps he prevented the other local fishermen from using it.

The Pig was my pet antagonist. He was so called because he rolled in the water, like a fat pig, when taking his flies. I usually fished for him from the opposite side, for it was easier casting and there was a chance of getting Jones Minor, whose beat came up to the Pig's. Our method of fishing, developed after my experience at Richardstown, was to grease the line and oil the fly well, and then wait till one saw a great nose break the water down-stream. One knew it would appear again and take another fly, about ten yards higher up. So, as soon as the nose in the distance was seen, the fly was cast in to the middle of the stream opposite with plenty of loose line, and one hoped that when the fish reached one's fly he would take it instead of the natural Mayflies that were always slowly drifting with the sluggish current. If he did, one of two things happened. If one had the self restraint to wait till the fish had swallowed the fly, there was a fierce pull, a mad rush down, deep down in to the weeds, and a sickening scrape against the thick stems deep below the surface. Then the cast came back, or some of it, without the fly. If one struck too soon, which was usually the case, there was a wild lashing on top of the water and one's fly flew up and fixed itself in the branches of the 'Sally' trees overhanging the stream. Often had I tried for the Pig and once I had scratched him on his way. Willie had hooked him once, he said, and lost him.

One year it occurred to me to try for the Pig from the near side of the river. On this side there was a dry ditch under a big willow tree about half way up his beat. From this ditch it was quite possible to get the fly onto the water, not casting overhead, for the boughs were too near, but with a sort of underhand switch, as nearly parallel with the ground as might be. There was just room between the willow tree and the next pollard to bring it off, but the high bank and thick vege-tation made it very difficult.

When, after tea, I had fixed myself uncomfortably squatting in the ditch, the Pig was feeding steadily and noisily. How hot I got, drying the fly in that narrow space, catching up perpetually in the sedges and bushes behind, climbing out cautiously (when the Pig had passed) on all fours to undo the fly. Casting again, lifting the fly gingerly when it began to get water-logged, repeating the whole process: while the Pig rolled up and down, snapping at the natural Mayflies but leaving mine untouched.

In daylight all our friends were wary enough and we had to fish with fine gut. But as it grew dark one used to change and put on a sea-trout cast – though it was not advisable to do this too early as it was apt to put them down. On this evening I was so excited I forgot to change my cast as the light failed. It was my undoing. About 9 o'clock the Pig made a mistake and took my fly. There was a tremen-dous pull, the Pig jumped six feet (it seemed to me) in the air. I saw a bar of gold a yard long fly above the lower branches of the 'Sally' tree and fall through with a resounding smack into the water – and that was the last I ever saw of the Pig.

I was down the next weekend and met Willie, who had a twinkle in his eye. He said in his soft Louth burr, so like Northumberland – is the Danish blood responsible for the likeness? – ' I cot the Pig, sorr – he weighed six and a half pound.'

I know I shall never see Ardee again, and that if I did I should be no better able to cope with those great trout – if they are there. Perhaps the new Irish Nation has bombed them all away, and proba-bly there was no other method of making sure of them. But always memory calls up the tall, gaunt Workhouse of Ardee, by which we passed on the way to the river. At irrelevant times it comes before my eyes – when I am shaving, at a dinner party, at a committee meeting. Then I smell again the peat smoke from the last houses of the little town. I see the broad high-road thick with limestone dust and the turning of the little stony boreen under the Workhouse wall by which one reaches the river, and the boggy meadow between the river and the Workhouse. I see again the Mayflies drifting slowly on the dark water, the bubbles left where the trout has gulped one down, my rod point wavering as my hands tremble with excitement while I watch the great nose poking up in leisurely progress towards my waiting fly. And all the while I am conscious that behind me, in the cold, grey light of an Irish May evening, there stands, watching sarcastic and aloof, the grey mass of the Workhouse of Ardee.

Maurice Headlam, *A Holiday Fisherman*

Fishing with Cecil

One day at Derravaragh early in May 1972, before the Mayfly was up (on an average year around the 19th), I saw the top trout man Cecil Gibson all tackled up and ready to go. Asking him if he had a spare twine (excuse) to start my Seagull, he offered to take me with him as his friend had not turned up. This trip turned out to be the most wonderful experience of my life on the lake.

The knowledge he had accumulated over a lifetime of fishing mostly on his beloved Derravaragh was told to me with obvious pleasure. His stories of the good old days before the Office of Public Works devastated the Inny (which flows in and out of Derravaragh) were marvellous. He was the first person to tell me the most closely-guarded secret of those years – when to fish the calm lanes where trout cruise, nymphing on insects unable to break the surface tension and when to give your attention to the sud lanes when different breeds of fly are hatching. It was his opinion at the time (and how right he was) that Derravaragh was on the way out. He could see the signs going up all over the lake but nobody would listen to him. 'Fishing is good today, so what?' was the attitude.

We were not long out of Donore towards Meehans when he boated his first trout of about 1½lbs which he returned to the water. Seeing how surprised I was, he said 'this is a great fishing day and the wind is blowing from the Raa Shore, I hope to catch my bag limit of larger ones than that.' He caught over twenty trout. When he had five 'kept' he really shocked me by the size of trout he was releasing waiting for a big one.

He got the one he was waiting for which brought his bag limit to 6 weighing from 2 ¼ to 5 ¼ lbs. He then turned all his attention to me, taking my three flies off and replacing them with three of his own. I had two trout caught at this time, neither of 2lbs. He showed me the angle to cast at and the correct speed to draw the flies in, which is dictated by the wind and the speed the boat is drifting at. In just over an hour I had my bag limit, one of 4 ¼ lbs.

There was a partition with swing doors in the local pub where he drank after a session on the lake. Cecil's car would pull up outside, and by the time he reached the front bar, the doors would be swinging – the local anglers had scrammed down to the back bar. Very rarely could they match his catch. He was top man OK.

There is an inscription on a rock at the weigh-in at Donore which reads Cecil Gibson 1919 to 1979, recording the number of years he was a member of the Derravaragh. If he were alive now to see the sorry state it is in, it would break his heart.

Jim Reynolds, A Life by the Boyne

Bungling on Belvedere

I had been asked to a supper picnic on Lough Belvedere, and my host suggested we might bring our rods on the off chance of finding a fish cruising for Silverhorns under the trees which line so much of the shore. Not very hopefully – it was August and the rise to big sedges should have been over – I put a box of dry flies in my pocket. There was, I knew, a cast in the lid but I had forgotten that the cast had been made up for small Slaney trout and was 2x tapered to 4x.

No trout were rising so we rowed out to an island for supper and sat on gossiping while the sun sank below the horizon. Just as it did so my host pointed to a patch of the lake about a quarter of a mile away and said, 'What on earth is that?' I looked. In a small area not more than three hundred yards square the trout were wallowing like pigs. In the rush, I had not even the sense to cut away the finer portions of my cast. When we arrived at the area of activity (it had shifted several hundred yards further while we made our preparations) we found it criss-crossed in every direction by the lines of immense fish swimming under water, coming up now and then to slash at the scuttering sedges. Trout often take a moving sedge with a bang. These trout took like runaway railway trains. I was broken four times in rapid succession by fish not one of which looked to be under five pounds. When I tried to fish with a free reel the barb of the big hook did not go home and the fish kicked off. Still I never thought of cutting down my cast to three feet which would have been quite sufficient in the growing dark. My companion, with a strong cast, was broken at least once but got a fish of over four pounds, while I did not land a single one. It was a quite ghastly bit of bungling.

T.H. Kingsmill Moore, *A Man May Fish*

A Day on Owel

Lough Owel bears little resemblance to her sisters, being surrounded by shores far more bold, broken and bare. Lying in a vast rocky basin, composed probably of limestone, its clearness and purity are remarkable. Over its entire surface myriads of bubbles rise from unknown springs, and, in fact, the lake is one vast fountain of delicious water. This, combined probably with the clean bottom, gives the trout the peculiarly silvery character that distinguishes them from all others with which I am acquainted. We found our boat drawn up on the south-east corner, near a circular fairy-like island, planted with larch and flowering shrubs, and, launching, pulled for the western side, in order to make our first drift towards a high headland on the opposite side.

Lough Owel was a special favourite with Willie, being, as he said, 'a place where a fish in earnest might be killed,' so I gave him a day; nor was it long before his line was sailing gracefully, far in advance of our humble bark. Here and there, at long intervals, the small circling eddy of some rising fish was seen as we glided on; but nothing came in our way till within two or three hundred yards of the rocky shore, when a trout sailed up, dexterously sucked off my fly, and disappeared. There was a momentary glimpse of a very broad tail. 'Out with the paddles, and over him again' but before the words were uttered, the folly of the order became apparent. The first dip of the oar would have driven the fish from his ground, so the boat was allowed to float silently on; accurate marks were taken, and on reaching the cliff, we pulled cautiously along its base before again taking our station far above the spot where the charming vision faded from our eyes. Every moment made me feel more and more certain of being in the exact line. Now the fly must be within five yards of the place – now within two – now within one. Can we have passed him? There is the smallest conceivable rise – a backward motion of the rod, and such a swirl! 'He's got what he won't get rid of easily. That's fine! Och, but that's beautiful! Ah, master! sure there's nothing like this in ould Ireland, any way at all.'

Thus spoke my faithful servant, instinctively charging his pipe, whilst a faint smile stole over his honest and sober face. Now rooting at the bottom, now rolling over the surface, again and again flying as if life depended on his speed, what a gallant fish it was! Little by little his efforts grew more laborious and less effective. Presently the broad tail which led to his destruction, scarcely possessed the power to keep that small head under water. More faintly still he fluttered from the fatal net, now it is over; nature can do no more, and like a log he is drawn slowly and steadily towards the boat; another foot and he is safe and on board. I would have walked all the way from Dublin for that one fish. 'Ten pounds and a quarter! No, not quite a quarter (our clerk of weights and measures was very precise) call him ten pounds lucky. That's something like a trout.'

Over and over again the same course was tried, in the hope of meeting another of the same class, but in vain. At length we resigned it reluctantly, and commenced a fresh drift over the broadest part of the lake in a line with Church Island. Half way down the shore of that low rocky reef a good fish rose right ahead. Slowly the fly sailed straight towards him. 'What's that?' My first thought was that Willie, who just before was sitting on the gunwale, had tumbled head-over-heels into the water. But no; there he sat, composed as ever. 'He's an awful monster, master; as big as a salmon.' To jerk the line out, reel sharply up, so as to ensure my companion fair play, was but the work of an instant. Had it not been for that startling plunge he might have been fast in a rock for anything I could see to the contrary. Fish have temperaments various as their captors; they are shy, bold, cowardly, volatile, sulky, or determined, and the one now under treatment combined the latter qualities in about equal proportions.

For a full hour we saw nothing of him, and all this time had been drifting deeper into the rocky and shallow bay beyond the island. 'Pull, pull, I'm fast! he's sat down. Oh dear, oh dear! what will I do? Pull, pull for your lives!' A few dashing strokes brought the boat over the exhausted monster; the line was free, and the battle over. There he lay on the bottom, with his great side leaning against the rock that refused him shelter. The water was barely 5ft deep; off went the net, on went the gaff, and then we found leisure to admire our prize. Perfect in make, exquisite in harmony of colour, in weight 13lb – truly he was a picture; glorious in life, beautiful in death, it may be long before his fellow is hung with such a thread. As may be imagined, all that occurred subsequently was tame. Two more, however, of 3lb and 5lb wound up the best day I ever saw with the blow line.

W. Peard, *A Year of Liberty*

Filling the Boat

With his account of one such day let me end this chapter. It came during high water in August eight or nine years ago. Patsey (who is a painter by trade) was professionally engaged at the Grey House (of which you will read later), and on this particular morning was crossing the lake to resume his painting. Of course he had his rod along with him; when had he not? As he crossed the big shallow he saw a trout feeding. He stopped, backed to the spot he had marked, and at the very first cast hooked and killed a nice fish. By the time he had come to the house he had four trout in the boat.

As he went through the stable-yard he met the master. 'Did you see any rises as you came over, Patsey?' 'I did, sir, and fine ones. Sure I killed four, they're below in the boat.' They went to see them.

'It looks like a good day; what do you think, Patsey?' 'Devil a finer, sir, have I seen these last five years; the water is an elegant colour.' They looked out over the lake. 'Never mind the painting, I'll get my rod.' They came in for lunch; duties prevented them from resuming sport for some further time, and they had to come in before dinner.

But in the short time they were on the water they took between thirty and forty trout, not one of which was under one and three-quarter pounds. As it was, Patsey lamented the time wasted, and he has never ceased to regret that I had not been his companion on that great day. 'Faith, you'd ha'filled the boat – and the Master fishing with a hook broke at the barb!'

F. D. Barker, An Angler's Paradise

August on the Suir

The next reminiscence goes back to about 1880, and has to do with a river in Ireland. The first time I saw this river was late in August. There were said to be trout, and good ones, and it was believed to be possible to catch some with fly earlier in the season, when the water was in order. The river had in parts a very wide bed, which when low it did not nearly fill. The water ran in all sorts of channels between beds of bright green weeds. Here and there was a long stream with a stony bottom, free from weeds, and now and then there would be a huge pool, full of peaty-coloured water of unknown depth, in which one or two salmon lay. One could wander for miles all day about the most extraordinary variety of water. The river was full of pike, and it was said, probably with truth, that the inhabitants of the district forked trout out of the weeds in low water with various agricultural implements. But there were trout enough for dry fly fishing. Half a dozen or so might be found rising near together, and then perhaps one would have to go several hundred yards before another one was found; a little sound would be heard presently, as if a small pebble had dropped in somewhere without a splash, and heard perhaps two or three times before the rise could be seen in such a large and curious river. Then there was a difficult stalk, probably through water and weeds, with the chance of going overhead into a big hole unawares.

I was warned that at this season of the year, when the water was low, I must not expect to catch any of these fish, but I cared nothing for warnings. The trout were there, and were rising, and though I saw at once that it was a case for dry fly and for that only, I had by this time been taught to believe that anyone who could catch Winchester trout, could catch rising trout anywhere. These trout, however, at first upset my calculations. They brought me face to face with a difficulty which did not exist on the ticket water at Winchester – they were unapproachable. Never was an angler more put upon his mettle. There were trout visibly and audibly rising, which had never seen an artificial dry fly, and would probably take it at once. They were evidently also big trout. There was splendid sport to be had, and reputation and glory to be won in catching even one of them, and yet so shy were they, that I could not get my dry fly to them.

For two days they defeated me utterly. I walked and knelt and waded and laboured and perspired under an August sun without success. Some of the trout were put down by my approach, some were scared by the first waving of the rod, and some, which had been successfully stalked, turned tail and fled when the gut floated over them without even the least drag; at last, on the second evening in a fading light, I hooked a fish which went off up stream at once with a mighty rush, and came to rest somewhere out of sight at the end of a lot of line. I waded carefully up in the twilight, keeping a tight line by reeling up as I went till I was over a great bed of strong weeds. Into this one hand carefully felt its way along the casting line, and touched at last the side of a great fish. Nothing could be seen for it was getting dark, and the weeds were too thick for a landing net to be used in them. I tried with one hand to arrange a grip on the trout, and very broad and hard he felt; but at the critical moment he made the most violent commotion in the weeds and dashed off somewhere.

When all was still I felt again and found in the weeds only the end of broken gut. There was nothing more to be done that evening, and I waded out and lay on the bank in the dusk. On the whole, I think that was the bitterest moment I have ever known in angling. To have come so near to success, and to have it snatched from me at the last moment, after keenness and effort had been sustained at the very highest pitch for two whole days, was more than could be borne.

But success did come afterwards, and in broad daylight; I found a place where, by wading and kneeling in the river on the shallow side, it was possible to get within reach of and opposite to rising trout without frightening them. Then the fly could be thrown some way above them with an underhand cast, so as not to show the rod; and being opposite and not below, I could let the fly float down a few inches on the near side of a rising trout, so that only the fly and none of the gut was seen. In this way I at last caught one or two trout, and then somehow, when the frost of failure had once broken up, it seemed more easy to succeed all over the river.

These trout were the shyest I have ever known. They were more difficult to approach and more easily scared by rod or gut than any others I ever fished for; but if the fly could be floated to a rising fish without frightening it, the fly was generally taken. On the best day that I had there I caught eleven fish. None of these weighed three pounds, but the first two were each over two and three-quarters. For such shy fish really fine gut had to be used, and there were many disasters in the weeds, but also many splendid struggles fought out in pools which were far too deep for any vegetation. It was the wildest and most exciting and most fascinating dry fly fishing that I have ever had. My experience of it has only been during late August or early September, but I can imagine that in May and June it might be the finest dry fly fishing in the United Kingdom.

Sir Edward Grey, *Fly Fishing*

The Sabbath Day

Once in the north of Ireland, when a very young man, I ventured after the time of divine service to put together my rods, as I had been used to do in the Catholic districts of Ireland, and fish for sea trout in the river at Rathmelton, in pure innocence of heart, unconscious of wrong, when I found a crowd collect round me – at first I thought from mere curiosity, but I soon discovered I was mistaken; anger was their motive, and vengeance their object.

A man soon came up, exceedingly drunk, and began to abuse me by various indecent terms: such as a Sabbath breaking papist, etc. It was in vain I assured him I was no papist and no intentional Sabbath breaker; he seized my rod and carried it off with imprecations; and it was only with great difficulty, and in exciting by my eloquence the pity of some women who were present, and who thought I was an ill-used stranger, that I recovered my property.

Sir Humphrey Davy, Salmonia

A Gillie Hooked

Pat did a very plucky thing on one occasion. There were several boats out, but nobody had killed a fish, although there were plenty of them in the water. We had been flogging away the greater part of the day, but the 'divil a tail we saw,' it was getting towards evening and the other boats were moving homewards over to Garrison. I proposed doing likewise, but Pat would not hear of it. 'Wait, yer honner, till they do be all away home and the sun down behind the Dartrey hills, shure didn't I see a big fish rolling last evening when the sun was off the water, in there betune where the two rivers run in to the lough and he'll not be far away this same evening.' And right Pat was; we dropped down very quietly over the spot as the last boat rounded Ross Point and nobody was witness to what happened.

I had a golden olive fly on the tail and a 'Lough Gill' on the drop, and up he came directly we reached the lodge, making a tremendous ring where his tail hit the water going down. 'In him' right enough, and the 'Golden Olive' had done the trick; he was a sporting fish and fought hard, but his runs were getting shorter and his jumps fewer. Gradually he came nearer and nearer, the gaff was in Pat's right hand with his left hand resting on the stern of the boat, nicely balanced to deliver the stroke. Suddenly the fish made a terrific plunge right under the boat and dragged the dropper on to poor Pat's hand – the hook entered the fleshy part between the thumb and finger! It all happened like a flash. Pat never flinched. There was only one way, he seized the hook and literally tore it away from the flesh, and there seemed to be at least six inches of stretched skin before the hold gave way. It was a horrible sight and must have caused poor Pat great pain, but he did not seem to feel any; it was soon all over, another plunge and the steel went truly home and a beautiful fresh twelve pounder lay on the boards at the bottom of the boat. We felt very proud as we paddled across to Garrison. The evening was closing in rapidly, but there was still enough light to show to all the anglers collected on the bridge that we had a clean bright fish. We had to answer all sorts of questions as to where we got him, what fly, etc., all the boatmen very jealous, or 'Was it on the troll I got him?' (we were not allowed to troll inside Rossinver Bay), 'or maybe it was a prawn yer honner had on,' etc, etc. The fish was much admired, but no one believed I got it by fair casting.

S.B. Wilkinson, *Reminiscences of Sport in Ireland*

A Blast at Reilly's

To reach Reilly's you have to climb through a fence and then walk up a little over a quarter of a mile, under a picturesque farm set on a knoll and through a clump of trees awkward to negotiate with two big rods on your shoulder.

This stream, though neither long nor deep, is very pleasant to fish.

The green bank on which you stand with your left shoulder towards the river is just the right height. The stream runs fairly fast with a sort of all-over ripple, and the bottom is of gravel and round stones. A fly is best in it, and the lower you go the further out you must cast, but your fly must swing right in under your own bank. For here there are three taking spots, and a most convenient line of bushes prevents your being seen.

It is best in pretty high water, and at one of my lucky spots, and if it was not so far away we should fish it more often. I once had a rather alarming experience there, which is what I really set out to describe when I began. Dick was fishing Gowra, and as the river was in good order for it, I tramped up to give Reilly's a try.

As I came out through the clump of trees and through the bramble brake on to the bank, I saw two men working in a small quarry which lies back about twenty yards from the river.

I passed the time of day with them and then began to fish. I remember I had up a small double-hooked Thunder-and-Lightning – I suppose the strain of subsequent anxiety impressed it on my mind.

At about the sixth cast I hooked an extremely lively fish, and at the same time one of the men shouted.

I thought for a moment it was merely his excitement at seeing a fish hooked. But he shouted again, evidently trying to attract my attention. I was annoyed, for what with the noise of the river, and my concentration on the antics of the fish, it was extremely difficult to hear. Realizing this, he strolled towards me, and what he said made me sit up.

'Listen now, Sorr,' he said. 'Tim here thinks you should know 'tis half an hour now since we put in a blasting charge and the bloody thing's hanging fire.' It was all delightfully casual. 'It might go off any time now,' he added, 'or of course it might not. There's no knowing, but I think we have it fixed.'

'Will I be all right here?' I asked with my head over my shoulder, and all the time hanging on to the fish, which had made an excursion across the river and was now trying to go down stream.

'Indeed an' you will not then,' he replied. 'The last time it threw boulders every way as big as your head; you can see some of them now on the grass beside you'; and with that they both made off into safety.

Here was a nice predicament. I could not give up the salmon. The only thing was to find what shelter I could.

Luckily the fish was pretty quiet at the moment, so I sat down on the edge of the bank and slithered into the water, which came up higher than I expected on my waders, and edged down stream, stooping as low as I could under the bank, with the knowledge that one false step would plunge me into deep water.

All the time I was playing the fish as best I could in my cramped position, and all the time half my mind was on that 'blasted' or rather unblasted quarry.

Then the fish again ran well out into the stream, and came round in a curve till he was directly below me.

That suited me in one way, as it meant that as I followed him I should gradually get more out of the direct line of fire, and nearer the protection of some big trees and bushes which grew thickly on the bank.

He was now in a sort of backwater, but still dropping down stream. If once he got into the strong current near the sheltering trees he would go right away from me and it was too deep to follow. I therefore held him hard, and still stooping low hurried down with the current, reeling myself up to him as it were as I went. The last bit I almost ran, if it could be called running in such deep water.

By holding my rod bent nearly double over my shoulder I was now just within reach. My long gaff was ready in my hand. Putting on all the strain I could, I held him stationary for a moment, and pulled it home, just as the strong water was beginning to lift my feet.

Somehow I struggled to the bank; somehow through brambles, thorns, and bushes I heaved myself, my rod and the fish out, and with it still on the gaff fairly ran through the trees until I felt safe.

The explosion did not take place till ten o'clock that night. But 'sure there was no knowing.'

G.D. Luard, *Fishing Fortunes and Misfortunes*

Black and Tans

Though Clarke's Water had, nearly all of it, those low banks which are so pleasant for dry-fly fishing, there was a deep high-banked stretch below where the local anglers extracted enormous trout with the natural mayfly dapped – often, I understood, cross-lining. At the top of this stretch there ran in a tributary, the Clodiagh, on which 'Arny' FitzHerbert (who had made the record bag of wood-pigeons, at Lord de Vesci's at Abbeyleix where his father was agent) had once caught, in mayfly time, eight three-pounders in one day.

At my last visit to Graiguenoe in 1921, after I had officially left Ireland, I determined to try this lower water if the mayfly was well up. The country was in a very disturbed state. I travelled to Thurles with Sir Charles Barrington who lived near Limerick, and we talked fishing. Afterwards I heard that, when he reached home, he found that his daughter had been murdered by Sinn Feiners on her way to a tennis party.

When I arrived at Graiguenoe I was told that bullets had been passing over the house all day: the Sinn Feiners were attacking the police barracks on the hill behind the house. I thought that the river would be the safest place, so at once put on my waders, in order to be below the line of fire. I had always fished alone, but several anglers had been kidnapped by Sinn Feiners and this time I took with me a small boy to carry my bag; I thought that, if the same thing happened to me, there would be someone who would be able to convey news of the incident. When we got to the lower river there was little or no fly, and no rise, either in the main river, or the Clodiagh. But I met a party of men with brand-new bandoleers and rifles though little other attempt at uniform. I was crossing the river at the time, with the small boy on my back, and shouted a greeting, thinking they were the 'Black and Tans' about whom certain circles in London were getting up an agitation. They answered civilly enough and walked on. When I got back to Graiguenoe I was told that they were not Black and Tans but the Sinn Fein patrol come down from the mountains, and that I was lucky not to have been shot or taken prisoner.

I never saw Graiguenoe again, for it was burned down shortly afterwards, happily when the Clarkes were away.

Maurice Headlam, *Irish Reminiscences*

Iar Connaught

High in the upland of Iar Connaught lies a small lake which communicates with the main river by a bog stream often less than a foot wide and half buried under coarse grass. White trout find their way up this runnel and into the lake which is mostly unfishable because of a growth of rushes spearing up from the bottom, sometimes dense, sometimes sparse, but always sufficiently close together to prevent any working of a fly. At one spot however a canal of open water, about 12 yards wide, stretches out from the shore and then turns sharply to the left. In shape this clear area is that of an inverted capital L the long arm being about 35 yards and the short arm about 15. At the shore end a big granite boulder, about six feet high but climbable, provides a casting platform.

Usually a white trout or two could be picked up here, mostly herling not exceeding a pound in weight. But this fish was no herling. It took some ten yards from shore and without a second's delay shot off for the far end of the canal. A biggish white trout is away the moment he is hooked and the first twenty yards of his dash is just one electric streak. My fish made straight for the rushes that rose like a wall at the far end of the open water canal. If he reached them he was safe. If I tried to stop him too brusquely there was the probability of a break. Very gentle checking slowed him perceptibly but he showed no sign of stopping. When he was two yards from the rushes I took a chance and clamped my finger on the reel plate.

Only two yards to go! He fought relentlessly to gain his asylum while I held on not giving an inch. It must have been two minutes or more before the strain suddenly relaxed and I was able to recover a few yards of line. But now he was off up the shorter left arm of the open water putting a long stretch of rush studded water between us. Owing to the height of the boulder on which I was standing it was possible to keep line and cast above the rushes which were not very tall, but there seemed no way by which to bring him back into the main canal.

I examined the area of rushes. Yes, there was one place where they grew more sparsely. A tired fish might, with luck, be skull-hauled, head above water through the obstacles and back into the long arm, but the problem was how to keep him in open water till he was sufficiently exhausted to make the experiment worth trying. If he chose to run towards me and into the near rushes he would be free in a few seconds. Luck was with me for, by keeping a steady strain I ensured that he would pull against the strain and towards the further fringes of the rushes. A series of short spurts varied by jumps further wearied him. Now he was opposite the sparse area of rushes and the attempt must be made. The first stage was to get his head above water which meant lowering my rod top as much as possible without fouling the line and then raising it to its full extension with my hand high above my head. Good, he was showing on the surface. Now it was a question of stripping in the line so rapidly that he became bewildered and for the moment ceased resistance, all the while steering him away from the denser growth. More than once the dropper touched projecting spikes but did not take hold and now, at last, he was in the main arm and completely under control. I could see him clearly, a fresh run fish of between three and four pounds. At the base of my boulder crouched the ghillie, a young man of 18 already an expert boatman and trained to net a fish by keeping the net well sunk in the water till the fish was drawn over it. I glanced down. There was the net a foot below the surface. In came the fish unresisting in a steady glide till at the last moment he saw me, checked and made to turn back. It was too much for my ghillie who took a step into the water and scooped wildly. The fish balanced on the edge of the net half in and half out, fell back catching the dropper in the rushes, and was gone.

The lesson is to net your fish yourself and this normally I would have done, but for the difficulty of climbing down from the six foot high boulder with a fish at the end of the line. The second lesson is never, never, allow your ghillie to scoop at a fish. Some boatmen are expert at landing a fish in this way but it is always more risky than allowing the angler to draw the fish well over the net and then raise it steadily.

T. H. Kingsmill Moore, *A Man May Fish*

140

In the Wet

It was one day on the river, good for nothing except butterflies or bathing, not a breath of air, and everything looked like copper, the river reflecting this tint looked more like red oil than water as it passed from pool to pool; my ghillie, Terry O'G., agreed with me that it was useless to attempt fishing. I had been some time sitting up on the shaded bank at Moss Row smoking and dreaming and thinking of the fine clean fish that Dr Peard describes as having killed on this throw in his Year of Liberty. I was asleep when my ghillie took up the rod and went down the few feet to the water.

'What in the world are you going to do, Terry?'

'Well, yer honour, sorra fish you'll ever get wid yer fly on dry land.'

'True for you, Terry. You fish and I will eat my sandwiches.' There was something about the fly that Terry did not like, and he sat down to choose another. By the time he had pleased himself I had finished and was thinking of something to wash down the sandwiches and cake when up came the head waterkeeper. We commenced to chat. Terry had waded out and was fishing very carefully, the fly falling on the oily surface as lightly as a feather, about ten feet below where we were fishing. Suddenly I noticed a displacement of the water, not broken, nor a sign of a rise, but an almost imperceptible bulging of the water. I shouted to Terry that he had moved a fish, and the waterkeeper agreed. Terry had seen nothing; he was too near the water's level, so we shouted to him to draw in his line by hand. He now began to fish the throw again, letting out a little by degrees; now the last yard had gone out and the fly was at the same spot where we thought the fish had moved. Up went Terry's rod, and he was into our friend. He had taken the fly deep in the water so we could not form even an idea as to size. It's a horrible bit of wading, big blocks of rock and deep holes. I would not go down until I had finished my pipe. Terry was roaring for help, still I did not go till at last his cries became so piteous that the waterkeeper said he would go out of his mind if I did not take the rod. I took in as much as I could of my waders with the belt round my waist in case of a dip, and went down into the water with the gaff. I took the rod from Terry, giving the gaff to him in exchange. The fish felt light to me, and Terry when asked agreed that it was not very large. I proceeded to lead the fish up to the limestone flag, and I had then to get over a low wall. For over a hundred yards he had been perfectly quiet, leading along without the slightest objection.

'Keep down a bit, Terry, and I will try and swing him into you.'

The words were hardly out of my mouth when this supposed small one of little account had turned round and the pace that we had to keep at, first on the flag, after that through the bad part, I never remember anything faster. We had no means of telling the pace, but it was very considerably faster than I had ever to follow a fish before. I looked for a pause at the lodge where he was hooked, but no, on he went, and I was very nearly out of line. If I could only make the little grassy bank at the end of the wood I would be all right. Alas, here it was that Terry let me down badly. I had tripped several times, but had been steadied by him; but now, not only did he fail to hold me up, but fell on the top of me! I kept the point of my rod pointing upwards, and made desperate efforts to get up, using – well, we will call it language – at Terry, he calling on every Saint in the calendar, the water pouring down my neck and into my waders. I made one last heave and flung Terry off me, and a still further effort and I had reached the grassy bank. Terry was only a second or two behind; we soon had all the bagging line reeled up and found our fish gone over to the south bank and rather higher up than we were, about eighty yards away. It was a big job he had given us; we could not get right across, so had to keep bullying him and not give him time to lie down; we kept moving him by slow degrees and took advantage of any spot that we could wade. I had very nearly had enough to it and would willingly have been rid of the brute: it must have been over two hours the fight had lasted. He was still fighting well, but I noticed his runs were not made with such vigour, and yet I thought it hopeless that we should ever be able to get him over to us; then by some lucky manoeuvre he had crossed into a stream that brought him to our side again! Now there was hope. I had him nearer, and presently under the point of my rod and never let him get very far away again. The end was getting nearer; he had already been on his side; Terry was down below watching for his chance; nearer, no not quite; he had floundered out again, evidently not liking the look of Terry; again he turned on his side, and I was able to give Terry another chance and he took it well, walking out of the water with the fish on the gaff and with a tight hold of his tail to stop his wiggling; a crack on his snout ended a terrific fight. He was a red fish in good condition with a big crummogue already indenting his upper jaw. Weight: twenty-three pounds. An excellent kipper. We produced the flask and each had a good three fingers, and deserved them. Tell that to the prohibitionists! The waterkeeper said when it was all over that it was as good as going to prayers to listen to Terry calling on the Saints. All the same, we might very easily have been drowned in that horrible bit of wading.

S.B. Wilkinson, *Reminiscences of Sport in Ireland*

PART TWO: COARSE FISHING

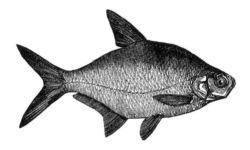

The Sporting Pike

As I consider it perfectly meritorious to destroy these fierce and destructive animals in every practicable way, except by nets, I propose giving the result of my experience, though I cannot say it is a kind of fishing I like. If you fish with frogs, kill them; and this is no easy matter, as you must knock them often against a stone before they are dead: have the fear of Lord Byron before your eyes, and don't hold the frog as if 'you had loved him,' but instantly put him out of pain.

The small trout, the roach, the salmon-fry, a small herring, the tail of an eel spangled and tinselled, are excellent; so is a small jack, and sometimes a good sized one; so is a gold-finch, a swallow or yellow-hammer. My method of putting up a fry, or small trout, or roach, is to have the hook come out in the middle of its side with a curve in the tail to spin. The head (when I was intent on real destruction) I fastened with another hook let slip down on the wire, or gimp, with a very small loop well armed, and this latter hook came out through the back part of the head. I have often taken more pike, and even trout, with the upper hook than the lower; for fish of prey generally make at the head. David Burke's method of catching pike was curious: he fished with a double hook, without swivel – put his chain through the fish's mouth, and drew it out at the navel – tied the chain about the tail, and left the double hook projecting through the mouth of the trout, or fry, or frog. In this way the bait was dragged tail-foremost; but he did not care, and laughed at any other method, and he always killed a great number of pike, and sometimes an odd salmon or so. He left the bait a very short time to any fish, and generally had him well hooked. This should seem an unnatural method, but it is a sure one.

They are a very whimsical fish, and the kind of bait must be frequently changed. I have often shot a pretty small bird for a bait, and killed large pike with it, when they would not look at trout or roach. A good-sized pike fly is often very good. The largest pike I ever killed was thirty two pounds weight; he had a trout of four pounds entire in his maw, which he must have taken only just before he had made at a small roach which I had on a single brass wire; and it must have been from sheer wantonness, or sport, that he seized it: he was only three feet four inches in length, but as thick as a salmon. Colonel R.G. Hare (who could not go with me that day to Dromore, but walked more than a mile to meet me) was astonished at him. Both of us guessed him at forty pounds, but he only weighed thirty-two pounds.

A pike which I had hold of on Lough Tedane, and lost (he having swallowed the chain and cut the line) was afterwards found dead and unsound; and the man who found him, and gave me back the hook, declared that he measured five feet eight inches, and was thick in proportion. Whether he told truth or not, I can't say. I have already given an instance of the rapacity of a pike in laying hold on a trout of more than six pound weight, which the late Master of the Rolls, Sir M. O'Loghlen, had on a cross-line; but this was a trifle to what I witnessed on Dromore. A large pike was hooked, and nearly exhausted, when he was suddenly seized and carried to the bottom. Every effort was made for nearly half an hour to bring this enormous fish to some shore (where we might perhaps have induced him to take a large roach) but to no purpose; when, finding our efforts unavailing, we succeeded at last, by making a noise with the oars, and pulling at the line. In getting up the pike we had been playing, it was all torn as if by a large dog; and this pike actually weighed *seventeen pounds*! The fish which held him so long must have been a monster, indeed!

The best time for catching these rapacious devils is the morning; and if hazy with little wind, so much the better. I mean on the lakes: for pike-fishing, a river without a boat is slavish and disagreeable work. The pike of Clare are very fine: the best way of dressing them is first to boil, and let cool; bone them quite clear – stew them after-wards with catsup, butter, a little red pepper, and a blade or two of mace; thus dressed, they prove a wholesome and safe fish to eat.*

Beware of thrusting your fingers between the grinders of a pike; they are dreadful even in death, and bite desperately. Have by you a short sharp stick, pointed at both ends, before you attempt to take out the hook. I always hold against a pike, and strike in a short time. As to bladders, trimmers, fishing with baits tied to the legs of geese etc, of all such I shall say nothing. I am for the rod and the sport.

O' Gorman, *The Practice of Angling*

* The late Doctor Edward McGrath, a kind and most experienced physician, an excellent friend and an accomplished orator, considered pike, eaten fresh, the very best possible description of fish, and the safest to eat.

Wondrous Tales

Wishing to vary my route back to Limerick, I took a car from Killaloe to Broadfield, a distance of ten miles on a bad mountain road, and not very picturesque. The latter is a very poor village, where I established myself for the day in a moderate country inn. Near it are some celebrated slate quarries; but my chief inducement in visiting it was to inspect two lakes, very celebrated for the enormous pike they contain.

They are situated rather more than a mile from the village, and are connected together by a short deep channel; their entire circuit may be about four miles. The shores are flat, the water dark, with an abundance of rushes and weeds; in fact, it is just the very place for pike, of which there are said to be an abundance of extraordinary size. Wondrous tales are, indeed, told of a monster killed some years ago which weighed ninety-six pounds! And, not long since, a man of the name of Crowe, who constantly fishes the lake, did really kill one forty-five pounds in weight. Crowe and I, however, carefully fished round both the lakes, without succeeding in rousing any of these Leviathans; I had only two runs of small pike, which both escaped.

By the way, I saw here great quantities of bream, which I had always understood not to exist in Ireland. The lakes, however, of this neighbourhood are full of them; and immense numbers are taken both by the rod and nets. There are, at any rate, I believe, no minnows in the Irish streams, nor moles among its animals, nor nightingales among its birds, any more than snakes among its reptiles.

Cosmopolite, *The Angler in Ireland*

No Unusual Event

In a country whose surface is covered with numerous and extensive sheets of water like Mayo, it may be considered that the angler will find ample occupation. Independently of salmon and trout fishing, to those who will employ themselves in killing pike and perch, the lakes and rivers here offer superior amusement. In the greater waters, Lough Mask, Lough Carra and Lough Conn, the coarser species of fishes are taken in immense numbers, and in the lesser lakes many interesting varieties of the trout tribe will be found, from the little speckled samlet to the large and curious gilaroo.

It is true, that the scientific angler generally confines himself to the use of the fly, and for salmon and trout, he will forego the commoner department of bait and float fishing. Hence, angling for pike and perch is usually an amusement of the peasantry; and to those contiguous to the banks of the large lakes, it yields occupation for idle hours, which might be less innocently dissipated, and occasionally supplies their families with a welcome addition to their unvarying food, the potato.

Besides the established system of bait-fishing, other and more successful methods are resorted to by the lake-fishers. By mesh-nets immense numbers of pike are annually taken; and with night-lines, and a very simple contrivance called the pooka, these fish, with the largest trout and perch, are constantly killed.

This latter implement is formed of a piece of flat board, having a little mast and sail erected on it. Its use is to carry out the extremity of a long line of considerable stoutness, to which, at regulated distances, an infinity of droppers or links are suspended, each armed with a hook and bait. Corks are affixed to the principal line or back, to keep it buoyant on the surface; and from a weather-shore, if there be a tolerable breeze, any quantity of hooks and baits can be floated easily across the water. The corks indicate to the fishermen when a fish is on the dropper, and in a small punt or curragh, he attends to remove the spoil and renew the baits when necessary. Two hundred hooks may be used on the same line, and the pooka at times affords much amusement, and often a well filled pannier.

There are no waters in Great Britain, with the exceptions of the river Shannon, where larger pike* are caught than those taken in Loughs Mask and Corrib. It would appear, that in these lakes the fish are commensurate to the waters they inhabit. It is no unusual event for pikes of thirty pounds weight to be sent to their landlords by the tenants; and fish of even fifty pounds have not infrequently been caught with nets and night-lines. The trout in those loughs are also immensely large. From five to fifteen pounds is no unusual size, and some have been found that have reached the enormous weight of thirty. The perch tribe appear the smallest in the scale of relative proportion. These seldom exceed a herring size; but they, too, have exceptions, and perch of three or four pounds weight have been

---

* About seventeen years since, when visiting the late Marquis of Clanricarde, at Portumna Castle, two gentlemen brought to the marquis an immense pike, which they had just caught in the river Shannon, on the banks of which they had been taking their evening walk. Attracted by a noise and splashing of the water, they discovered in a little creek a number of perch driven on shore, and a fish, which, in pursuit of them, had so entangled himself with the ground, as to have a great part of his body exposed, and out of the water. They attacked him with an oar, that by accident lay on the bank, and killed him. Never having seen any fish of this species so large, they judged it worth the observation of the marquis, who, equally surprised at its magnitude, had it weighed, and to our astonishment it exceeded the balance at ninety-two pounds; its length was such, that when carried across the oar by the two gentlemen, who were neither of them short, the head and tail touched the ground.

sometimes seen. Within fifty years, this latter fish has increased prodigiously, and, in the lakes and rivers where they abound, trout have been found to diminish in an equal ratio. If any doubt remained touching the fecundity of the perch, some of the Mayo waters would prove it satisfactorily. Half a century since, I have been assured that pike and perch were almost unknown in the rivers of Belcarra and Minola, and the chain of lakes with which they communicate, and that these waters were then second to none for trout fishing. Within ten years, my cousin tells me that he often angled in them, and that he frequently killed from three to six dozen of beautiful middle-sized red trout. Now fly fishing is seldom practised there. The trout is nearly extinct, and quantities of pike and perch infest every pool and stream. The simplest methods of taking fish will be here found successful, and the lakes of Westmeath will soon be rivalled by the loughs of Mayo.

Mr Young mentions that, at Packenham, Lord Longford informed him, respecting the quantities of fish in the lakes in his neighbourhood, that the perch were so numerous, that a child with a packthread and a crooked pin would catch enough in an hour for the daily use of a whole family, and that his Lordship had seen five hundred children fishing at the same time; that, besides perch, the lake produced pike five feet long, and trout of ten pound each.

W. H. Maxwell, *Wild Sports of the West*

An Enormous Pike

To the Editor [of the *Limerick Chronicle*].

Sir, As the following may not be uninteresting to some of your readers please insert it.

Mr Patrick Sheehy and Mr John Norton trolling for pike near Derry Castle, on Lough Derg, on Friday last, became entangled (as they thought) in a rock. It blowing at the time a very stiff breeze, on letting the cot drift back, to get their line clear, they were surprised by a pull, which nearly took the rod from Mr Norton's hand, and at the same time took all the wheel-line they had, which was about 30 yards. After all the line being run out, they were obliged to pull the cot in the direction the fish took, which happened, fortunately, to be with the wind. After two hours hard work, sometimes pulling after him, and at other times coming within a few yards of him, they succeeded in getting him into shallow water, when they both jumped out, and brought to land the largest pike, I believe, ever taken in this lake; his weight being 90½lb; his length was 5ft 8in. The bait he took is a common brass shoe-lift.

Hoping I have not trespassed too much on your space,

I remain respectfully yours,

John Sheehy

The Limerick Chronicle, 13th May 1862

[Fred Buller believes this report to be factual. I see no reason to disbelieve him – TF]

The First 20 Pounder

I had taken over with me to Ireland that year a large-mouthed glass bottle containing spirits of wine, in which was pickled a few dozens of Thames bleak and gudgeon. They had been some years in the spirit and were shrivelled, but the bleak, which had turned yellow and had lost all their silveryness, proved a far more deadly bait for pike and trout than the most gorgeous of artistic artificials. I used to spin them on a Chapman Spinner, for by no possibility could they have been put on any other form of spinning tackle. It was with one of these mummified Thames bleak that I caught my largest Irish pike.

Jim Brady was rowing me. The time was about the middle of October, the pike were at their primest, and we were slowly working along the edge of the big shallow which is dominated by the ancient castle near the mouth of Scariff Bay. Suddenly there was a good substantial pull at the end of the rod, and I roundly abused Jim for taking me into all too shoal water, which is a small depth for pike fishing in a big lake like Lough Derg. The rock on which I had caught soon began to move, not in a very lively fashion, perhaps, but in a steady, resolute way, to which I dared offer little resistance, for my tackle was fine.

Strong was this Irish fish, you may believe me, but certainly within fifteen minutes I had him up to the side of the boat, when Jim gaffed him near the tail. I am ashamed to say that the handle of the gaff was old and unreliable, and fearing a break I got Jim to hold the gaff while I put my fingers in the eyes of the fish, and we brought him in together – I should say 'her,' because it turned out to be a female. There she lay at the bottom of the boat, as beautiful a picture of a pike as an angler could wish to gaze upon – small in the head, thick in the shoulder, and without that great pot-belly which is the defect in most large pike. I was very anxious not to injure her appearance in killing her, and the killing was a matter of no small difficulty, for she showed certain vicious propensities, and failing to catch hold of any of our legs, grasped one of the timbers of the boat and scrunched it up between her teeth.

The end soon came, and she now rests in a glass case over my dining-room mantelpiece; and I hope the epitaph which Mr Williams, the clever Dublin taxidermist, has placed in the corner of the case is more truthful than such inscriptions usually are, for he states her weight to be twenty-five pounds, and I had no means of weighing her myself, though I made a feeble attempt in that direction with the spring out of a steam launch pressure gauge.

To give an idea of the frequency with which monster pike are caught in such lakes as Lough Derg, where they are popularly supposed to abound, I may add that I could get to hear of no pike so large as mine having been taken out of the lough for several years.

John Bickerdyke, *Wild Sport in Ireland*

The 40-Pounder

Our old friend the forty-pound pike of Ireland may, and probably does, exist. He may even have been caught, but his alleged captures do not so far bear investigation. I would strongly advise persons who land these monsters to say nothing as to length and girth. Many a forty pounder would have had a place in history had not the captor given these particulars, and thus thrown doubt and discredit on a story in which he would otherwise have figured as hero.

A striking peculiarity of these great pike is that their bodies are never preserved. One I investigated – it was a fifty-pounder by the way – had been torn to pieces by dogs. Surely such venerable fish deserved a nobler fate, and far be it from me to suggest that had their illustrious corpses been produced, their weights would have been found wanting. However, he who being a pike fisherman has not a yarn of a monster up his sleeve is no true angler, so, for my credit's sake, I feel bound to spin one.

My new acquaintance, from what I could gather, was an Englishman who had lived for many years in Ireland, and apparently passed his whole time in fishing; but I was able to tell him of certain modern methods of pike fishing of which he had heard nothing. By-and-by he began to get communicative, and finally I ventured to ask him why the weighing of the pike had so disturbed him. Without hesitation he told me the following story:

'From a boy,' said he, 'I was an enthusiastic fisherman. I need not trouble to tell you now how I caught salmon in Norway, gudgeon in the Thames, trout in the Test, and enormous grayling in the Hampshire Avon. I fished whenever and wherever I could, and nothing however large or small, came amiss to me. But one thing I had never caught – a really large pike. Even in Sweden I never took one over 30lb. This nettled me, for many were the tales I read of monsters, particularly in the Irish lakes. One morning I read in a sporting paper a letter from an Irishman – a tackle dealer, so I afterwards

153

ascertained – asking why English anglers did not come more over there. In the lakes in his neighbourhood there was fine pike fishing. Thirty-pounders were common, and they got a forty-pounder or two every season. Here was exactly the information I wanted. I told some friends about it, but they only smiled. I said I would catch a forty-pounder before long. They replied that there was no such thing as a forty-pounder alive or stuffed. Well, the end of it was I made a bet that I would go to Ireland and before I returned I would catch a fish of that weight.'

'I began badly,' he continued. 'I wrote to the man for details of these loughs he mentioned, and received a reply from his widow, he having died soon after writing the paragraph. From the poor woman I could get no information. She said she had no idea to which waters her husband referred; in fact, she knew of none. Then I put a letter of inquiry in the sporting papers, and received many replies from persons, some of whom were possibly not altogether disinterested in the matter.'

'I came to Ireland armed with tackle such as would hold the largest pike that ever lived,' he continued. 'At first I was hopeful. What tales they told me, to be sure! There was one of a big pike caught in Lough Derg, or, I should say, was killed by some workmen who were digging drains near the lake. The Bishop of Killaloe was reputed to be fond of pike, and to him the fish was taken. It was so large that half its body dragged on the ground as two men carried it, slung on a pole, to the bishop's palace. When the bishop saw it, he told them to give it to the pigs. "I am fond of pike," said he, "but distinctly decline to have anything to do with sharks." Ah! what would I not have given to have caught that fish!'

'Well, I fished here and I fished there, first trying all the large Shannon lakes, and then visiting Corrib and Cullen. Thence I went to the North of Ireland, catching now and then some fine fish, but never even a thirty-pounder. The more difficult I found it to attain my object, the more determined I became to succeed. Ay, and I shall succeed yet, too! Let me see; it is now twenty-five years since I came to Ireland. Why, I must have killed thousands of pike in that time. That one there is the largest of the lot; in fact, the largest I have seen killed by myself or anyone else. This is my second great disappointment. At Athlone I thought I had succeeded. That was a big fish. We took him to the station, and weighed him there. "Forty-three pounds," said the station-master.

'A Major Browne, who was looking on, began to prod the fish with his stick. "Something hard there," said he; "let's cut him open and see what he had for dinner."

'I would not agree to this, as I wanted the skin entire; but the Major squeezed him a bit, and up came a lot of swan-shot which my scoundrel of a boatman had evidently poured down his throat so that he might earn the reward I had promised him if I caught a heavy fish. But at last I really have found a monster pike – the catching of him is only a question of time. Not a quarter of a mile from this cabin' (there he lowered his voice to a whisper) 'is a deep, reedy lake. The priest has a boat on it, which he lends me. I was rowing along the other evening, when something struck the boat with such force that I was thrown from the seat and nearly capsized. It was in deep water, and there are no rocks in the lake. I had rowed right on to a pike as large as a calf.'

He said the last sentence lowly and earnestly. I expect I showed real interest in the statement, for, like the old man, it had long been my ambition to catch a really immense pike. 'Well,' said I, 'let us go and try the lake together; I should like to help you land such a monster.'

'Ah! But you might catch him and not I. How then?' And he gave me a very unpleasant look out of his deep set eyes.

We said nothing for awhile, when my companion suddenly startled me by asking if I was aware that he was the Emperor of Germany. I said I was not, and another unpleasant silence ensued. Mrs O'Day had made up two leather beds for us on the mud floor, and without undressing we each stretched ourselves on our moorland couches. Just as I was dropping off to sleep, my companion got up on his elbow and said gravely: 'Hang me if I don't believe you're a pike. I'll have a triangle into you tomorrow morning. Good-night!'

There was no doubt of it; he was mad. I dared not go to sleep. I made a pretence of it until the old man began to snore, which he soon did with much vigour, and then sat up by the fire until daybreak, when, leaving some money on the table for the voluble Mrs O'Day, I sped over the moor in the direction of Ballycracket Hall.

John Bickerdyke, *Wild Sports of Ireland*

The Cow's Horn Spoon

In common with a good many other anglers, I want to catch a leviathan pike, but hitherto the fates have been against me. Twice, at least, I have been very near the realisation of my ambition, but, you will say, those lost fish always are monsters! A man of my acquaintance suffered from the big pike mania to such an extent, that he, being possessed of ample means, devoted his whole time to the search after one of these monsters. And what is more, he captured one at last, and has lived happy ever after. This is how it happened.

Two of us made a serious effort to beat the Irish pike record, and the fact of our attempting such a task shows how badly we were bitten by the craze. The loughs of Antrim, Derry, Donegal, Sligo and Mayo were each and all tried in turn, and great was the slaughter of *Esox lucius*, but nothing over 20lbs did we get. A few grand trout fell to our pike lures, and of these fish a 14lbs Lough Neagh trout took a 4-inch gold spoon!

Well, to get on with this true pike story. We finally laid siege to Lough Derg, of whose mighty pike the oracles of Killaloe are never weary of discoursing in London angling papers. Here I did get hold of a veritable monster, hooking him in thirty feet of water, on a huge spoon; and after having him on for upwards of an hour, he either weeded me, or else got round a rock, and it took the united efforts of two men to break the tackle. This fish only showed himself once, and he was 4ft 6in long if he was an inch. Next day my friend killed a 20lb pike, spinning a pound perch for a bait; but we were in search of forty pounders, and our man Mike vowed that the lough was just paved with such monsters! He further assured us that when the salmon smolts came down on their way to the sea, these big pike moved in a pack to the neck of the lough, where the Upper Shannon enters, and there congregated in thousands, to feast upon the young samlets. This story we repeated in due course to the man whose life was dedicated to the capture of a mighty pike.

Forthwith he equipped himself, as if about to start in search of the North Pole, and off he went to Ireland. We heard of him first from the quaint old town of Neenah, and then he was lost to us for many months, until one day a telegram arrived, saying, 'I have got him at last, 35lbs.' This grand fish was killed on a large spoon bait, of native manufacture, carved out of a cow's horn! I saw that pike, after it was mounted, and it took me months to recover from the attack of envy, hatred, malice, and uncharitableness, which the sight produced. In fact, there has been a coldness between us old cronies ever since. You can forgive a man almost everything else, except beating you at fishing. After all, it was only an Irish pike, and 35lbs was nothing of a fish for a country whose pike had swallowed greyhounds when swimming in the lough, and who thought nothing of a 10lb. salmon for a meal. At least, that is what several Irish boatmen have assured me; and if they are not to be implicitly relied on, our confidences in such matters are nowhere safe!

C.W. Gedney, *Angling Holidays*

Garvin's Record Pike

Extract from the *Fishing Gazette*, 27 November 1920:

53lb Lough Conn pike wins the Fishing Gazette reward:
It was when, in the intervals of salmon and trout fishing on Lough Conn, trying for pike in that deep, 'pikey-looking' bay just below Pontoon Bridge, between Conn and Cullen, that I got the idea of offering a reward of ten guineas for a pike of 50lb taken in fair angling, with 6d. per lb additional for every pound over fifty. It was owing to the tales of monster pike which our delightful Irish boatmen told Mrs M. and myself as they rowed us about those fine loughs under Mount Nephin.

'I hear there are big pike in this lake?'

'Plenty, yer honour.'

'Any over 50lb?'

'And bigger. Yer honour sees that bit of a bay there, with the sedges? Well, we heard some dog barking there one day and found a monster pike there and no dog. Presently the barking began again, and it seemed to come from the old pike. We cut him open, and by jabbers, as fine a little black and tan terrier as you would want to see jumped out.'

'How much did he weigh?'

'Oh, we never bother to weigh them, your honour, but he was as long as my oar, here.'

So I offered the reward, and it appeared in the *Fishing Gazette*, in *The Field*, and in Irish papers: and, curiously enough, it was from Lough Conn that the prize-winner came. The terrier was missing, but in his place was a tidy salmon which would have the pike pull down the scales at over 60lb, had it been weighed in the pike, as surely it fairly might have been. If you are weighed at your club after a good dinner, you do not allow a discount for that!

It was on August 28, 1920, that I [Mr Marston, Editor of *Fishing Gazette*] had the first note about this 53lb pike, as follows:

Mr Arnold K. Mellor, of Castle Gore, Ballina, sends me this interesting note:

'Dear Mr Marston, I heard some eight days ago that a very large pike had been caught on Lough Conn, but was more than doubtful. Yesterday, however, I made it my business to see the man, John Garvin of Cloghans, who caught it. The fish was taken on a 2-inch copper and silver spoon, and took just over three hours to kill. The trace was of snare wire. When brought to land it was observed that the fish obviously had some other fish in it, and it was cut open, and a salmon 2ft 6in. long taken out of it. This is the length of the salmon just as taken out, headless, the head having been digested and the softer portions of the body. The tail-fins were 9in. across. After the salmon had been taken out of the pike, the latter was weighed and measured: weight 53lb; girth 36in; length 4ft 3in. These are the dimensions as given me by Garvin yesterday. There are no trains now, and he had no means of getting the fish away. So he cut it up. The head is, I believe, in Ballina, and I hope to see it to-morrow and, if I can, get it. I am most distressed that I did not know about it in time, as I could, at any rate, have photographed it. If there is anything else I can find out about it provided that you are interested, as I am sure you are, I am at your service. He killed another of 30lb the same day. If I can I will measure the head, even if I can't get it, and try to get a few scales for you.

Yours sincerely,
Arnold K. Mellor

Writing to me on September 26, 1920, I got the following note signed by John Garvin:

'Dear Sir, – I beg to claim the reward which you have kindly offered for a pike of 50lb or over, killed on rod and line. I killed the pike, the head of which you have seen, on or about July 18, on Lough Conn. It weighed 53lb. I enclose the trace and spoon on which I killed it.

Yours faithfully, (signed) John Garvin.
Cloghans, Ballina, Co. Mayo, Ireland.

I sent Mr Garvin a cheque for ten guineas, and congratulated him on getting such a grand fish.

R.B. Marston, Editor of *Fishing Gazette*, 1920

[The redoubtable pike investigator Fred Buller, has established that Garvin's great fish was, in all probability, caught on July 20, 1920, not July 18. He has also, to my mind, demonstrated that that there is no worthwhile evidence to suggest that it was taken by other than fair means. – TF]

Even Patsey Wouldn't Miss

More often than not I have found the tail of a fish not yet past the throat when I have taken him with a bait representing another fish. I am tempted to believe that the pike will kill merely for the sport, for I have never found more than one fish pouched at a time. No wonder our pike are fine fish and lusty with such feeding as they have – the very best trout, perch and roach with an occasional indulgence in poultry by way of a change. That is not a joke. I have found the feathers and feet of a water-hen in one big pike. It was after this that Patsey said to Frank, 'Keep away, you with your dog, from Lough Namara; 'tis no place for him at all. Sure this day we were after killing a pike that had been eating coots – the likes of him wouldn't think twice of a dog.' I have, however, found a piece of blackthorn nine inches long and with seven spines on it in the stomach of a pike. The fish was very much wasted in consequence, but the wood was dissolving and I feel sure that he would have recovered. No doubt this piece of wood was dabbling in the water when the pike took it, for a pike will not, I am certain, touch anything unless it appears to be alive.

On my next visit, then, I came prepared to carry out a vigorous campaign against pike, setting up as my ambition the capture of a thirty-pounder. I had been greatly impressed by the proportions of that dead monster and had no experience to guide me. Strength was, I felt, the first consideration. Well, the rod that I bought fulfilled that requirement. It was a stiff cane trolling-rod, twelve feet in length: I have that rod now. When I first displayed it to Patsey he exclaimed, 'Begor; faith, sir, 'twould hold a horse.' I honestly believe it would, or a tarpon; certainly it takes a man to hold it. Then there was a big Nottingham reel and a great length of line. The traces corresponded with the rod – I was impressed with the importance of strength in everything. About lures I knew nothing, but I bought a copper and silver spoon that did not err on the small side. Indeed, it was a weapon rather than a lure. That spoon accomplished great things. I have it no more, but I know where it is. It lies in the rocks opposite the island in Lough Namara. Originally there depended from the tail a portentous triangle, admirable as an anchor. This I soon abandoned for a much smaller triangle, around the shank of which I wound red worsted. A nice, quiet, unobtrusive bait it was, of scarlet, gold and silver; but it worked. The fish may have been unsophisticated in those days. Another bait I got was an artificial minnow which put Nature to shame, a good eight inches in length and most sumptuously decorated in blue and gold. That, too, had its day, though it seems to me now more likely to frighten the fish than to lure them.

Since those early days my taste has grown quieter. A spoon certainly – for our water copper is the colour. It must not be too large, and the triangles must be on the small side. Small triangles hold best. Very small triangles – such as are mounted on three- or four-inch minnows – are deadly holders in the gums between the teeth; a hold I have never known to yield. Moreover, the bait stays outside the fish's mouth and escapes mangling.

That first rod of mine, known familiarly as 'Sampson,' is still in use. With it, not long ago, on a light single-gut trace and a three-inch minnow, I killed a pike over thirty pounds. I admit that towards the end of the conflict I noticed that the rod was heavy; but a stiff rod gives confidence in handling a heavy fish. Though I possess other rods, somehow it is Sampson with which I have taken the largest fish.

The drought held for a week after our arrival; the great masses of cloud that came sweeping in from the Atlantic failed to gather. But there came a morning with lowering skies and Patsey confided to me that it would be a good day for Lough Daun, and we might get a big pike. We crossed the lake to the tiny cove where we first beheld Inchicrag, then up the hill to the stile by the roadside. Not even the eagerness of the fisherman in search of a big pike kept me from looking back at the view. This day, under the heavy sky, it was beautiful; the white hood on the mountain hung streamers down the little glens, merging indefinitely into the black larches and the deep bronze of the beeches. There were banks of ruddy yellows in the lower slopes, and here and there a dead tree ablaze with tinted creeper. Wood Island was a mass of reds and yellows, and close beside it the Slate was golden-brown up to the dead-white line of the bare rock. The lake itself, alive with flashing lights from a crack in the clouds, was flecked here and there with tiny white caps.

To Lough Daun is the traditional Irish distance – 'about a mile' – across dry, springy turf and down a terraced bank to Kelly's house, where the oars are kept, and numerous little Kellys, hiding behind mother or peeping over the half-door. Might we have the oars? 'Sure you can, sir, and welcome' – with that inimitable Irish mixture of friendliness and dignity. The craft would float, and there were two boards across the gunwales. So far it was a boat – but it had no further conveniences. Pat groaned at the absence of stretchers.

Lough Daun is, roughly, a round lake, mostly shallow, into which flow four streams – the largest being that from Inchicrag – and from which the river proper has its beginning. The outflow is through a cutting – made many years ago – which considerably reduced the size of the lake. For the most part the bottom is of fine sand with round boulders scattered over it. The deep is small in extent, but there is a fine cover of weeds along three parts of the edge, which makes trolling dangerous. The salmon come up as far as this, and there are splendid trout as well – said to be the largest to be found in all the lakes; but never one have I been able to rise.

That Patsey was right in saying it should be a good day for this lake was proved before ever we had reached the deep. Playing with a minnow on a very short line, to see how it would spin, brought about a great rush through the weeds and I hooked a very respectable pike; I am sure he came a distance of twenty feet for that minnow. It was a running fight, for the water was scarcely three feet deep – and a jumping one, too. An onlooker would not have gathered the impression that a pike was a slow-playing fish. This one came out of the water again and again with either a leap or a rush in which he would cover a clear yard. Since the boat was so unhandy, it was for me to keep the fish in the right direction – that was when 'Sampson' showed his quality. I had my fish very tame before I swung it in for Patsey to gaff, which he did successfully.

Patsey is, as I have said, a conjurer with the net, but with a gaff he can miss a fish in nine different ways. For a time he could not make up his mind whether to attack from above or below. He compromised by beating the fish – a method which left much to be desired; and when I looked my disapproval or hurled a remark at him, he would laugh – 'Sure I have no practice with those coarse fish at all' – or, ''Twas too small for the gaff entirely, sir; get into another!' Only on great occasions did he take coarse fishing at all seriously.

We had not completed the second round before the long-deferred rain came down, very gently at first, putting the fish in rare good humour – particularly the perch. They were a fine lot, those perch, some scaling close upon three pounds apiece. There were four pike in the boat, averaging about eight pounds, and we decided to give the top corner just one turn before we went home. Neither of us had waterproofs. I think that we got as wet that day as ever we did in all our fishing.

The top corner held a good pike for sure, and he wanted that big spoon with the worsted tail. He took it and then set back – never a move out of him – merely rising slowly to the draw of the line. That, I have come to know, is ever the way with a big pike. As this one came to the surface he lifted his great head, his jaws wide open, and gave a mighty shake to rid himself of his trouble. How I trembled lest that one hook by which I held him should yield – but it held. With a great lumbering thrash he drove down, and then I got my first taste of how a line could go out when a pike was really in a hurry. Forty yards and more in one straight run. I managed to get some in before he was off again, this time keeping deep down, to come to the surface for another vicious shake of his head, followed by a lunge clear of the water, a mighty splash, and down again.

This sort of thing went on for a long time and all the while it was pouring with rain. When I told Patsey that the water was running down my back inside my shirt, all I got in reply was 'Ptcha! Lift him, sir, lift him 'til we have a look at him. Faith, he's having it all his own way entirely.' 'Having it all his own way, is he?' I retorted – 'look at the rod, will you!' Down went the point and away went the line, while I put as much check on the reel as I dared. 'Now, Patsey, how would you stop that, and that?' 'Ptcha! Sure it's a small fish – bring him in!' By this time we were both laughing, for, wet as we were, we were very happy. I did bring him in, but not all at once; and when he was alongside he was too far gone and too big for even Patsey to miss with a gaff. That ended the fishing for the day and the pike fishing for the season.

F.D. Barker, *An Angler's Paradise*

Stone Dead

That evening after dinner Patsey came in for a pipe and a chat. He related the following story:

'Well, I'll tell you what happened to myself and Jackie – my brother, sir, he's since dead.' The speaker eased the draw of his pipe by a double blow on the palm of his left hand, took two or three explosive draws and resumed: ''Twas an old copper spoon of my own I had on the same time, made from a powder-flask, a piece of the very same, sir, you have this minute in your box. I was after cleaning it with some sand that was in the boat, for the day was dark, and was still letting out the line when I got a pull and gave him a good welt. Faith, I'm not over-tender with a savage, as himself well knows. There was nothing, sir, remarkable in the pull at all, and I started to wind on him when down he went and a devil a-stopping him, down to the very bottom, sir, and there he lay with never a stir out of him. Jackie was pulling the boat – nothing would stop him – and that only took more line, and I not having too much of it all.

'Raise him, Patsey, can't you raise him?' says Jack.

'How will I raise him?' says I; 'can't you see the rod for yourself?' – and it doubled on me.

'Oh, raise him, man, don't be playing with him at all. Raise your hand, Patsey; what have you but a small jack?'

Jackie, I'd be telling you, was rough on a fish – any fish at all – 'twas come in or break with him, rod or line. Well, sir, not a stir could I get from him; and all the line I got in was when Jack backed the boat to him. Then, sir, he came to the surface as quiet as you like, and he was *stone dead*. The two sides of him were cut nearly to the bone; and that fish, scaled sixteen pounds. Faith, sir, 'twould be a queer sort of pike that would be after doing that damage; sure a bulldog wouldn't have a worse grip.'

F.D. Barker, An Angler's Paradise

At Last

I had set the thirty-pound mark as my ambition with the pike. That I did it in utter ignorance, knowing nothing of the difficulties and disappointments before me, goes without saying. However, it gave Patsey the opportunity to indulge in some quiet laughter at my expense; he also pointed out that, though they undoubtedly did exist, never a pike of that size had been taken with a rod in that neighbourhood – at least to his knowledge. Still, as thirty pounds is a nice round figure, I stuck to it. It was as good as another.

In the meantime I was resolved that there should be no cluttering of the walls at home with mounted fish of meaner proportions. It was a harmless sort of an ambition and caused me no unhappiness. Indeed, it slumbered for the most part, except when the Colonel would greet us upon our return from the lake with his 'Well Patsey, have you got that thirty-pound pike?' To which Patsey would answer, laughing, 'Faith, we haven't, sir. There's more than himself looking for a pike of those dimensions. Don't you know, sir, it's not to go out and kill a thirty-pounder just when some one wants it; no, sir, nor a *twenty*-pounder. But', with a side nod of his head and closing his right eye, 'there's desperate fish in Inchicrag, sir, *that* I know.' 'Anyway, Patsey, see that you get him!' and off would go the Colonel, his stick tapping, down the hall to his study; and Pat would send after him, 'Devil a doubt, Colonel, but we'll have him.'

It must have been the third or fourth spring at the Grey House that the great event came to pass. March had been excessively dry, and when we arrived, towards the end of the month, we found the water down almost to the summer level. With us there is no close season for pike; so, until the rains came, I devoted myself to their reduction. I think that it was the last day before a great storm broke that we were on Inchicrag looking for pike. We had lunched on Wood Island in the shelter of the trees, for already there were heavy squalls and showers of sleet driving across the lake from the west and northwest, raising miniature water-spouts that bounded along the roughened surface of the water, singly and in platoons, to break on the rocky shore opposite.

We were in no hurry to quit the protection of the wood, for the squalls were bitterly cold; besides, there was a bright fire blazing in the corner of the old tower and there is always plenty to talk about. But towards half-past three we roused ourselves, trampled out the fire, and got into the boat.

While still somewhat sheltered I got out the trolls: Sampson with the 'Shovel' on the inside and a large blue and gold minnow on the other – it was still the era of large baits. To clear some outlying rocks it was necessary to give the north end of the island a wide berth and then to turn sharply to the south along the western shore. Just as we were about to turn, a squall struck the boat, taking the way off her; the baits caught the bottom and had to be taken in; the boat, meanwhile, was headed into the wind. When we got going again I put out the 'Shovel' only. We came down the shore somewhat farther out than we had intended, as there was a big sea running and the wind was difficult to anticipate. Half-way along I got a pull, such a pull as caused me to give line and call out that I had again got a rock. Patsey at once stopped rowing, intently watching my bent rod. 'I never knew a rock so far out as that, sir.' Then, looking at the point where my line cut the water, he cried out, 'Look out, sir, look out; your rock is moving!'

It was moving, but so slowly and heavily as to lead me to believe that, instead of a rock, I had hooked a water-logged bush. Then there rose to the surface what looked to me like an enormous pike. 'Good Lord! Patsey, look!' 'Faith, he looks more like the devil, entirely!' The first demonstration was a most vicious shaking of the head. Could hooks hold against such a thrashing? Then the huge fish flung itself clear of the water, coming down with a splash that sprinkled us.

I gasped and Patsey gave a cheer. That time the fish went down, I think to the very bottom, taking line at great speed in spite of the pressure I put on the flange of the reel, and giving Sampson a curve I had never dreamed possible.

The fish was still running when a squall struck us broadside on, and Patsey had all his work cut out to keep off the rocks, scarcely an oar's length away. To add to the excitement, down came the hail. So hard did it drive that one could not face the slashes, and I thought that we must touch the rocks before Pat could get the boat to move. In fact, I got ready to jump. And all the while I was attached to a pike somewhere down below, but I did not know where; I only knew that I was still giving line, and could feel the fish jigging. The blow lasted only for a few minutes. When it was over I began to get in line, but very slowly – lifting the fish with my rod and taking what offered as I lowered the point – until the pike was again on the surface taking a rest, after the manner of his kind, not twelve yards off the boat. Another puff of wind caught us, this time on the starboard side, swinging the boat half round and setting us down upon the fish. Then it was that Patsey moved, more swiftly than I have ever seen him move before or since, and did an exceedingly smart bit of work. He let go his oars, reached for and seized the gaff, and gaffed the fish before it could get down. The pike, but half played, was almost beyond Patsey's power to handle and its mighty thrashings gave Mary a thorough wetting before he and I together got it into the boat. Instantly Pat was at his oars again, just pulling clear of the rocks, and for some time that pike took charge of the boat. No harm was done beyond snapping the upper triangle, but we got some idea of the strength and energy in that huge body. In one of its springs it seized the seat next to that I occupied and retained its grip even after I had severed the vertebrae.

Once we had cleared the shore we were at liberty to admire this very beautiful fish; in fact we admired it all the way across to the Grey House and long after we had landed. Not satisfied to admire it by ourselves, we sought the family and advised them of the great event, and their admiration and wonder added to my delight. Clearly we had to be photographed – 'himself' with the rod and Patsey with the gaff, standing at attention. My ambition had been reached; it had been exceeded; the measurements were – length forty-five inches, girth twenty-four inches, and the weight was thirty-two and a half pounds. How many potential pike perished then, who can estimate? With the spawning season yet a month away, that fish carried something over two gallons of roe. So far as we know, that is the largest pike taken with a rod in our country.

F.D. Barker, *An Angler's Paradise*

Conn Man

I have had a couple of good stories connected with Lough Conn pike told to me by a Glass Island boatman named Johnnie, whose tongue was loosened with a few shots of the local mountain dew known as potheen.

Lough Conn was the lake on which the largest pike was ever caught – the fish had a nine pounds salmon inside it, and his captor, John Garvin of Ballina, was awarded a prize of ten pounds sterling by the late Editor of the *Fishing Gazette*, Mr R.B. Marston, for being the first angler to kill a pike over fifty pounds in weight. It appears that shortly after Garvey caught the big pike there were rumours that there was even a bigger one at the entrance to Massbrooke Bay that smashed the tackle of every angler who hooked it.

One local enthusiast who saw the opportunity of earning a reputation, decided to have a go for the fish. He procured an unbreakable steel trace, a ten ply hemp line and a set of forged steel trebles on which he mounted a two pound trout, and set out in a small boat not much bigger than a canoe.

He started trolling around the bay and after some time he fastened in the fish. The fish towed the small boat up and down the lake for half the day, and in the heel of the evening the fish began to weaken and the speed of the boat reduced considerably. The angler was in a collapsed condition also, but eventually he managed to tow the fish into a small bay where there was a small island near the shore with a single tree growing on it. He fastened the line to the tree and he looked around him for help. Eventually he saw a man ploughing in a field, and he went up to him and asked him to bring down the horses and traces to the lakeside to beach the pike, and when he came down Johnnie said: 'What do you think happened?' I said; 'Maybe the pike was gone,' and Johnnie said: 'Gone be damned! The tree and the island was gone with it.'

Johnnie told me another pike story. It was about a tinker's wife who was washing her red petticoat in the deep pool at the Bridge of Pontoon when a pike as big as a sow came out of the depths and grabbed the petticoat, and as the pike dived into the depths again the tinker's wife shouted after it: 'Bad luck to ye for lavin' me with a cold rump for the winter.'

Laurie Gaffey, *Freshwater Fishing*

The Gander-Fished Frog

One of the most novel methods I ever saw of catching pike was at a small lake near Athleague in County Roscommon, at a place called Ballinturley. It is quite close to the River Suck, with which it is connected by a river. The method adopted was to convey a large gander to the far side of the lake and attach a live frog or sometimes a live roach to a short wire trace, which was made fast to the gander. Then the bird was let into the water and hooshed off in the direction of the flock of geese which were grazing in the field at the far side of the lake near the farmhouse. Naturally, the gander swam across the lake to his flock of concubines, who were watching his progress. As a general rule the gander didn't make much progress in his journey before a pike seized the live frog or roach, and then the fun began. The first sign that the battle was on was when the gander started flapping his wings and screeching like mad. This state of affairs went on for some considerable time, but eventually the gander started to make a little progress towards his eventual destination, and when he was close enough to the shore, two of the farmer's sons rushed into the water and secured the gander and proceeded to relieve him of the ferocious companion that he picked up on his journey across the lake – a six pounds pike. Naturally, I was dumbfounded, as I thought: 'Is this a case for the Society for the Prevention of Cruelty to Animals?' But, I'm not well enough versed in the law on the subject to discuss that point. However, if I was asked for a ruling on the case I would dismiss it with costs, as there wasn't sufficient evidence to prove that the gander suffered any damage or pain in the encounter with the pike. The boys assured me that they had been engaged in that method of catching pike for years, and as they had no boat to fish from and the edge of the lake was too weedy to rod-fish it, they had no other option: besides, they enjoyed the fun. They also assured me that the antics of the gander after he made contact with the pike was a sure indication of the probable size of the fish, for with small fish he only gave a few flaps of the wings and then swam back in triumph, while with the bigger fish he had to battle with them for a bit, so as to subdue them into being towed in. Both the boys really believed that the gander was fond of the sport and that he enjoyed it as much as a terrier would chasing a rat, or a ferret bolting a rabbit.

The anglers on the Westmeath lakes shoot the pike when they are spawning in the reed beds in May. There is a lot of exaggeration attached to most of the big pike stories that are floating around the lake-sides that is due to enthusiasm, and the desire to entertain visitors. Every boatman on Conn, Mask, and Corrib has a good stock. Judging from the lack of emotion I saw two Lough Mask boatmen displaying over the capture of a twenty-five pounder that took a small spoon that was being trolled for trout, it must be an everyday occurrence for those boatmen to see twenty-five pounders coming into the boat. It's good fun to see a boatman playing a pike on a hand line. Talk about treating him rough. He skull drags it and shows it no mercy. The boatman doesn't believe in giving him line. It's a battle royal with no quarter given or asked for.

It was to Ballinasloe on the river Suck, a tributary of the Shannon, that a party of anglers came from Manchester for a week's fishing in pre-war days, under the patronage of the Irish Tourist Association. I happened to be in Ballinasloe at the conclusion of their visit and some of them were in my carriage coming up in the train. I never met such a crowd of enthusiasts. They painted Ballinasloe red, and the natives were quite amused at some of their antics. One of them had a big pike in a sack: it was about a week out of the water and I said to him: 'What's the use of bringing that fish to Manchester, it is stink.' He said: 'Stink or no stink, I'm bringing it back. I've a bet on that I would catch a fifteen pounder and that one is nearer twenty pounds, so I have to have proof.'

Laurie Gaffey, *Freshwater Fishing*

The Pordge

1932 was one of the driest summers in living memory, the year of the Eucharistic Congress and the water was low and clear by the time the raft reached Higgins'. The Pordge Kelly, with his uncanny eyesight, soon caught sight of a huge pike so all work was forgotten and all energies were directed to 'get that big so and so out of there.' All the rest of the day there was no other sight of it. Word got around that night and some other fishermen arrived the next day including the water bailiff. There were as many as twenty people there armed with long hazel poles to prod the weeds. It was in the afternoon before the Pordge got close enough to stick it. Jimmy Higgins weighed it on a scales he used to weigh wool and other farm produce, and it pulled the scales down to fifty four pounds. The hook used in situations like this was made from the grain of a hay fork by Paddy Brady, a blacksmith in the Rathmolyon area, who was an expert in the art. It measured four inches across with a barb and a flat back to enable it to be tied to a hazel stick. Lower down from the flat part about thirty yards of strong picture cord was attached. When the fish was stuck it pulled the hook from the stick and after a run or two was hauled in without much ceremony by the cord.

After a couple of hours there we would drift downstream 'watching our corks' while Jim stood up in the boat throwing casts at moving trout, until we came to the huge expanse of dead deep water backed up from the weir at Newhaggard. This was always an exciting place. It was here that Jack McKenna caught a pike of 43lbs and on another occasion one of 33lbs. A veteran of the Boer War and the 1914-1918 war, he was to be found on the river every day the whole year round except when conditions were very bad. From Christmas he fished a large Wagtail. At that time it was illegal to fish an artificial bait of four and a half inches or under without a salmon licence costing £2 or to use a spinning reel, carry a gaff, or more than one worm on a hook. With the advent of the fixed spool reel and nylon line and the increase in the number of fishermen, this law became unmanageable and was abandoned. From May on he never used anything except a full-size frog which he bled to death by cutting one of the balls of its toes with a sharp knife or razor blade to give it a golden-green colour. He rigged it up with a large eel hook through its head and treble down at the end of its belly, one smaller treble at each knee. All the line he ever had was the strong flax white line which sold for five yards a penny in Billy Sweeney's. (He was such an expert at throwing out the frog he always landed it right side up and when he drew it in with jerks one would think it was alive and swimming. He never fished it with lead but always on the surface). If it were sinking he would blow air into it with the aid of a straw. His pal Gonnie Rochford would walk up Tier's bottoms as far as the Mereing Ditch to give him a hand home with his catch. It was a nice sight to see them walking home, each with a bough of timber on their shoulders, and puffing out smoke like two steam engines.

Jim Reynolds, *A Life by the Boyne*

CHAPTER NINE: PERCH

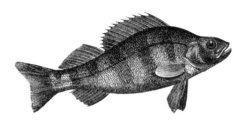

Perch on the Troll

Lough Erne is famous for the size and quality of its perch; one was caught that day, by trolling with the loach or callagh, which weighed four pounds; they run also to five and six pounds; it was as broad as a well-fed carp, and was as handsome a fish, with its scarlet fins and white scales, and as good as ever was placed on a table. A successful mode of catching perch is, also, by trolling with four or five high crimson or ruby-coloured flies, the foot-line being loaded lightly with lead, so as to keep the flies moderately sunk in the water; more than one or two fish may be thus taken at a time.

The angler not conversant in trolling for perch, (which is a pleasant substitute occasionally for trout angling) should be told that this fish generally moves in skulls, or gregariously, and when the boat comes over one of these skulls, the angler should not immediately quit the spot, but return upon it, slowly and transversely, bringing his bait among the fish while they continue to take it. His foot-line should be furnished with two swivels; one connecting it with the wheel-line, and the other about two links from the bait. The best preparation of the hook (or rather hooks) and the mode of affixing the bait, are as follows: unite three hooks, single or double B, by their shanks, so as to point from each other, triangularly, one rising a little above the other two; attach these to a strong link of silk-worm gut, having a loop at its other extremity, for the purpose of being united to the main foot-line by a similar loop.

Some anglers affix a running weight of lead to the wheel line; others, the necessary loading, according to the waters depth, to the foot-line itself. The best mode of fixing on the bait is this: with a long darning-needle, or one made for the purpose, to be had at the fishing-tackle shops, draw the detached link through the bait, entering at the vent, and coming out at the mouth, and when fully drawn, the shanks of the hooks should be hidden in the vent - it will be well to tie the mouth of the bait with a thread, to prevent its gaping. The advantage of this mode is, the economy of bait, if scanty, as the moment the fish is hooked, the bait runs up the line, and may take several fish successively without being mangled. If the water abound in pike, it will be prudent to have six or eight inches of silver gimp (being the least showy) next the hook. The bait to use, are the callagh or loach, the minnow, gudgeon, trout or perch sprat, or even, in extremity, the small fins of the perch itself, shaped with a knife to the size of a small sprat. Most anglers attach importance to the bait being alive, but, without being affected by morbid sensibility, I implore my scholar not to unite unnecessary cruelty with his sport, but let the bait be dead before it is impaled. Any degree of life is not essential to its efficacy; the purpose of the swivels is to make the bait spin in the semblance of animation, and thus attract the prey. It will be useful to the reader to tell him, that the best fishing hooks are now made by Phillips of Ellis's quay, Dublin - bad hooks cause sore disappointment to the angler, and draw down his maledictions on the maker.

Having instructed those who needed the instruction how to catch a perch, it may not be amiss to tell him how it should be dressed, so as best to invite to its being eaten. The abundance of small bones, lying in the range of the back, are an annoyance, if the fish be not divested of them, previously to being dressed which is done by two cuts of sufficient depth, drawn collaterally along the line of the back, and inclining inward, so as to meet at the depth of the two cuts: that strip separated from the fish will take most of the small bones along with it. For the most common ways of dressing perch, the scales of the fish should be carefully scraped off. By the process I have mentioned for extracting the small bones, the perch will be spit-cocked, and is then fried. It is sometimes dressed as is the mullet; and sometimes is substituted for lobster; being first boiled, then cut in small pieces, seasoned in every respect as a lobster should be - that is with good butter, in the absence of fine pure oil, cayenne pepper, lemon cut in slices, a glass of madeira wine, and a little grated nutmeg - an artificial redness may be imparted so as to resemble the tinge of the coral. There is one other mode of dressing perch, which the ingenious necessity of rude and simple life discovered to me. I was with a party once fishing lake Derevaragh; we landed, in an interval of our sport, to dine on shore, at one of those beautiful spots consecrated to my memory. Our cloth was spread under the shade of a hawthorn in full blossom shedding its odours around. We had caught a noble perch and felt inclined to add it to the materials of our repast. We asked a person who attended us from an adjacent cabin with boiled potatoes, if we could get the perch boiled or fried.

'Troth no, we have never a gridiron or frying pan.'

'Have you a pair of tongs?'

'Sorrow bit sir.'

'O! then, we can't eat the perch.'

'Troth can yez, and well too I'll roast it, so sweetly in the ashes, that yez never eat the likes of it!'

He made good his promise, and I attended the process. After cleansing the inside of the fish, which he did without opening it much, he rolled it up well in cabbage leaves, thrust it into the ashes of a turf-fire, keeping up not too great a heat, and when brought, piping hot, to our arcadian sal de manger, the fish separated from its scaly skin like a nut from its shell; while smoking on the dish, we added some butter, a little pepper and salt, and I pledge you my word, most worthy, admiring, and, perhaps, mouth-watering reader, that a morsel of it was not left.

Gregory Greendrake, *Angling Excursions*

Perch on the Paternoster

The morning had been sunny and bright, and Mick and I devoted ourselves to catching perch fry, for these were our standing bait, and, as I have said, very superior to the worms used by the Irish, and called 'blueheads.'

For some reason or other, probably because they had been harried by the eel boys, the young of the perch were disinclined to come over the spritsail which we lowered under water for their special benefit; but before lunch time we had obtained enough for our purpose, quickly got under way, and were carried by a soft, southerly breeze up to Coos Bay.

As soon as the anchor had been let go, and everything made snug, we jumped into the fishing boat which we had towed behind, and Mick brought me to a great patch of weeds standing out in the lough about a furlong from the shore. It was desolate spot. Bare rocks showed up above the surface. Here and there the stony shores were fringed with a scanty growth of reeds, and rolling moorlands trended up from the water's edge. Not a tree, nor, if I remember aright, even a cotter's hut, broke the monotony of Lord Clanricarde's great peat bogs. A few wild ducks, with their broods of flappers, swam about, and now and again a grey crow would come down to the water's edge and search for such food as the barren shore afforded.

The local method of catching perch is to have one or two hooks at the end of a fine hemp line, with a lead (as likely as not, cut off a piece of composition piping, or the sheeting used on roofs), placed a foot or two above them. I found our ordinary English paternoster answer far better than this rough contrivance, and very soon had one overboard, baited with two small perch, each about an inch long.

In sending the paternoster smartly through the water, an experienced hand can feel when the lead hits the bottom, and even judge whether that bottom be of rock, or sand, or mud. But on this occasion I was puzzled to know what the bottom was like, for the feeling of the lead was different to anything I had ever experienced. But there was a bite almost immediately, and, reeling up, I found I had two perch, each of about three-quarters of a pound, on my paternoster. That was a good beginning, and, without much doubt, the brace of fish flew at the bait before the lead reached the bottom at all. Mick smiled, as he always did when our endeavour bore fruit, quickly re-baited my hook, and down went the paternoster again among the shoal.

This time the lead was allowed to reach the bottom, but no sooner was it resting than there came that pleasant double knock on the end of the rod, and, striking, I found I was in another fish. And so the sport went on, sometimes one, sometimes two fish being brought into the boat at once, and, at the end of two hours, I had six dozen as fine perch as an angler could reasonably desire. Few, if any, were under half a pound, but, I believe, none were over a pound; the majority were three-quarter-pounders. Suddenly there came a subtle, curious, and indefinable change in the atmosphere conditions. It was not colder, nor had the wind shifted so far as I could see, but I made a remark on the subject to Mick, saying I would not be surprised if the fish left off biting now there was some change in the weather coming.

My prophecy of evil was verified, for never another bite came to me that evening, the fish leaving off as suddenly as they commenced. But what reasonable being can wish for more than seventy-two perch, mostly over half a pound each, in a short evening's fishing?

John Bickerdyke, *Wild Sports in Ireland*

No Childish Thing

Perch are the most widely distributed fish in Ireland. There is hardly a lake, river, canal or pond between Fair Head and Cork, where they are not to be had for the asking. Yet how seldom it is that this truly sporting fish attracts the attention of any but the schoolboy angler. With such indeed he is the favourite quarry, and in the summer months there are few pastimes more popular among the 'gossoons' of the countryside than 'catchin' perches.'

I for one can never forget those glorious days in the summer vacations that I spent on the banks of the mighty Shannon, or the countless hours of pleasure that the friendly perch there provided me with. And I am proud to say that 'when I became a man, and put away childish things,' I did not put away perch fishing as a childish thing, but learned instead to look on it as a sport worth following, as amusement to be elevated into art.

Since those far-off days I have fought the lordly salmon and the silver sea-trout in the rivers of the west; I have landed speckled three-pounders from the dry-fly waters of County Cavan, but I still look forward to a day's perching with something akin to the old thrill, and still I doubt if there is much greater joy in all the field of sport than the joy of seeking and finding a shoal of feeding perch.

These words are being written in a barrack-room in 'Command Headquarters,' and if at this moment I were told I could go on a Magic Carpet, the spot for which I would exchange this dusty parade ground is a certain lough in the west of Ireland, where close to the peat-bog shore the perch will even now be feeding around the water-lily beds. What sport we used to have there.

C. E. R Sinclair, *Coarse Fishing in Ireland*

It was no use

On one occasion rumours of an immense pike were spread abroad, and I determined to have a go for him myself. Having sent my servant out in the morning to fish for baits in the canal, I joined him beside the pike's lair about three o'clock in the afternoon, my friend the County Inspector having promised to bike out to see the fun. He was a simple soul, and I fear the butt for many of our boyish witti-cisms, or what we thought witticisms: jokes which the good man never resented, and seemed in half-an-hour's time to enjoy as much as we did. Selecting for my first essay a rudd nearly half a pound in weight, I attached a huge float and commenced operations. After some two or three swims down, I had just plucked the bait from the water to send it forth again, when a voice behind me exclaiming, 'Well done, indeed!' gave me such a start that I dropped it in the field behind.

'Well done, old chap,' said the old gentleman, hurrying up to the fish.

'Why, my dear friend,' I answered, 'that's my bait.'

'Oh dear! Oh dear!' he sighed. 'You are, indeed, the most wonderful fellow that ever came to the Depot. Why, even your bait is bigger than any fish I've ever seen any other chap catch in the Liffey.'

One afternoon a young subaltern given to angling for pike returned to mess early. On being asked how he had fared, he replied: 'Oh! it was no use: I couldn't get a pike: I kept on catching some of this sort of fish, so I gave it up and came home.' On examining his bag we found therein five perch, which weighed within an ounce or two of fifteen pounds. Truly 'some have greatness thrust upon them.'

Arthur Mainwaring, *Fishing and Philandering*

A Strange Feeling

There was a very deep stretch of water from the weir up to Brennan's Lock. It was the best perch hole we knew of. To catch a can of gudgeon in the head race and fish live gudgeon with a cork at the end of Brennan's Lough was an experience never to be forgotten. In the evening we could catch as many big perch here as we wished. If one fished live minnow here some of the perch would not be so large, but with the gudgeon all would weigh between one and a half to two and a half pounds. Paddy McCormack, one of our gang, caught one here of 3lbs 5oz.

One Sunday morning early in the season in 1938 I hooked my biggest fish ever. Mick (Dripping) Corrigan, chauffeur for the Wilkinson family who lived at Newtown Park at that time, saw this huge fish rising after a flood under the house and told me. It was in the big holding pool where the head of the old weir used to be. The following morning I went there and within a few minutes of my first cast it was hooked. It took me quite close to the bank and it was so heavy it was like getting stuck in the bottom. It didn't move for about a minute but the rod was jumping as if it were shaking its head, then it moved out to the centre of the river and came to the surface before plunging. When I saw the size it was I lost my head and put too much pressure on with the result that the wire trace snapped.

I'm not going to speculate on what weight it was. Every time I think of it, and that is quite often, a strange feeling comes over me. I wish I could forget it, but that is something I cannot do.

Jim Reynolds, *A Life by the Boyne*

Coarse Fishing in Ireland

There are several species of freshwater fish in English rivers, of interest to the angler, which do not occur in Ireland. These are the grayling, barbel, chub, bleak and ruffe. Dace and roach are found only in the Cork Blackwater, where they were introduced from England over sixty years ago, and are now well established. In size and number, however, the Irish coarse fish more than compensate for their lack of variety. This applies particularly to pike, bream and rudd. Rudd, which has a rather local distribution in England, is widely distributed and attains a large size in Ireland, where it is commonly named roach. The only districts where coarse fish, with the exception of eels, are not found are West Kerry, Connemara west of Lough Corrib and Donegal. This distribution is probably governed by geological conditions, limestone being absent from these areas. The huge size of our record pike shows the richness of the great lakes, and if complete records of bream, rudd and perch were available, they would doubtless tell the same tale. It is very surprising to find that there are no records of large rudd, only five of perch, and very few of bream. This is undoubtedly due to the fact that the type of angler who would be likely carefully to weigh and record his fish attaches no importance to these species. In fact, the art of catching coarse fish has not been developed in Ireland to anything like the same degree as it has in England, owing to the extent of the salmon and trout fishing which is available. Only the most primitive methods of fishing are practised. The great size and sporting qualities of the pike have made it somewhat of an exception, but only so far as the recording of large specimens is concerned. The great majority are caught by trolling. The only form of live-baiting for pike in vogue is the use of trimmers. The method is to attach the bait, usually a perch, by a hook through the skin of the back, and a short line, two or three yards long to a float such as an empty tin can or petrol tin, or lump of wood. If a pike swallows the perch, it is allowed to play itself out. This method, which is very deadly when practiced on a large scale, can hardly be regarded as a sporting one. Perch are also caught by the use of living perch fry as bait, a method known as 'sniggling.'

Anglers' Guide, 1948

A Doctor Waits

It was one of those days, so rare in Ireland, when the sun pours down with full midsummer force; were such days more frequent, we should hear less of the troubles of Irish peasants and Scotch crofters. The broad Shannon looked very beautiful that morning. In the distance the round tower and the ruins on Holy Island were reflected in the still water, and more to the right I could just discern the rocky shores along which Charles O'Malley sailed for his life after his famous duel. Not a sound was to be heard, save the cooing of wood pigeons in the larch wood which lined the rocky shores of the bay, and now and again the whistling cries of merry little dabchicks disporting at the edge of the great reed beds some hundred yards or so from the yacht.

I was just getting interested in one of Samuel Lover's tales of Irish peasant life, when my man, who had been rambling along the shore in search of firewood, came on board in a state of excitement, with the news that great shoals of fish were swimming about on the shallow behind the reed bed. Would I cast a fly over them? To this I said 'certainly,' provided he would tell me what the fish were. He did not quite know. Anyway, they were not trout; some people called them roach, and the captain once caught a pailful with his fly rod.

The last remark was enough for me, and in a very few minutes I had my ten-foot Farlow in fighting order and was very quietly poling the dinghy over the shallow towards the reed bed behind which were the 'roach.'

I soon reached the spot, and there was a shoal of fish, indeed – the water seemed alive with them. Mooring the dinghy to the edge of the reeds I put up one moderate-sized fly, a governor, dressed after the late Mr Francis's pattern. My first cast yielded somewhat astonishing results. Every fish within a circle of ten yards seemed bent on taking the fly, and there was a general rush for it. I struck at once and hooked nothing. When next my little governor went flying through the air and alighted near the shoal, I profited by experience, and let the fly rest until the line tightened a little, then struck, and hooked a good fish. I gave him the butt strongly, for the bottom was smothered with a thick mass of weeds, which came to within about six inches of the surface. There was in consequence a good deal of kicking and plunging, and I was not sorry to see his gleaming bronze side turn up to the sunlight. I soon had him on board, and my roach proved to be a handsome rudd of about 2lb weight. I quickly caught others, not quite so large, but after two or three had been landed, the shoal would leave the shallow for a few minutes, only to return to go through the same performance.

The rudd does not, as a rule, rise like a trout. The fly should be cast as near the fish as possible, allowed to sink a few inches, and then be drawn slowly through the water. A slow swirl coming towards it shows the approach of a decent fish which may or may not suck in the lure and be duly brought to basket. One is very apt to strike too soon, especially if accustomed to trout fishing. The best plan is to watch the line carefully and to strike the moment it begins to straighten out.

My first fish was not the only two-pounder I caught that morning, and by twelve o'clock I had some twenty or more handsome rudd kicking about the bottom of the dinghy, for in my hurry I had brought neither basket nor landing net. About that time my man hailed me that the doctor was on the quay waiting to come aboard; but as at least the whole College of Surgeons would have been required to induce me to leave such a good bit of fishing, I shouted word back that I was exceedingly busy, and begged he would excuse me for awhile. The shoal, which had been taking one of its periodic cruises in the deeper water, made its reappearance, and the antics of a large rudd which seemed to have strong conscientious objections to keep out of the weeds when hooked, caused me to forget for awhile all about my would-be medical attendant. In a few minutes, however, I espied him, escorted by Captain S., scrambling over the rocks towards me. Captain S. was a fisherman, so took in the whole state of affairs at a glance; but the doctor seemed a trifle annoyed when he discovered the 'business' which had caused me to delay making his acquaintance.

However, he sat down on a rock and quietly waited, watching me. I had not previously caught so many heavy fish with the fly in so short a time. But then these fish were absolutely unsophisticated, and took the fly greedily. There were, of course, some small ones, but the large majority weighed over half a pound.

At the end of the half an hour I felt I could not decently keep the worthy disciple of medicine waiting any longer, so took him on board, and had to explain that an angler may, under certain circumstances, have a somewhat quick pulse without it denoting disease of any kind. Then he went away, remarking that he really did not see the necessity of sending me any medicine at present. There had been no time to wash out the dinghy, and as I bade farewell to the doctor at the quay I noticed that his trousers glittered like a harlequin's dress, the spangles being some hundred or more scales from defunct rudd.

That evening there was a great distribution of fish among the peasantry, one of whom assured me that rudd were 'grand eating entoirely.'

A more or less modern hunting song propounds the axiom that there is 'only one cure for all maladies sure,' which is, 'the sound of the horn on a fine hunting morn' but I venture to assure the writer that thirty rudd, weighing 30lb, caught in two hours and a half, is to some persons a better cure for most of the diseases to which flesh is heir than the sound of a thousand horns, or even a blue pill.

John Bickerdyke, *Wild Sports in Ireland*

A Noble Sport

For eels I have a special method which I have only seen in one place in Ireland, the noble sport of eel-switching.

It was pursued in a lake, which had not originally been a lake, but the dammed-up waters of a considerable stream which flowed, as is not uncommon in limestone countries, out of the rock a few hundred yards up the valley. The dam had been made to supply power to the distillery, now long disused, of which many great walls remained standing. The ruins seemed to occupy acres of ground – the distillery dated from the lavish, careless Ireland of the eighteenth century, when stone and labour were cheap – and though it had served as a quarry and much of its debris had been carted away to build cottages elsewhere, the high walls still rose like a prison. And, (it was typical of Ireland) though one could walk through a gap on the north side, the south door was always kept carefully locked.

It was so long since the dam was built that it scarcely looked arti- ficial. Everything grows (except rhododendrons and azaleas) on limestone; and the ashes and sycamores were great trees, up the rocky banks at the sides, and on the dam itself – hiding, almost, its man-made curve. The top end had silted up, and in many places the fine white mud was only a few inches below the water. By the dam it was twenty, even thirty feet deep; but so clear everywhere that, on a calm day, one could see the least thing at the bottom, and did not realize the depth. And this gin-clearness, while making it possible, was a great handicap to our eel-switching.

The eel-switch is a long, thin, gaff-stick. To the end is lashed a knitting needle, and on to the knitting needle is lashed a cod hook. On the still days, when there was no wind or ripple, one drifted silently over the water, the switcher kneeling on the bottom of the boat with his eyes glued on the bed of the lake till he saw an eel, either inert, stretched at full length or curled up, or with his head under a weed or stone, and his tail and body waving in the water as he hunted for worms or shrimps. Then the switch went over the side very cautiously till the hook was within an inch or two of the eel's body. A sudden jerk, and (if the switcher was an expert) up came the switch and a writhing, astonished eel was wriggling amidst our feet.

It seemed to me incredible that the hook should go into that slippery, narrow strip of indiarubber as if it were butter – but so it was, when an expert wielded it. Even I got one occasionally, though the owner of the lake switched four to my one – and mine were always those that were still. He could switch them as they moved, or strike at exactly the right place in an unseen body when only a tail showed from under the weeds. He was even quick enough, on rare occasions (remember this was Ireland, the home of poachers), to switch a trout. He never miscalculated his distance in the clear water, as I did, and struck above his quarry: he never timed his strike too soon, and caught a weed – or barked his knuckles on the gunnel, or let the eel drop off the hook as he brought it up.

And he was equally good at the night switching, which was even more exciting, as is anything done in the dark; and more difficult, because the eels are more lively at night and apt to be scared by the electric torch. For eel-switching at night requires, not only a dead calm but an electric torch, held downwards on to the water by an assistant, who searches the bottom and keeps it steady on the eel while the switcher makes his stroke. We sometimes got as many as a dozen eels, though never any very big ones. But, of course, the smaller they were, the more difficult they were to switch. Apart from the skill required and the pleasure of picking one's prey suddenly out of the deep, the great merit of this form of eel-fishing is that there is no extracting of the hooks from the inside of the eel, and no unravelling of a slimy line.

Though I have had much fishing since I left Ireland, I have never had a chance to switch an eel.

Maurice Headlam, *A Holiday Fisherman*

Bobbing, Snouting, Tom the Longliner and Major McVeigh

Occasionally one still hears the story of the big eel that was hooked by Paddy Farnan, Ned Thompson, Tight Arnold and Micky Cahill one summer in the mid 1960s. The first two named didn't have very heavy tackle, but the 'Tight' always used a strong hazel pole, heavy chalk line and a rabbit snare as a leader. With him it was a case of 'it's either me or you for it; I'm coming in or you're coming out.' In this particular case the eel won. The very strong line broke.

Micky Cahill was pike fishing with a gudgeon and cork during the smolt run and had his salmon outfit, rod, 35 breaking strain Cuttyhunk flax line and a 40lb. Hardy trace. The eel he hooked was as strong as the one mentioned above. The line broke in this case also.

People who witnessed these hookings were of the opinion that the eels were between five and six feet long. There were no 'loners' among the fishermen in this area in those years. They always travelled in twos and threes because it was easier to carry the catch when there was more than one person. In mid-Summer when conditions were right you would see anglers making their way home at dusk with a branch of ash on their shoulders and the catch of eels, pike and perch hanging on it.

In my youth, eels were very plentiful and very much sought after. There were numerous ways of catching them. The traditional method was to fix in a gap or eye of a weir a conical net called a coghill net. As the eels make their way downstream they find their passage blocked by the weir and eventually a large number will swim into the conical coghill net.

The invention of the eel trap which was part of every weir did away with the coghill nets. The eel trap worked by passing the water of the river through an opening in the weir and the eels were stopped by a grating and then passed along a trough with flowing water into a live eel house, where they were stored until required for market.

Eels were worth more than £100 each year to mill owners on the Boyne and Blackwater in the 18th and 19th centuries. They were exported live as far as Billingsgate in barrels without water and always arrived in good condition. Silver eels are always marketed alive, dead eels only satisfying a poor class trade.

In the 1700s and 1800s the lot of the agricultural labourer earning a few pence a day was not an enviable one. He had no job security, seldom had money in his pocket and was hard put to exist in the Winter months. Hay-making, harvest time and potato digging were the most rewarding, but also the hardest work. His wife and children were paid even less than he, but had to work hard in farmhouse and field. Eels meant a lot to these poor people, and they had various ways of catching them. The most successful was bobbing. Bobbing was carried on from about mid-August to the end of the year, on the first nights of the new moon, preferably with a small flood in the river. Eels ran in huge numbers on such nights on their seaward migration.

A bob was a large cluster of slobs or dew worms caught on wet soft nights with the aid of a light. They were strung together with a large darning needle and strongest thread to form a round lump about the size of a cricketball, a piece of lead to keep the bob down, a strong piece of picture cord and a strong pole of either ash or hazel ten or eleven feet long. Spread on the ground would be a large sheet made from flour sacks. Three or four chaps held pieces of bull-wire about 3.5ft long while another person held a strong sack. A sod of turf soaked in paraffin oil would usually be stuck on the grains of a fork to supply the light at the farthest corner of the sheet from the river.

The bobber raised the bob up and down until he felt a bite and then lifted it out. The eels could not let go as their teeth are facing backwards. When they were dropped on the sheet the bull-wire went into action striking the eels and paralysing them long enough to get them into the sack. Sometimes as many as five or six were landed with one pull, some large ones up to 5lbs. It wasn't unusual to catch as many as a hundred if conditions were right on one night's bobbing.

Some were given to needy friends, some eaten fresh, and considered by many as far superior to any fish or flesh. The biggest part of the night's catch were skinned and cleaned and placed in pickle for nine days and then hung up a chimney to smoke. Pickle was made by dissolving coarse salt, 1oz of saltpetre and water, until an egg would float in it. Coarse salt could be bought in any grocer's shop up until a couple of decades ago at one penny per lb, and was used extensively by farmer and cottager alive, in curing home-made bacon. It was known as 'hard salt.'

Eel skins were cured by rubbing salt into them and were worn on the wrists to guard against and cure pains. When the eels were considered smoked they were hung in an outside shed along with sides of salmon (treated the same way), sides of kid goats and rabbits. Each family had its own recognised bobbing stand handed down from generation to generation and nobody fished there without seeking permission from the family with The Right. Recognised as the best standing was Tommna Faughlins which was at the tail race of Kennedy's Mill, (right in front of the hall door of Mrs Gilsenans' Mill House at Watergate Bridge) now filled in by the O.P.W. The holes in the wall to allow surface water to drain away (which are still there) were stuffed with old sacking and straw and very few eels escaped from this standing. Kennedy's weir was almost intact except for an opening at the Head of the Weir but the eel trap there wasn't working. With only one eel trap up the river, it's no wonder it was referred to as The Best Standing on the Boyne.

When the eels were hibernating in Winter and up to mid-May, a snout was used to catch them. A snout was a strong hazel stick with another piece a little thicker than a pencil tied at right angles at one end, and a piece of strong line and an eel hook baited with a worm. The hook was lightly stuck on the end of the snout and the line was run around the joining and up the handle. The snout was then poled into holes in walls. When an eel was hooked this way it was always a struggle to get it out.

A very successful way to catch eels as used by Fuzzy Maguire was to stuff a barrel sack with straw and tie the mouth round a short piece of drain pipe to form an entrance; put some slobs or dew worms, a rabbit, chicken, offal, sheeps' bellies etc. amongst the straw and fix large stones to the barrel sack to keep it in position in the water with the opening downstream. After about eight or nine days take out quickly and empty into a barrel. Surprising amounts were caught this way.

A Scottish eel 'longliner' known as 'Tom the Fisherman' arrived at Ballyhoe Lake in the middle '40s and built a tar barrel one-roomed hut for himself and his wife and proceeded with the business of catching eels. I rowed the boat for him on several occasions both 'setting' and 'hauling in.' He could manage the 'hauling in' on his own if the wind wasn't too strong and his wife usually rowed when 'setting' unless there was somebody who wished to go for the crack.

As he retrieved the line, he coiled it neatly in a round box with the droppers hanging outside. With the two small fingers of his right fist he held a knife with the blade pointing downwards. He drew in the line with his left hand and the thumb, index and middle fingers of his right hand. As each eel came aboard he cut the dropper with a flick of his wrist leaving the hook in the eel which slithered up and down the boat with its luckless companions.

He was a wonderful chat (when one could understand him). He never took a drink but worked very hard and long hours looking after his equipment; catching barrels of dew worms on wet nights; gathering moss to keep them fresh; baiting 600 hooks on a mile of line; set one and haul in another each day; bring the catch to Kingscourt railway station twice weekly; collect the empty containers and bank his cheques. He gave all the smaller lakes a try with a shorter line and when fishing Lough Ervey he had an enormous catch of huge eels. 'Me and my father before me fished most of the lakes in the British Isles, but we never experienced anything like this,' he said. He thought he was made up. Barrels of eels left Kingscourt station but none of them reached their destination alive. They died and rotted so quickly and the smell was so atrocious that the railway people threatened not to transport any more for him. He couldn't explain why this happened but on enquiring he found that none of the locals ever fished that lake.

Tom found Lough Ree a great eel lake and had set up at different parts of it before a terrifying experience forced him to leave. He was fishing out of Derrynagalliagh near where the River Inny flows into the lake. The locals told him that that part of the lake was haunted. He paid no heed to them, thinking they were annoyed by the amount of eels he was catching, and wanted him to move on. The last day he fished Ree he was about a mile out when he boated a huge eel which twisted its tail around one of the struts or runners of the boat near the bow and started to force its body around it which loosened one of the boards of the boat and water started to trickle in. Like the majority of people reared around boats he couldn't swim. He dropped all and started to pull for shore like he never rowed before, while keeping his head turned to see how the eel was doing. He kept staring at the eel and it kept staring back at him, and when he straightened up to get all his strength into the oars there was a dead man sitting on the back seat staring at him with the same eyes as those of the eel. The poor man was in such a blind panic he didn't know how he reached the shore. When he did he ran as fast as he could to his cabin, pitched himself on the bed and couldn't leave it for two days. His wife hauled in the boat with the eel still hooked to it. When weighed it topped seven and a quarter pounds, the largest eel he had ever seen. When I heard him tell this story he visibly paled and his voice trembled.

One afternoon in the late fifties, Major McVeigh came into my shop and while waiting for his order he overheard a chat between The Gael, Paddy Canty and Garda Egan about a big eel that had been caught in the traps at Newhaggard weir. At that time Mickey Brogan had the traps leased from Eddie Malone. The eel was estimated to be in excess of 7lbs weight, but unfortunately, it had escaped when being taken from the eel house. It was so big it got its tail against the iron rim of the net which gave it sufficient leverage to burst its way through the sackings.

Major McVeigh then told a story of how his workers or their families would never go near one of the two lakes on the Drewstown estate, as the old people would tell stories of monsters being seen in it. Once when he was home on leave from India as a young officer, the herd at Drewstown poisoned some dogs that were worrying the sheep. As it was Spring and the ewes were yeigning, he was too busy to bury them, so he dumped them into the 'haunted' lake. Some time afters, two monstrous eels were found floating on the surface of the water, dead.

When Major McVeigh described the size of the eels, there was a lot of laughter and wisecracks such as 'give him the belt.' (The belt was an imaginary Lonsdale Belt conferred on any person in the Trim area who spun the most atrocious yarn. It was usually won by an employee of either Smyths or Spicers!) This grand old gentleman who claimed to be a friend of the great T.E. Lawrence was so annoyed at their laughter that he asked them to meet him again the following morning. When he arrived the next day he was armed with a photograph complete with frame and picture cord and also carrying a diary. The photograph showed the McVeigh family; the butler and all the staff gathered around looking at two eels draped down the pillars of Drewstown House. The diary said the year was 1907 and the larger eel measured just over twelve feet, had a girth of twenty five inches and weighed forty one pounds. The other one was ten feet long, had a girth of nineteen inches and weighed twenty nine pounds.

Jim Reynolds, *A Life on the Boyne*

The Bountiful Quoile

Less than twenty miles south of Belfast in Co. Down, and near to the historic town of Downpatrick, there is a river which may one day rival in reputation the now well-known Blackwater river in Co. Cork, and the Fairy Water in Co. Tyrone.

The Quoile river, as the lower reaches of this long meandering river are known is, in a sense, almost a dream river for the beginner. Broad, shallow, and gentle of flow, it is ideal for float fishing. There is also just a hint of colour in the water, and a pleasant reediness along its banks, that somehow suggests that its fish will not be too hard to catch.

Those anglers who have fished long and hard for little reward in some of the crystal-clear, difficult waters of England, will find the

Quoile a great morale booster, for it teems with rudd which fall readily to slow-sinking bread-flake.

There are no complications of fast, contrary, currents, and very little bottom reed. The river flows slowly and smoothly down to the sea below Downpatrick, and there are many miles of water in which you may fish, and no-one is likely to bother you.

Catches of rudd can be large. Ten, twenty, or thirty pounds of rudd are by no means unusual; and some of these rudd are good, big fish. My best scaled one pound twelve ounces; but it is probable that there are rudd in excess of two pounds in the Quoile.

Not too far away there are other waters in which rudd are plentiful too. Amongst the best of these is a small lough known as Loughbrickland, and adjacent to the main Newry to Banbridge highway.

Loughbrickland rudd are not, in my experience, of such a good average size as those of the Quoile River but they are present in vast numbers, and I would say that, providing conditions are favourable, it would indeed be most unusual for anyone to fail to catch some rudd from this lough.

Fishing is easy, for although there are extensive and dense patches of lilies along one shore, there are also plenty of open shallow places which can be fished with a loaded float and slow-sinking bread-flake. Like the rudd of the Quoile, Loughbrickland rudd will take small worms; but bread-flake is a sure killer.

This lough is seldom fished, except by local boys, and is but one of many waters in this locality. By travelling south from Loughbrickland, and on through the town of Newry, it is possible to reach the Newry canal, another water that holds large quantities of rudd.

This canal flows through some beautiful wooded countryside, and is easy to reach and fish. More than that, local anglers seldom bother about it, and its population of rudd remains almost unknown, and untouched.

A few miles distant is another vast lough of great natural beauty called Camlough which is quite free to holders of the ten shillings angling license, which you must have to fish anywhere in Ireland.

This lough, like Loughbrickland, holds vast quantities of rudd and rudd-bream hybrids; but it is a much bigger lough, and its water is exceptionally clear, and also very deep in places.

During a walk along one of its many reedy bays I saw the water quite literally boiling with fish as a vast shoal of rudd and rudd-bream moved out from the shore. These fish provided me with some hectic and quickfire sport before they moved out into the deeps later in the day; but they are not always as easy to locate, and some days can be disappointing, as they often can in large open waters such as this.

All these waters hold other coarse fish too; and in the case of Camlough, and the upper reaches of the Quoile River, trout too. But it is mainly for the sport I enjoyed with their rudd that I remember these waters; and most of all, I remember the Quoile – that most bountiful and beautiful of rivers. I shall certainly fish it again.

Ken Seaman, *Angling,* March 1966

A Great Weight of Bream

I suppose it is the ultimate aim of most bream anglers to catch either an outstanding specimen, or such a memorable weight of bream that they can look back on it, and perhaps gloat over it for many years afterwards. There are waters in England where one might achieve either or both of these ambitions; but I would say that Ireland offers greater opportunities, for while this pleasant land is admittedly deficient in some species of coarse fish, it has some outstanding bream waters.

Many of these waters are located in Southern Ireland; but there are two great loughs in Ulster – namely Upper and Lower Lough Erne – that offer the visitor some outstanding bream fishing. County Fermanagh is still, to my mind, a place where one can savour the best of what Ireland has to offer: good fishing, freedom to roam where you wish, idyllic surrounds as yet unspoiled by those who are concerned only with exploiting its beauty, and waters where you may never see another angler. It is a paradise for the seekers of peace and

solitude, a place where one day can slip easily and almost imperceptibly into the next, and time is no longer important.

I made my initial visit to Upper Lough Erne in 1957 with two
friends. Since then I have been back several times and I can honestly
say that not once have we been disappointed with our catches. On a
few occasions these catches have reached truly memorable proportions.

I do not seek to give the impression that vast quantities of fish
came to our nets every day. Some days only a few fish were caught,
sometimes we caught nothing at all. Such variations have to be
expected and endured, especially when fishing such enormous
waters as these: but after some initial disappointment, totally blank
days became less and less.

Lough Erne bream are of good average size. Fish varying
between three and five pounds are quite common, while individual
specimens often exceed five pounds. Even bigger fish, in excess of
six and seven pounds, can be caught sometimes and total weights of
a hundredweight, or even two hundredweight, of these fish are not
impossible to achieve.

For any one man to talk of catching such a weight of bream
himself might seem highly improbable to those who have never
experienced one of those days when the bream are really 'on,' and I
have listened to many expressions of doubt concerning the stories of
big bream catches that come from Ireland.

I assure readers that such catches are possible and are made
every year by individuals, or by groups of anglers. Individually, and
collectively, we made catches of bream that could not be contained
in one ordinary net. One catch totalled some 250 pounds.

Much prominence is given to the use of worms as a bait in Irish
waters and there can be no doubt that both lobworms and brandlings
are excellent bream baits. But maggots and bread baits will take
bream too, if persisted with. My biggest fish, and most impressive
catch of both bream and rudd, fell to bread-flake fished as a slow-
sinking bait, most of the bream taking the bait well off-bottom.

The anglers who have never before fished waters of this nature
may feel intimidated by the sheer size of Upper Lough Erne and the

task of locating the bream in the seemingly endless miles of bays and inlets. There is no need to allow a defeatist attitude to mar one's chances though, as the bream usually stay out in the deeper channel and are not often found in the shallow bays, except at spawning times.

A boat is necessary to reach many of these swims, which are sometimes marked by stakes driven into the water by local fishermen who catch coarse fish for sale. These spots are obviously good ones, as they are often well-baited. Heavy groundbaiting is usually necessary in the first instance to attract the bream shoals and then it is simply a matter of concentrating. The worst thing the visiting angler can do is to give up a good swim just because it does not produce fish at once.

Bream that live in these large, open waters often need a lot of time to find the groundbait, unless they are already occupying the chosen swim. By moving away you may leave the swim at the very time the bream are moving in. Once you have located a good swim, fish it consistently for two days at least, as in my experience the first day is not infrequently a blank one.

For this reason, it is a good idea to bait the swim up and leave it until the following day, if possible. Trout fishing, of which there is plenty, will provide sufficient diversion meanwhile.

Opportunities for good bank fishing exist in several places; notably at Enniskillen – where anglers can fish right in the town centre if they wish – and at Corry Bridge, an excellent stretch of water situated mid-way between Enniskillen and the town of Lisnaskea, where bream can also be caught in the slower moving stretches of the Colebrook River.

The best of the bream fishing commences around mid-June, and gets progressively better until September, which is often the best month of all, in the opinion of the local fishermen.

Ken Seaman, *Creel*, June 1965

Prosperous Days

Bream behaviour depends largely on the depth and type of water in which they live. The Grand Canal varies tremendously in water quality, flow and colour. Back toward Dublin the water was almost gin-clear, with great expanses of lily pads providing cover. Those sections were known rudd and tench habitat. Colour only crept into the water beyond Prosperous, past the village of Allenwood. It was, and still is, generally accepted that canal water needed to be chocolate in colour before it could be classed as holding bream. Such conditions prevail at the stretch where the narrow-gauge railway crosses the canal from the peat bog, en route to the power station.

Another fish-producing swim was where water flows into the canal from a pipe that emerges from the peat briquette plant. There was never much flow, but seemingly enough to create conditions that attracted fish, though rudd always seemed to dominate.

From Ticknevin, onward to Shannon Harbour, the Grand Canal remains a wild, almost natural fishery. The only positive change that I've seen over fifteen years consistent fishing has been the arrival of roach. Some authorities claim that these fish have swum in from the Shannon, crossing the width of Ireland for nearly 80 miles; others insist that pikemen introduced the roach in the years that livebaiting dominated the fishing scene. Either way, the roach are taking over from rudd – which I don't consider a good thing. There are at least three major river systems in Ireland that contain and can support vast shoals of roach, whereas the rudd, that made for traditional sport, are fast disappearing from those waters in which we expect to find them. It is as though roach arrive through one door and rudd depart from another. Perhaps the competition for food and territory is won by the more active species.

One advantage in the arrival of roach on the canal is that they provide winter sport for anglers, something usually missing in a shallow water fishery, rapidly affected by temperature change, where only rudd and bream are the mainstays.

Our fishing session produced nearly 50lbs of bream for

Dickinson, while I had 20lbs or so made up of a few bream and a lot of rudd. I hadn't quite got the hang of the bream biting characteristics, something Gordon seemed to detect by a kind of angling witchcraft! I didn't even see half of the bites he had. It was as though he expected a bream to be mouthing the bait, rather than knowing it by seeing a registration at the float. Obviously he was totally familiar with his tackle and technique. He never filled the swim in. His groundbaiting was a small, initial feeding before his tackle was set up. Then he waited until fish came before putting anything else into the water. After he had caught a few fish, he would feed golfball-sized lumps, at about ten-minute intervals, with loose-fed maggots thrown before each successive cast.

Hooking a bream produced a rhythm in his tackle handling. The fish was drawn away from its feeding area by a smooth sweep of the rod, lifted to mid-water and fought out within an arc of 20 feet of the net. I never did see Gordon allow a fish to splash on the surface, apart from the last flurry that most fish make when they see the rim of the landing net. He kept the swim peaceful and that, I now know, was his secret for keeping it productive.

I continued to visit Prosperous regularly, introducing many friends to the fishing. Although we always tended to return to familiar swims, we began to travel around, taking in far more of the canal than I had ever previously fished.

I had a memorable experience on the canal about five years ago during the second week in May. While walking along the bank beyond Ticknevin, where the waterway crosses a huge area of bogland empty of roads, I noticed from a distance that the water surface was agitated. Getting closer, I saw a mass of bubbles bursting up from the bottom, spreading across the water for what seemed at least a 100-yard stretch. The bubbling identified the position of a massive shoal of bream. There must have been thousands, probably concentrated in a spawning frenzy, although the vigorous bubbling display suggested that many were preoccupied with rooting around in the bottom detritus. I doubted whether these fish would take a bait; the specimens occupied with sexual activity certainly wouldn't, and who could blame them?

There was another occasion when the lift-bite and soft-take theory went haywire. John Woods and I arrived in early April to find the canal swept by blustery winds that created waves at least a foot high. Difficult conditions in which to shot a float down carefully! We decided to tackle up with wagglers, carrying a lot of weight, that could ride fairly high in the water, and threw quite an amount of feed into our swims, reckoning that there wasn't much chance of good fishing and that we might stop a few fish in front of us for long enough to get them to feed. There were offers straight away, both from bream and rudd, which made bold bites that slid the floats away purposefully. We could hardly see the bites clearly. Only the strongest pull had any effect as the floats rose and fell on the troubled water. John was hell-bent on changing to a quivertip, although, after some argument, he had to agree that we were probably catching as many fish as the tip might produce by continuing to feed, little but often, while offering three or four maggot-size hookbaits.

Five hours fishing gave us over 100lbs between us – not easy even in calm conditions. It may well have been that the bream were avidly feeding prior to the arrival of the spawning season, and perhaps that movement of the bait was, in the conditions prevailing, acceptable to them.

Michael Pritchard, *A Sporting Angler*

The White Roach

Yet, apart from the fact that the so-called 'white roach' inhabits Lough Erne and is intermediate between rudd and bream, little is known scientifically about it.

From examination of one specimen weighing 32oz, sent to the Museum from Newtownbutler, it was found that it had 17 branched rays in the anal fin against 29 in the bream and 13 in the rudd. It was similar to colour to the bream without the red pigment of the fins, or the eyes of the rudd. Yet it seems hardly feasible that the remarkable abundance in Lough Erne's waters should be attributed only to chance meetings, even if the breeding seasons of both species do coincide.

Although there is no apparent reason to doubt that both bream and rudd are indigenous to Ireland, it would appear that many species of fish in Irish rivers and lakes have been deliberately introduced. At the turn of the century the then Duke of Abercorn released 100 true roach, taken from English waters, into the lake at Barons Court in County Tyrone, in order to feed the pirate pike there. A thunderstorm in an ensuing winter caused the lake to overflow its banks, spilling its fishy contents in the River Strule close by; they disappeared mysteriously for over half a century. Then in 1957, strange to say, a tributary of the Strule, known popularly as the 'Fairywater,' was found to be alive with roach.

E.V. Malone, *Creel*, February 1965

200

PART THREE: SEA FISHING

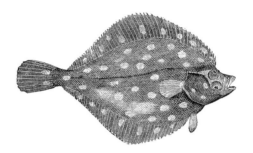

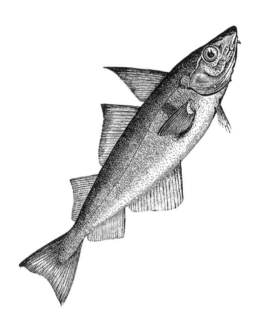

Out from Black Sod Bay

I think Belmullet must be the genuine original 'Back of beyond.' You leave 'civilisation' at Ballina and turn the car due west. A few miles later you come to the village of Crossmolina and then you are on your own for mile after mile of peat bog and mountain, driving it seems for ever into the rays of the setting sun. There is one distraction on this lonely, beautiful road and you come upon it suddenly, like some dragon's castle in a Tom Thumb landscape. It is a power station, complete with giant cooling towers and grid lines and you stare goggle-eyed at this vast anachronism, wondering how on earth it exists so far from river, sea or railway line. Then you see the proud notice board, proclaiming that the colossus gobbles peat, and then it is gone, a rapidly receding image in the rear-view mirror.

Belmullet lies at the centre of a T-shaped peninsula in the far west of Ireland. It is surrounded – literally – by a wealth of sea fishing, to the north and east the sheltered waters of Broadhaven Bay, to the west the Atlantic Ocean, and to the south Black Sod Bay. Whatever the weather you can go fishing at Belmullet and there are fine fish to be taken in both bays.

The Belmullet Sea Angling Club have prepared a chart of the area and have marked it with the species that have been taken in the past year or so. It is already quite detailed, showing the presence of great skate, tope, shark, cod and many others but perhaps the real fascination of this area is the scope for exploration and discovery.

My hours at Belmullet in 1965 were all too brief but in a mere half-day of fishing I struck on quite fantastic sport. I went out with Bill Heneghan and Ted Sweeney, from Black Sod, in a small but seaworthy outboard craft. Scorning the placid waters of the bay we motored for over an hour, until the islands of North and South Inishkea loomed up. Soon we were pitching in the Atlantic swell, close into the west shore of South Inishkea.

Bill, to my surprise, did not anchor. 'Too rocky,' he said, 'but we won't drift far in this tide.' Looking at the foam-flecked rocks only

200 yards away I hoped he was right, and of course he was.

I set up a running ledger on 35lb line with a yard of nylon-covered wire trace and a size 6/0 hook. Ted Sweeney, feathering, was soon into mackerel and hauling them in six at a time. Some were enormous, too, but I had scant time to admire them for my own line was running out. It was a typical tope run and I hit him hard, only to feel an immense solid resistance and almost immediately the mackerel strip bait came back.

Within minutes of re-casting the same thing had happened, but before I could work this one out Ted was on his feet, rod bent double, his big fixed-spool fussing and grinding under the unaccustomed effort. I thought I knew what had happened: had I not witnessed this same comic-opera of a tope on feathers with Denis Wilkinson at New Quay? I was only half-right, for Ted had not one, but two tope on his hooks. One of them, the larger, escaped as he drew them to the boat, the other we got on board and it scaled 25lb.

We fished off the back of Inishkea South for four hours, until the sun was just a red ball on the horizon and mist began to creep across the hills of distant Achill. In that time I lost count of the fish I hooked and lost. I ranged through bait size from mackerel strip to whole fish of two pounds and more. I shortened and lengthened the trace, using strains of up to 70lb in an effort to boat a fish. Twice, to all accounts, I succeeded. A smallish cod came in from one drop down and once I fought a great tope to the side of the boat. It was a very big tope and it was a very small boat so we cut it loose, counting it as caught.

On nearly every other occasion I was broken, often around the great rocks below us, sometimes in a straight test of strength as I struggled to stop the fish reaching them. Were these creatures all tope? Perhaps they were, but Bill and Ted spoke quietly of great shark they had seen at this very spot.

We departed that bewitched water as dusk closed in. I had not a lead left in my box, nor a swivel either. But I am going back to resume the contest and this time I shall be ready.

John Nixon, *Creel*, March 1966

The Contrary Mullet

On our return from the White Strand to Waterville, a new kind of sport had presented itself. The mullet, which at this season of the year congregate around the entrance of the river, had formed a black mass at the embouchement of the lake. It was impossible to use a net, the shore being covered with rocks. Neither bait nor fly had the least attraction for them; and, although they might be seen in the sun as shoals of myriads, and as closely packed together as was consistent with their power of motion, no means had yet been devised of securing this excellent fish. Their annual visits, therefore, were always paid with impunity. I was angry at this, and spent some hours in endeavouring to allure them with flies, worms, bait, all to no purpose. On inquiry, I found that Segueson had taken some by salmon-flies; not in the usual way, but by accident. He had hooked them in the side gills and tail. An idea struck me that such a system might be available; and, stringing together about twenty stout pike hooks, I awaited the bubbling which indicated the presence of the shoal. I threw over them with a long rod, and jagged the line after it had sunk amidst them. This plan was comparatively simple, and I had the pleasure of adding to my fish-dinner, in which my friend, the surgeon, was generally joined, the exquisite mullet.

Cosmopolite, *The Sportsman in Ireland*

Mullet at Courtown

Here is a story of frustration. I first saw the mullet off Clone strand, swimming close beneath the surface where the river joins the sea. Greenish ghosts flashed silver as they rolled. It was hot and still and the Irish sea was lapping the sand in a quiet, restful way, unlike its usual determined assault on the land. I thought they were bass and I tried every damned thing in the box which spun or wobbled and even a sea trout lure left them cold. And then the penny dropped – of course they were mullet!

I had nothing to offer, not even a bit of bread from a sandwich and there were no worms for the digging, or little soft backed crabs, on this almost tideless coast where the range of the tide is about 4 feet. I gazed moodily at the rocks which bound the strand and memory stirred. Did not I read somewhere that they will mouth floating weed?

The rocks were bright with green ribbon weed and I had some small triangles. A bunch of weed was soon tied around the hooks but casting with a general purpose rod and a monofilament line was not easy. However, I managed to get it out about twenty feet and the slight current from the river carried it on. It was very difficult to see the weed among the less lethal bits which were coming out of the river, but I did see a sort of bulge on the surface – you could hardly call it a rise – in the general direction of the bait. I struck and there was a hell of a commotion. The fish put up a splendid fight, moving parallel with the shore and keeping a fine curve on my light rod. Two small boys and a dog materialised out of the air, as they always do just when you least want to be disturbed, and were aghast as a very rude word signalled the parting company of me and the fish.

But the method worked; I felt full of self-confidence with the rest of the day in front of me, and saw no known reason why this delightful state of affairs should not continue. I managed to beach a fish of three pounds; my net was thirty yards away by the time I had him whacked and my waders were full of water. There he lay, a great powerful fellow with the sun gleaming on his scales. Oh, what a happy calling, and who cares about squelching waders. Three more followed before they faded out; something to do with the tide, I thought, or could it have been the association of the flashing rod with the departure of the late lamented? Anyway, they went and the sea was dead, no sign of life except a derisive tern who dived and soared over his own shadow.

Back in London, toiling away at the tail end of the rat-race, I relived the happy time with my uncle, who also fishes.

'Well,' he said. 'You seem to have got the mullet taped.'

And God help me, I thought I had, while we discussed greased tapered fly lines and various other methods of getting the very un-aerodynamic weed to the fish.

As I write now, with veils of snow sweeping across the hill, and Courtown harbour in a grey murk, that summer seems very far away and long ago. Since then I have come to live in this lovely place. Of course I have tried Clone many times with hope in my heart and what I reckoned was the ideal outfit for fishing the 'weed fly.' The only snag was that the mullet and I never synchronised our time of arrival.

So I tried Courtown. There was no question of not finding the fish here; one or two grandfathers almost always lay suspended in the shadow of the boats moored on the east wall and they owed their continued existence to the complete disdain with which they regarded any votive offering from the fishermen who come to worship at their shrine.

At the north end of the small harbour there is a bank which dries. During the last half of the flood, as the water stirred the ribbon weed on the stones, the mullet hurried in from their fishy business in deeper water to see what the new tide would reveal on this happy hunting ground. You could always see them furrowing the water and flashing like new shillings as they rooted among the weed. I used to stand on this bank, close to the wreck of an old pram, and they used to mouth my bread or dough or bacon or any other bait in the book, causing my float to do all sorts of exciting things, including becoming airborne at frequent intervals, as I struck with mounting exasperation. And when the water covered the handle of the pram I knew it was time to make for the steps if I wanted to avoid full waders.

Eventually I gave it up. Who wants silly old mullet, garbage eaters, scavengers. My wife said she would not cook one if I caught it, and had not I anything better to do than stand in the middle of Courtown harbour like a dyspeptic old heron, soliciting lively comment from the trippers?

But I often found the car wandering thataway and one lovely evening I saw a figure fishing from the wall with a nice shiny rod and the usual crowd of small boys in attendance.

'Hah,' I thought, 'Another poor mug.'

I sauntered over and passed the time of day. The man was on holiday from the north of England and was soon telling me how to catch mullet.

'What chance has the fellow,' I thought. 'And fancy telling me how to ensnare these impossible fish, when I have tried every legitimate ruse known to man.'

I forbore to tell him that he was wasting his time with that great hunk of bread floating about and his entourage of gawpers who must have been in plain view from the fish below. Let his hope die slowly, his excitement die a lingering death as it did in me. I sometimes think that I am not a very nice person.

Just as I was turning away a great blunt head appeared and two white lips engulfed his bread. He struck and was playing a heavy fish which he eventually brought alongside the steps and netted expertly. It was all done in the most nonchalant manner as if the whole sequence of events was a foregone conclusion. He gazed lovingly at the fish, which must have been all of four pounds, lying on its side and feebly waving its tail, and then gently returned it to the water.

'Moolet are not bad to catch if tha knows how,' he observed. He caught another before he met his Waterloo in the shape of two girls who descended the steps and waded about below, despite his entreaties and eventual threats. I too wished their little pink toes would be grabbed by a crab or that they would step into a hole. We exchanged glances.

'Wimmen,' he said.

R.H. Connell, *Creel,* February 1966

A Seatrout from the Sea

Ravensfort stands on an arm of water which runs up behind the cliff-girt mass of Curranbenny; and at low tide the whole is stripped bare, a lovely expanse of clear sand, save for a channel, no broader than a good sized river, which skirts the headland's inner shore; and toward this drains through the sand another small trickle of water. The morning was beautiful when Billy the boatman and I walked down along the short grass of the links on the Ravensfort side to where his curragh was lying bottom up above tide-mark like a huge black slug.

Raising a side of it, he slipped under the gunwale and lifted the craft on his head and shoulders, I trailing the oars with one hand and steadying the nose of the boat with the other, for a strong breeze out of the west was blowing.

These curraghs, as most people know, are made of tarred calico stretched over a hooping of willow rods; the whole kept in shape by a frame of timber, which it was Billy's pride and profession to manufacture for the neighbourhood. In Donegal they build them pointed sharply, with well defined bows; elsewhere (and in Tory Island) they are, as one Ravensfort man said to me, for all the world like a washtub; and these rougher craft are propelled by paddles. But in Donegal they use oars, with small light blades, but made clumsy in appearance by the flat broad piece of wood nailed to the oar itself and pierced with a hole for the thole-pin. The whole equipment costs about £2:10s., and it will carry two rowers and two passengers in almost any sea – the passengers sitting in the bottom, bow and stern. A lady aboard is a danger, for the small high heels of her shoes may go through the calico between the interstices of the wicker-work; and Billy told me a story of a lame man, with a raised heel to his boot, who was helping to fill a boat with herrings, when the water began to come in more than could be accounted for. Luckily other curraghs were near by, the hole where this fellow had in the hurry put his heel through was plugged with caps and handkerchiefs, and a good weight of herrings being piled on, no one was the worse and the night's fishing not interrupted. After all, if you are accustomed to have nothing but a strip of calico between you and a wild sea running under huge and unscalable cliffs, why should you fuss, because instead of the solid calico you have a makeshift of miscellaneous wearing apparel?

These boats do not divide the water; they go over it, much as a bird swims. Billy put down his burden at the nearest point of the small tributary trickle, and sent me along the sands nearer the main channel. He came down sidling like a crab, rowing across the breeze which was taking him fast by itself. A curragh will float in about four inches of water, and he was dextrously keeping off the places where there were only three. But when he came abreast of where I had found a kind of pool, he gave a pull of one paddle and a backward swirl of the other, more like the movement of a fish's fins than of oars – swung her clean round on her axis, and then, with almost the same motion, drove the blunt stern firm on to the sand. I stepped in, and, still sidling, we slipped down between long stretches of sand-bank which rose from the blue strip of water.

Once we were in the main channel these banks became peopled, for we were now a good mile from houses. Tall curlew were there, brown on the tawny sand; herons, too, silhouetted strangely against the sky where they stood, a couple of feet higher than our level; gulls were there, common gulls and herring gulls, in the white and grey plumage; and above all, dozens of sea-pies or oyster-catchers, the dandies among birds, with their smart black and white dress, neatly set off by red bills and red legs, and with I cannot tell you what elegant absurdity in their small twittering run.

All this while, of course, we were fishing, sidling down the channel or pulling up it, and I, unaccustomed to the work, was uncertain whether various tugs had been merely the strain of tide and wave or a fish's bit. However, Billy avouched them for bites; but in the meantime we were getting nothing. I had just hauled in my bait to make sure it was clear of sea-weed, when a sudden darkness came up, and lash of rain with it. Well knowing that, on a river, this would put a stir on fish, I hurried to get my bait working, when the line, with the natural perversity of things, caught in the hitchers of the rod and refused to move. In a curragh you must sit down and stay sitting, and the joint was wholly out of reach; I had to run the butt in under Billy's arm and free the line, while the bait hung almost under the boat. As I was in the very act of doing this, down went the line taut, the rod-point bent, and I thanked Providence that I had been just (if only just) in time. By the time I had the rod in its proper position the fish was fifty yards away and still running. We followed him, but not before he had got out nearly the last turn of my eighty yards. And a pretty dance he led us; making, I should be afraid to say how many of these long dashes and never showing, so that I put him down for six or seven pounds at the least. When at last he did break water, I could scarcely believe my eyes. The back which emerged was small to begin with, but one is prepared for that: the colour startled me. It was bright brown in the blue water, – but brown does not suggest lustre, and this was lustrous colour, like the reddish amber of a certain sea-weed. Frankly, in my ignorance, I was afraid that all this fuss had been about a pollock, but Billy heaped contempt on my suggestion. And when, after a full ten minutes' hard play with salmon rod and tackle, we backed the curragh in and got out to land our prize, he was evidently a fish of under three pounds – but, as we had guessed already, hooked outside the mouth, so that he could keep his head down and his jaws tight in running.

It was no great capture; but for any lover of fish, the colour and shape of that trout as he lay on the sand was a sheer delight. His back was hardly darker than his belly, and the colour that was on it cannot be defined in words – except by saying that he was precisely the colour of a new-caught sand-eel. After he had lain in the boat a while, the blue began to appear, and by the time we brought him home he was just like any fresh-run white trout you may catch in the river – or very little sheenier. But when he came out of the water his back shone like the sun.

Stephen Gwynn, *Fishing Holidays*

Digging Sand Eels

Sand-eels, of course, are not eels at all (the English name, sand-lances, is better), but simply the most exquisite fish that swim in these waters. To see them in perfection it must be (and the chance is not common) when they are coasting about in shallow water by the sand's edge, yet with rock or weed making a dark background; and the sun must strike sideways, not vertically, then they appear like little rainbows adrift in the blue. In your hand they are iridescent and wonderful, pure silver underneath, on the sides greenish, as it were overlaid with some nameless sheen between silver and gold; but the rainbow crimson that shows in the water wholly disappears. Indeed the whole colour fades and changes on all fish taken out of water; but the peculiar hue that is on sand-eels, and on sea-trout when you get them in sandy channels, vanishes more utterly than any other. Flatfish have in water the colour of sand under water; they fade or rather darken in the air to the colour of damp sand. But the sand-eels and the sea-trout while swimming take on the colour of shallow sun-lit water over sand – the most radiant and indescribable of all things that I have seen.

The spot for our fishing was a narrow arm of the bay which ran up two or three miles between steep shores and was floored with the purest sand imaginable. Low tide stripped it bare, save for a little winding channel scoured by the outfall of a stream from off the lower slopes of the big gable-ended mountain which closed our view to the left. It is a place to dream of, not to tell. But I was there to catch fish, not to dream, and it was a good sign to see gulls busy over the nar-row flow. Bare-legged and bare-armed we began our fishing.

At first it seemed a chimerical project. Each of us had an old blunt table-knife, which was plunged into the sand at a venture under the water or near the brink, brought it through from right to left, and pressed down the left hand to meet the edge as it came up. But after a few desultory sweeps I felt a faint wriggling resistance of some-thing (fishing trains the sense of touch very nicely). Half a dozen more trials and I brought up a little silvery creature, held between the blade and my palm. At the end of a quarter of an hour I was quite proud to have captured some seven or eight, since my friends had not yet achieved the knack; but also I perceived that we should not get enough to do more than bait a few hooks with at this rate of going. Possibly the fish might be in greater numbers elsewhere, and I walked along the warm sandbank towards where some gulls were hovering.

Fifty or sixty yards down I saw suddenly a whole fleet of golden-brown shadows shooting away from me like shuttles. A little farther and I saw more. Then I realised our error. We had crossed the chan-nel, splashing through it, and had begun to fish where we waded and downstream from that (the tide still draining out), and we had made, relatively speaking, a solitude about us. I slipped quietly in at a very shallow place and working across and up perceived that I was driving a shoal before me. The bottom was uneven, and the sand above swirling holes was, of course, looser; and in these easier places of entry the fish buried themselves. I began to fish now systematically and carefully, and soon I was catching an eel with every sweep of the blade – sometimes two together.

The working of the thing is quite simple. Sand-eels swim naturally head on to the stream; they burrow as they swim; you fetch your blade across at right angles to the current, and when it strikes it pins the soft body against the half-solid sand and forces it through; your left hand, coming down and covering the edge just as it emerges into free water, holds the fish.

Working this way up-stream, three of us abreast, we caught and caught till bags grew heavy, interrupted only by a huge brown flounder, who shot up and down distractingly, and we tried to stalk and pin him; but untrained eyes could not distinguish his lodge in the sand, and he was always too quick away.

Finally, one of us gave up and went to bathe; the two who remained meant to give up fishing, but went on and on, always in the hope of getting something bigger even than the biggest we had got yet (some must have been a foot long), and I did not stop even when I had captured four at one lucky swoop. This was in a narrow place where the driven shoals seemed to have gathered, and the sand was honeycombed with them. When at last in sheer weariness we gave over and I poured the take together into one bag – there was fifteen or twenty pounds weight in it – we walked home triumphant.

Disappointment came at dinner. The creatures looked like a very ambrosia among dishes, and they are reputed exquisitely delicate. I found the small ones, say four inches long, as good as ordinary whitebait, but no better; the bigger ones had an acrid flavour without substance, like a mouthful of sea-water.

Stephen Gwynn, *Duffer's Luck*

The Wriggling Brute

Congers had still to be pursued, and at half-past nine there was Mike, with the motor car's tail lamp, to lead us over a rubble of rocks and stone walls to where the boat lay. We dropped down stream a bit, and our host inquired if it was not the case that conger fell back with the ebb. Mike agreed and suggested that we could go down to the lower pool and fish there; we could get back by two o'clock. At that point some of us revolted. My expressed opinion was that if we shot rapids in the dark with heavy coats on, we might see more of congers than we desired; at best it was too like an all-night sitting. So, reluctantly, our host and leader consented to fish where we were; and the lines, baited with half a herring, were tossed overboard. It was a new fishing to me, and I was uncertain as to distinguishing the bites with that heavy weight on; but I need not have troubled; it is like the tug of a terrier. I struck too soon, however, at the first, but happily a conger is not easily deterred, and if he is scared off one bait goes to another. Someone else got him, and to see Mike gaff that wriggling brute as he came aboard in the dark – or rather to be aware that he had done so – was an education in the fisherman's business. Then came much banging with a stretcher, for a conger bites whatever his jaw touches and does not let go; and the jaws are formidable. The biggest we got was nearly five feet long, and the pull against one at first was incredibly strong. Then the line came in with a mere dead weight till suddenly the strain began again; he had got his grip now on the boat-keep as on the rocks at starting. I cut my fingers with the line in that hauling. Six conger made the last item in our mixed basket, and these, I admit, we did not attempt to eat. But we learnt how they are prepared for eating. Mike brought us down next day one of the previous captures; it had weighed seventeen pounds, but now was little more than half that. Split open, it was thrown into salt and made its own pickle; in a couple of days it was taken out and hung up, to be steeped in water when it was wanted, and then cut into steaks and fried. The cured fish was perfectly supple, and rolled into a ball like a lady's muff.

Some say that this eel has other uses, and that the green lumps which float in turtle soup are no other than the flesh of conger. But of this Connemara knows nothing, nor I either. What I do know is that people who, instead of slavishly adhering to the orthodox and accredited types of angling, vary their routine with whatever fishing comes to hand, are the real fishers; for the essential part of fishing is not throwing a fly but learning how to catch fish. And folk of that disposition, who take holiday in the West of Ireland, may defy wind and weather; come rain or come shine, they will always knock pleasure and adventure out of it.

There was never a better man to knock pleasure or adventure out of anything than that host of mine: and I am very sure that he knew them both to be the utmost in the last moments of a brilliant life, till a German bullet suddenly stopped his flight, high over the lines in Flanders.

Stephen Gwynn, *Duffer's Luck*

Bass from Dingle

For years shore anglers have chosen the long yellow strands of the Dingle Peninsula as their favourite fishing spot. High among the many reasons must be the sheer exhilaration of being pounded by the streaming Atlantic surf of these storm beaches. Built up by mid-ocean storms, the creaming breakers roll steadily in to the strand. In the breakers, within sight of an angler, the scaly bass flashes to and fro in the glistening water, constantly searching for worms and sandeels forced out from the sand as each curling wave spends its energy on the beach.

Surf fishing has an added ingredient for the men who fish the littoral waters of Ireland's west coast. Standing in the moving water, watching and feeling the line as each rolling line of surf breaks around protective waders, the angler is keenly aware that he is only a small part of the ecosystem, surrounded by other life forms. Power is the key to the marine world – the power of the ocean and the wild winds that drive the huge surface swells in to pound the shoreline. Tide streams and currents are mere children of that awesome force formed so far off in tropical and arctic waters. Wading into the rushing water to let loose a baited rig, one feels so tiny and alone in a world dominated by the sea and the endless sky.

Many years ago, driving out from Tralee, I had my first glimpse of the golden sands that ring Brandon Bay. There on the north side of the peninsula, beyond the tiny hamlet of Castlegregory, where a finger of sand dunes juts out to a mass of tiny, rocky islands, the strands lie open to the sea. At the western end of miles of beach, the mighty hump of St Brendan's mountain marks the beginning of a series of indented bays that shelter small, solitary whitewashed houses and stone jetties, from which the people of the peninsula set out to fish.

Dingle spells bass, which have a natural liking for clean, clear water that has been warmed by currents spilling off from the North Atlantic Drift. It is one of those rare shorefishing locations where bass can be found in any month of the year, although their average size has never been very high. My largest weighed 8½lb and I haven't often seen bigger fish from that part of the south-west. This may be because bass, in western areas, feed on the open grounds in fairly wild water; perhaps their life is one of constant swimming activity and battle against the elements. Bass found in harbours and stillwater lagoons seem to attain larger body weight, suggesting that the life of a scavenger, feeding on shore crabs, sandeels and detritus, provides more nutrition with less energy expended.

There is one particular day that I shall long remember. It started with a protracted bait-digging session at Clogharne, made difficult by an incoming tide that continuously forced us to retreat from the sand-mud mixture that held the larger lugworm to weeded, shallow areas which produced only stringy worms, though we added a few useful clams to the bait bucket. We washed our worms, cleaning them in the rush of fresh, tidal water, then covered the wriggling mass with bladderwrack, as a necessary precaution against the drying heat of a sun that promised a perfect Dingle day.

We had decided to fish the open strand at Kilcummin, reached by driving back toward Castlegregory to where a stony boreen inclines seaward. This shore mark is identified by a solitary wooden post, jutting out from the sand at low tide, said to mark the remains of an early wreck. A shallow stream follows the lane down to the shore and there it spills on to the gently sloping sand.

We spread ourselves out at either side of the post. Clive Gammon, an extremely knowledgeable bass angler who now lives and works in America, chose his hotspot next to the freshwater flowing over the beach, muttering that 'bass are always to be found around freshwater running off the land.' Kevin Linnane was first out into the surf, making purposeful strides against the pressure of the breakers. He always liked to be in thigh-deep surf, where he could gain the extra few yards to his casting – at the risk of a wet backside. I must confess that I have a natural aversion to being soaked, especially at the junction of my legs, so I try to find a fishing position where current pulls the bait round with strength. I know that it can be hard to hold the ground, even when using a griplead, but bass seem to search for food where the water is wildest.

Our arrival coincided with the last hour or so of the flood, perhaps not the best time to begin a bassing session, yet bites came almost immediately. Kevin, who was probably fishing farthest out from the sand, struck hard. Moving back quickly, with a faint shout on the breeze to tell us that he was 'in,' Kev picked up the slackish line that bellied between him and the fish. His rod arched over, then straightened, as each rolling breaker put its pressure against the moving bass. I have always found it difficult to maintain that 'tight line contact' that is vital in keeping a strong fish headed my way in tumbling water. Kevin's fish seemed a good one, so we all put our rods into rests and ran along the shallows to get a sight of the first of the season's Dingle bass. It played hard in the last 20 yards of flat water, careering sideways along the water table with vigorous head-shaking, intended to dislodge the hook.

With a practised hand, born of catching hundreds of bass in his time, Kevin played the fish on the rod. Then it lay, floundering, in a few inches of water ahead of his boots. A couple of strides and Kev put himself between the bass and the incoming line of surf – always a bright thing to do with a fish that, in its last desperate lunge, can shake off from the hook. The usual congratulations were proffered and a few hands stretched out to give the hard-scaled body a purposeful rub – establishing a kind of affinity between man and the highly prized quarry!

Back we all trooped to our respective rods, which stood like sentries in their rests. Some of us immediately took the rods down to hold them tightly across our chests. I admit to enjoying holding my bass rod throughout a tide of fishing. Clive Gammon, during my nursery days when I fished alongside him in West Wales, convinced me of the value of always holding the rod with the nylon crooked over my little finger. He believed in an intimate contact with the slightest vibration that might be transmitted back along the reel line – almost willing fish on to his bait!

Bass fishing can certainly be tiring, what with the constant to and fro of the water that shifts fine sand, undermining one's waders and enforcing a change of stance after each table of water weakens and begins to run back to join the surf. Most times I prefer to stand facing the breakers, hoping to see birds working the surf or, more rarely, actually to catch a glimpse of bass swimming along inside the turning wave. As this stance becomes tiring, I turn my back on the sea, still holding the rod across my chest. From this position it is much easier to react to a solid bite. One can strike by punching the rod away and at the same time take up slack line with a couple of hasty strides, up the strand, toward dry sand.

Within the hour the tide started to ebb, with a noticeable slackening of power. The turning breakers eased, although a slight off-the-water breeze kept a ready curl to the rolling surflines. I do not much enjoy fishing on an ebb tide. On surf beaches, it never seems to yield more than a few schoolies and flounders – yet, the ebb is still far better than a surfless day!

We fished for another hour or so before Dennis Burgess, a newcomer to the Kerry sands, gave a shout and turned to display a quizzical grin, as if seeking confirmation that his detected bite was from a bass. It was his first time in Dingle and his first bass fishing session. We had all lectured him on the wide variety of bites that he could expect, and the trembling tweak he'd experienced was hardly the promised lusty wallop that we had all assured him spelled bass. As soon as his line tightened, however, Dennis himself realized that this was no flounder, or even a school bass. Once again an audience grew behind the angler as the fight progressed. Inundated with ribaldry, and an element of advice, most of it useless to a tyro bass angler, he did the right thing by keeping a tight line to the fish that swam 60 yards out in the rough water.

It is always a pleasure to watch a fisherman handle a fish well. This battle was no exception. Dennis may not have caught a bass before but he had mastered many good winter cod and difficult freshwater species. Another and possibly more crucial thrill in bass fishing is getting the first glimpse of the fish, watching it respond both to the pressure on its head and the surge of water rolling landwards. Dennis' fish surfaced and ran along the edge of a turning breaker as though it was surfing, speeding from one breaker to the next, disappearing momentarily into the troughs.

Roars of 'tight line' issued from the gallery, while I was busy with my camera, trying for the opportunity of a picture of the fish cutting through the water tables. Like seconds in a boxer's corner, the lads kept up their chatter until, in a few inches of creaming water, Dennis was able to reach down and lift his first bass by the gillcase. Amid the excitement he did not notice that he had cut himself badly on the sharp spine on the fish's gillcase. The fish weighed 8lb 4oz – a creditable performance and a splendid beginning to Den's bass fishing career.

A few smaller bass came our way on the weakening ebb tide, but we soon agreed to leave the strand until the beginning of the evening flood. Les Moncrieff, Dennis and I decided to fish later in the day somewhere in the area beneath the sand dunes at Stradbally. Clive Gammon, with Kevin Linnane and Ian Gillespie, were making their plans to fish at Inch, a west-facing storm beach that juts out at right

219

angles into Dingle Bay. This strand had always proved reliable for a catch of bass when there was anything like a tickle of surf running. After a leisurely meal in the village, we divided into two parties and left for our respective fishings.

Les had chosen our fishing spot on the basis that Stradbally was a 'sharp corner' of Brandon Bay. Evidence of the sweeping, tidal action was indicated by the rounded pebbles that are only found on this part of the 14 mile-long strand. As Clive remarked: 'There is only one beach in Kerry that looks like Dungeness – and Moncrieff has found it!'

We expected fish fry and other littoral-water food to be driven into Stradbally. Feeding bass should have been grouped up as the evening light dwindled and the flood got under way. As it turned out, I waited for an hour before the first distinct knock came, from a smallish bass, a schoolie that weighed a couple of pounds. In the next hour, before true darkness, each of us took many similar sized fish. Our flood tide, on the northern side of the peninsula, lacked the benefit of a wind behind it, so the offshore swell was gentle and only a soft tickle of surf ran on to the strand. In conditions like that I prefer to fish in the darkest hours, as I cannot ever remember having a good catch when there was practically no water movement. In daylight, with the added ingredient of bright sunshine, absence of breakers gives the angler no chance. In such circumstances bass stay out in deepwater that offers a darker environment, with increased security from predators. Only at night will these fish venture right up to the tidemark when there is only a slack surf.

In those days Leslie was unrivalled as a long-distance shorecaster. When he bent into a rod, he could outcast both Dennis and me by at least 40 yards – with bait on! Proof of his ability and his control of a multiplying reel, that lacked any of the modern breaking devices, came after dark. Even though we couldn't see the flight of his lead, we judged the trajectory by the sound made as the spindle rotated in its bearings. Suddenly he shouted that he had hooked a bass that wasn't behaving at all like the book said. In a couple of minutes he had the first of a dozen or so spurdogs lying on the sand. Since Dennis and I continued to catch bass for an hour or more without a sign of a spurdog ravaging our hookbaits, we concluded that Leslie's baits were fishing many yards beyond ours. I think that the crafty spurdogs were farther out than the bass, making sneaking runs into the shallow water to pick up the unwary fish that were too preoccupied with their own feeding in the shallows. When we opened our bass, they were filled with small sandeels and minute, partly digested creatures that felt like gritty sandhoppers.

By one o'clock in the morning we were just about ready to pack up the gear when a shout, from atop the dunes, heralded the arrival of the Inch fishers. They hadn't done so well; in fact, Clive admitted that they had ceased fishing early in favour of some convivial drinking 'behind the onion factory.' So, accompanied by our giggling companions, we left Stradbally for the warmth of our Castlegregory guesthouse.

Michael Pritchard, *A Sporting Angler*

The Sands of Raven Point

You will hear the call from your friends along the line, an odd fish or so shortly after the tide begins to rise, then two or three on at the same time. From then on you know the bass are feeding mad. As quickly as you can bait and cast you can be sure of a good fish each time.

Where is this fabulous place? Daniel F. Curtin's article in the February issue of *Creel* set me dreaming of the wonderful times I've had around Wexford, on the south-east corner of Ireland, where the beautiful Slaney meets the sea. There are many good and expert anglers who are not keen on boat fishing. The famous Splaugh Rock is not for them. Then why not a day on the Raven Point at the mouth of Wexford harbour? Miles and miles of beautiful silver sands, not a snag on any part of it, on a good summer's day a place of peace, of plenty.

But as with all the good things of life, there is a price, a fair enough price, a walk of two or two and a half miles along the soft yielding sands from the nearest point of entry at Curracloe. Ask any of the locals; they will direct you to Raven Point. Bait? Rag, of course – also lug if you have to wait for the proper point of the tide. There are some fine flounders to be had on lug. But, once the tide sets firm, then it's rag on your two-hook paternoster, the bottom link two to two and half feet long. Soft crab are a good stand-by.

Well out from high-tide mark at the Point is a sand bar, running parallel with the beach for about three-quarters of a mile, then a break over which the rising tide runs into the channel. It's a fast tide, but no matter. The bass love it. Fish into the deepest part of the channel, and, as the tide rises, lengthen your cast. I can never recall a blank day at the Raven Point.

Farther along at the end of the channel, where it empties into the harbour, is a place they call 'The Gut'. A pair of thigh-waders, a good medium split-cane rod, 10 or 12 lb b.s. monofil with a long trace and single hook, plus the knack of unhooking a lively 2½ or 3-pounder while standing in a foot or two of fast-running water, a small bag for bait high on your chest, and a belt around your waist with hooks and loops of string on which to hang your fish – and, believe me, after a few hours of that you will be well satisfied to retire before the rising tide. You will have a good harvest of some of the cleanest and best-conditioned fish to be had anywhere.

Perhaps you are more fortunate and can spend a few days there. Then set a tent in the hollows of the dunes, where the rabbits have cropped the grass as close as a bowling green, where the turf is so soft it almost covers your uppers as you walk over it. Icy cold spring water to be had for the asking from the good friendly folk in the little thatched cottages among the dunes at the road's end, and a small shop or two which will produce all a man can need.

A soft balmy summer's night with just a little wind from the south or south-east to put an extra bit of push into the breakers on the sand bar, then have a night session on almost any part of the beach where a channel has formed. Fish just beyond the first line of breakers before the tide runs deep in the channel – but watch it. If you decide to wade out to the sand bar at low tide, that channel can be deceptively deep very shortly after the turn, as I know only too well. It's not finished by any means when you retreat up the beach. On the rise or fall, with just a short breathing spell between tides, that channel will yield a good harvest of prime fish. Then as the dawn of another day begins to show faintly grey and eerie in the east, hey presto, they are gone. Who knows where?

Thomas O'Byrne, *Creel*, October 1964

The Delights of Kinsale

I have known Kinsale for three generations: I mean that literally. My grandfather was a good amateur painter and, being a Victorian, he was influenced by the Italian Craze (there was one even in those days); therefore when he could not go and paint in Italy he went to Kinsale because it reminded him so much of Italy. My mother also had a great liking for the place and she, too, said it was like Italy. A friend of mine, a rather nationalistic Italian priest, on seeing Kinsale admitted to me that well, yes, one might perhaps say that it does look like some bits of the Riviera or of the Lombardy lakes; of course there is not all that sunshine, and not so many flowers, and the blues of sky and water are not quite the same; those conical Irish yews are

not so slim and tall as cypresses; all the same, the place was far too good for a benighted heathen like me.

There are houses climbing up on the hills round the little harbour, narrow irregular streets giving glimpses of blue sea and white sails. The town must have been a finer sight when grandfather went there to paint; even within my memory beautiful old houses have gone, and the aristocratic Georgian atmosphere has faded away a little. There has been an improvement lately, and luckily those accursed 'developers' have been kept within bounds. Most of the new constructions have not done too much damage to the attractive old-fashioned appearance of the town, nor ruined the landscape of the Bandon estuary. Summercove still retains its Italian air, while Scilly and Sandycove look prettily and unmistakably Irish, with whitewashed cottages and fuchsia bushes. May the Irish planning authorities preserve them as they are for long years to come! And may they receive the support of all tourists endowed with good taste and good sense!

Kinsale has its place in history. The famous battle of December, 1601, ended the old Clan system of life, and slowly turned Ireland from a chaotic hotch-potch of contrasting tribes into a nation. For a thousand years Kinsale was an important port, worth defending with imposing fortifications, whose ruins are still there to see and visit. It was an important fishing port, too, always full of drifters and coasters. The town also serves the agricultural district around it, and perhaps that is why there are good shops and plenty of pubs.

It is no place for wild living, though, not even of the mildest sort: no fruit machines, no candy floss, not even (mercifully) juke boxes. You may have a chance of seeing at the local cinema the film you missed three years ago at home; there are three different shows every week – no long runs in Kinsale. The shops are surprisingly well supplied with goods: clothing, hardware, footwear are there in plenty; and if you want souvenirs, useful and useless, you can buy indestructible hand-woven Irish tweeds, Aran jerseys, Connemara rugs, Kinsale pampooties, Waterford glass, Belleek china, hand-turned teak bowls, as well as all the leprechaunery and shamrockery you want (or don't, I hope). There's a grocer with an astonishing selection of the oddest delicacies, and pubs with special clienteles: one may be full of gourmets, another of anglers, a third of folk singers, and so on. There are posh hotels and homely ones, boarding houses, good and average restaurants; if you want information about accommodation write to the Information Office in Main Street. There are, I said, posh hotels and plain ones; you can get the moon, but don't expect to get it for sixpence; if you want a lot, you must pay a lot. If you dine on Lobster Thermidor you'll have to pay more than for fish and chips – after all, you can get fish and chips for the price of fish and chips.

This is all fine, you may say, but what about the fishing? Well, the fishing is great, some of the finest in Europe. Some people told me that they had their doubts about it, because they just could not believe advertisements talking of swordfish and tunny, marlin and sailfish, or claiming 73 different species of sporting fish to be caught in Kinsale. These Doubting Thomases were justified, of course. The different 'species' are only about 50 (enough for you, I trust), but the advertising agents thought that specimen meant species – well, some advertising agents are like that, you know. And others, when they say that swordfish and tunny are to be found (and supposedly caught) south of Kinsale, forget to state how many hundred miles south – we are all absent-minded sometimes, are we not? Forget those doubts then, and believe me when I repeat that Kinsale is one of the finest angling resorts in Europe. One of the finest in Ireland too, but not the only one. Once Ballycottin was the only one known to British anglers, now it is Kinsale. Let me whisper to you that there are others, all first class five star places, ready to be discovered by you. But in Kinsale the angling is organised better than in any other Irish resort. Again, you can get the full treatment, the big fast boats, the fighting chair and the rest – but at a price. That 'full treatment' costs a lot, and it must be charged heavily; if you don't want it or cannot afford it, you can go out cheaply with local anglers or you can hire a small boat; you may hook a 150lb skate, even from a rowboat, but for your sake I hope you won't.

There are shops which sell fishing tackle in Kinsale, therefore don't load yourself with half-a-hundredweight of leads, and pay excess baggage rate on your plane ticket, as somebody I know did. If you want advice on tackle ask the local anglers or go to Mrs Green at the Trident: and don't think that a woman could not know; she probably knows what is right for Kinsale a darned sight better than you do.

If you don't fancy going out into the Atlantic, you can catch good fish from many parts of the shore. It is not an easy shore to fish, mind; it is rocky and very weedy, and you must know your job at spinning, as Tom White knows (don't forget to go to see him: nobody can give you better advice). If you cannot spin properly, you won't catch many fish and you'll lose plenty of tackle. If your line is casting heavy spiked leads over sandy bays, go to Garrettstown, 11 miles away, where you can catch bass and flatfish. Don't wade far out, because those sands are full of gullies, and there are strong currents. For full information on the fishing write to the Secretary of Kinsale Sea Angling Club (E. Hurley, Pearse Street, Kinsale), who also can give you information on the Irish Shark Club and on the competitions run by the two clubs. Try to go out with the local anglers: they are good sportsmen, and apart form the fun you'll learn a lot from them.

Lastly, if the weather is too stormy for fishing, spend a quiet hour in the little local museum: it contains things of interest for all visitors, such as Kinsale lace for the ladies, and ships' models for the men, a pretty ancient piano made by the great pianist Clementi, the harpoon used on Captain Scott's expedition to the South Pole, old maps and charters, and lots of other things.

Professor A.F. Magri MacMahon, *Creel,* May, 1967

A Day for the Head

Sea fishing has a history – just about. Although the sport, in any real sense, is not more than 100 years old, there are certain places where you can legitimately say to yourself – here, sea angling history was made. And for me, at least, this is always exciting, if not indeed moving. Filey Brigg, where early attempts at light tackle fishing from the shore took shape, is one such place. And I cannot visit Scarborough without thinking of the epic tunny fishing battles of the thirties or Ballycotton without remembering the British Sea Anglers' Society and the birth of heavy bottom fishing.

So, when I went to Achill Island last September, I felt a special kind of excitement which went back to boyhood and my eager reading of what was, until after the war, the classic text-book on sea angling, the volume of that name in the Lonsdale Library. It is completely out of date now, of course: the invention of nylon has seen to that. But there is one section that I still read with great interest – the notes that the Marquis of Sligo wrote about the remarkable series of big porbeagle that were taken off Achill Island, Co. Mayo in the 1930s. Keem Bay, you may recall, is where the Marquis and his friends operated, and the most successful angler of them all was Dr O'Donnell Browne who caught the 365lb porbeagle which, in spite of all that has been said, remains the biggest porbeagle shark ever caught on rod and line in European waters (and indubitably caught, let me stress, by fair angling).

And so there I was, on this September day, off the Point of Moyteague, very close to where the Doctor hooked his great fish, with the steep sands of Keem Bay in the background, the black curraghs still to be seen there drawn up above the tide-line. I won't deny that this was a moving moment.

I hadn't thought to have been out there at all. For me, last summer was a disaster, weatherwise. I shouldn't like to count the times I had been shore-bound by bad weather and other accidents, the times someone had said to me 'You should have been here last Wednesday week', or its equivalent. And so, travelling across Ireland with Des Brennan and Mike Prichard after trout fishing in the Midlands, I wasn't at all surprised that the wind howled all the way with us, and put our chances of getting out to sea the next day very low indeed. And at Achill itself, as we humped our gear into the Amethyst Hotel, we could hear the surf exploding on Keel Strand. I climbed into bed to the rhythmic creak of the inn sign, not an unpleasant sound in itself, but a pretty bad omen. I didn't even bother to put my gear ready.

Which caused some panic in the morning, I can tell you, what with

Brennan and Pritchard dancing about, impatient to be off and myself cramming sliding booms and leads and hooks into a bag, desperately sorting them out from lake trout casts and the odd pike spoon. Outside, the sun shone, the sea sparkled. The sign had stopped creaking. Before my breakfast was well down, along came Percy Huet, in whose boat we were going to fish, with the news that the shipping forecast was of that splendid 'light, variable' kind and we were all of us loaded in the car, bouncing along to the little harbour of Purteen to meet James and young Pat Keane who were going to handle the boat.

Even then, taking no chances with the fishing Gods who might be listening in, I said to Mike, 'We haven't caught the bait mackerel yet.' There were frozen mackerel aboard, of course, Percy had seen to that, but I am never entirely happy with them for deep sea work though they are a good bit better than nothing. Just outside the harbour we stopped for a quick drop down with the feathers. Nothing except pollack. I permitted myself a thin-lipped smile. 'Away to the Black Cove,' said Percy, and we headed close along the high black rocks to Keem Bay, cutting the engine just opposite a deep cavern in the rock of Moyteague Point, the classic ground where O'Donnell Browne had taken his porbeagle. James, who hadn't said a word since we left Purteen, picked up a feathering rod and eased the weight over the side, slipping the gear lever of the big reel to let it plummet down fast. As he started to haul, his cigarette began to waggle about in his mouth and, impeded by this, he gave out with a few high-pitched yelps. He'd found the mackerel. So had Pat, and the bait box began to fill with an iridescence of the most beautiful fish in the sea, seven at a time.

Every season, if I may be permitted a digression, we hear from the Willy Wetlegs who wants to ban the feathers. I can see the point that there's no sense in catching mackerel by the boxful just for fun and if they are going to be thrown away at the end of the day, but when I go deep sea fishing I want bait and I don't want to be short of it. I like to feel that I can use a whole side of mackerel at a time, even a whole fish at a time if I want and, supposing myself to be biteless after a quarter of an hour, to cut a fresh bait for a new drop down. I want to do all this without the feeling that I am depriving someone else in the boat of the bait. Obviously, when fresh mackerel are short, then they have to be rationed. Otherwise I take advantage of the sea's bounty and fill a box before the real fishing starts. I don't expect feathering for mackerel to be sporting – neither is digging for lug-worm, which is in the essence the same thing.

It didn't take James and Pat very long to get us an ample day's supply and I began to get the feeling that, after all, it was conceiv-able that the luck had turned and we might get the odd fish. 'Where do you fancy now?' I asked Percy. 'It's a day for the Head,' he replied, in the happy tone of a man who could see that things were going to go well. Achill Head, that was, a ferocious amalgam of seven tidal currents, where the sea boiled over rock islets, then fell away to thirty fathoms, a broken uneven bottom where almost any-thing could turn up. We'd have a couple of hours there before the tide grew too strong to fish.

As we motored up, we rigged the kind of all-purpose bottom gear it is as well to start with when one fishes unknown ground. A short nylon link above the lead first of all, a simple blood loop that took a 2/0 hook. Then a sliding boom to take the lead, stopped from fouling the upper hook with a bead. Below, the sliding boom was stopped with a swivel, to which was attached a 12" hook link of stainless steel, nylon-covered wire armed with a 6/0 hook. A 12" link can lead to trouble if there are tope or shark about, but for the moment it would keep down the risk of getting foul in the bottom too often. We were going to drift, and on this ground that meant allowing the lead to tap the bottom, then reeling up a half fathom. A small skep of mackerel went on the top hook, a whole, luscious side on the bottom.

Before we started, James took time out to check the drift of the boat. No sense in chancing anything among those fearful teeth of blackened limestone where an unexpected swell from outside could pick you up and drop you right on the rock if you were on the wrong side of it. Then we picked up a safe drift and the engine was cut.

The bottom was a long way down, I felt, as I eased the tackle down slowly, to avoid the hook links fouling. I was waiting for the first tap to get the trace out of danger. Then – 'Hell,' I thought, 'I'm fast.' But the bottom began to heave about unmercifully and I started to haul my first fish of the day and heavy going it was. 'Pollack!' says Pritchard; 'Conger!' says Brennan. 'No!' says I, 'a big cod!' 'Ling' says James, and a ling it was, fighting all the way up, as good ling always do. There was no time for any more comment, Brennan, Prichard and Percy Huet were all into fish themselves as we drifted over what must have been a really splendid ling mark.

And so it went on, all through that first drift, with perhaps a hundredweight of fish coming aboard. Not all ling. Once I thought I had the mother and father of all ling but it turned out to be two good pollack on at the same time.

It's one of the great pleasures of sea fishing, I think, when everyone in the boat is hauling fish and good fish at that. A wild excitement reigns. You begin to get the feeling that anything could happen, that the next knock could produce something fantastic. Everyone finds it necessary to shout and laugh, with a slight edge of hysteria. Or something like that. And everyone is standing up.

Then we found clean ground, and the good bites stopped. This was no day to fool around. The motor started again and we found a new drift. This one was different. No ling but good pollack and, all the time, bream rattles. I can't resist bream if they are big ones. I sneaked a long-shanked No.6 on the top link and baited it with a fine strip of mackerel belly, tapped bottom and started to reel up slowly. A series of hard snatches, then the thumping, diving weight of the bream, fierce enough even on the solid gear I was using, and I wished then for a spinning rod in the boat so that I could do justice to these fine little fish. Red, silver and orange, I swung the first bream aboard, and there were plenty of them to follow, not monsters but many over three pounds.

A half hour sufficed though. When one is on ground like this, there's a strong desire to experience everything that is going. We tried a drift outside the rock, on patchy ground. More bream and pollack, then Percy started to haul one that suddenly multiplied its strength by ten and started to move off down tide. A tope, of course, and as he came towards the surface and we could see him clearly in the clear water, we realised that he was not alone, that there were two others with him. Mike, landing a bream, stopped to let it swim there for a while. Screech went his reel. Des did the same. Screech again, and so for another spell we were wholly occupied with the tope. Landing three at the same time can be hilarious.

Our fishing at the Point had been over for some time, for we had drifted well out from the rock. There was no going back to the Head now, the tide would be too fierce. With the time we had left we would motor back towards Moyteague and try a drift out to sea over patchy ground. This is where we would hope to get good cod and pollack, and that is exactly what we did. Mike took the honours with a 20 pound cod, but good fish came into the boat all the time. And that was our day. Four hundred pounds, roughly, of mixed fish, most of them good eating fish, as they say. Sixteen species. And four anglers who moved with determination into the bar of the Amethyst, well knowing they'd earned this one.

Clive Gammon, *Creel*, December 1965

A Sea Filled with Bass

Brennan had seen it once before, he said, at Rosscarbery. But it was the first time for me in twenty years of surfcasting for bass. There had been odd times, of course, when there were bass breaking the water as I waded out to cast. But never anything like this.

The surf was whitening a hundred yards out or thereabouts, and there were odd, big rollers; but there was no consistency in it. This was a ground sea, bred somewhere in the Atlantic, not whipped up by a localized wind off the sea – there was scarcely a breath to be felt at all, just a few light airs from the south-east. We had started fishing where you can drive a car down a stony boreen almost to the sea, and twenty minutes went by without a touch before we decided to move a couple of hundred yards up the beach to where a small stream flowed in. The three of us, Roy Haggar, Des Brennan and I, were not particularly optimistic over our chances. A ground sea rarely seems as attractive to bass as a true, wind-whipped surf, and the first, blank twenty minutes seemed to confirm the idea. But there was no point in giving up so early, and there might be the odd fish around the stream mouth; we had good, lively ragworm, and this, after all, was a Kerry beach in early November.

We spread out a little, waded in to cast. Brennan gave out with a wild, Celtic cry which eventually resolved itself into the message that he had disturbed a respectable shoal of bass working close in. Then there was another wild, Celtic cry (Welsh variety) from Haggar whose rod was plunging as he made contact with a lively four-pounder. First bass of the trip, beautifully conditioned as only Kerry bass are at this time of the year, with the fat summer's feeding on sprat and sandeel behind them. I'd stuck my rod in a monopod to help Haggar beach his fish, then turned to see it bounce over hard. But I was given a second chance, and as the rod went over again, I grabbed it and struck by the emergency method of running back up the beach for a few yards with my thumb in the reel spool. A good fish, this one, a really good one. It brought me with it down to the water's edge, then sheered off to the right. Bucking and kicking as it was, I side-strained it into shallower water where it flurried and swirled until Haggar, wading in, could slip his hand under the gills and beach it for me. A quick hoist on the spring balance: just nine pounds, an excellent start. Brennan, meanwhile, torn between duty and pleasure, had chosen the path of duty and was fumbling for his camera. And then I saw them. Thousands of bass were out there, regiments of them, armies of them. As the farthest breaker toppled, I could see them in the bright green water, travelling along the wave, grey and silver, twisting sinuously, riding with the surf. I stopped dead as I waded out to cast again. Never in the whole of my sea fishing had I see a sight like this. Out rang a third wild Celtic cry, as I put everything into a long, powerful cast. Then stopped dead again as I realised that the whole sea was filled with bass, not the far breaker alone. There were bass swimming head-on to me, no more than twenty yards away. And suddenly there were bass all around me, inshore of me even. I recovered line slowly, with little bursts. No takers, even though the bait was passing through bass all the time.

For the two or three hours that we fished, the bass were there, passing and repassing in mighty shoals. But though we took fish, there was no free taking – considering, that is, the numbers of fish that were out there. We ended, I think, with sixteen between the three of us, enough to make my fish bag look inadequate, but far fewer than we would have taken if the shoals had been feeding well. An interesting point: most of the bass we landed were good ones, between six and nine pounds. I am fairly certain – though appearances in the water are deceptive – that the shoals were made up of 2-4lb fish. Were the fish we caught, therefore, not part of the shoals at all? It became clear after a while that long casts were giving the best chance of a fish. Were the shoaling bass merely playing, or were they feeding on something that we could not detect in the water? There was a good deal of floating weed about, and the fish seemed to be moving toward the thickest patches (which, naturally, we had to avoid). The weed might contain maggots (it had been rotting onshore before the tide had picked it up) or some other small form of life with which the shoal bass had become preoccupied.

Then, confident, excited, conscious of the already formidable task of carrying our catch back to the car, we made a mistake and packed up while the bass were still taking spasmodically. The morning's fishing had been an afterthought, for we had stopped overnight at Tralee and were on our way to Dingle to fish the beaches there. Since we had to drive parallel with the Castlegregory beach it had seemed a good idea to spend an hour or two there on the way. And a very good idea it had been, we thought, as we loaded the catch into the back of Brennan's car. But there would be more fishing that night at Dingle, at the Black Strand possibly, and if the fish were in at Castlegregory, they would probably be there also. Had we not been so pleased with ourselves, we would have noticed what was happening to the weather. The light airs from the south-east, even as we were loading the car and kicking off our boots, were becoming gusts and shifting to a true easterly direction. By the time we drove into Dingle, there was a steady, cold blow that would kill the surf and put the fish right down.

Every angler, one time or another, has heard the old couplet about when the wind is in the east, then the fish will bite the least. And I, for one, am quite sure that no truer word was ever spoken – with odd exceptions, of course (an easterly in summertime, for instance, will sometimes bring fry inshore in calm seas, and the bass with them, and east coast beaches sometimes benefit). But by and large, the cold, chilling easterly finishes the fishing. The fish will not take. This is not due, I think, to the temperature of the water becoming lower: often, the fish go off the feed long before the wind can have made that much difference. And trawlermen find the same thing, that an east wind brings bad catches. Possibly what happens here is that the easterly is a clearing wind, the water becomes less cloudy and the fish can see the net. It's a bad, black wind for anglers and commercial fishermen alike.

There was no surf when we went down to the Black Strand that night, and no bass, only dogfish, flounders and small plaice. Jim O'Sullivan told us we should have been there a week before, to catch the end of a big nor'westerly they had had. There were plenty of fish on the Black Strand then. He has had the remarkable experience of two nine-pounders on at the same time. But with the bad wind and no surf, the night was hopeless. We decided to hit the Castlegregory beach again next morning.

There was more weed. We could see that at once, broken fragments of red, offshore weed that would cling to the line and make fishing difficult. It made it impossible, in fact, and we had to drop down the beach from where we were the previous day. The big shoals were still there, though, in greater numbers if anything, and we tackled up and cast confidently. But this time there were no outriders to take our bait. We tried clam instead of rag, and Haggar got out a spinning rod, but that was no use either. The wind blew cold down the beach. The previous morning we had had to shed coats. This time we looked for extra sweaters. We kept going and after lunch, just at the top of the tide, Des Brennan scored our solitary success, an eight-pounder that took clam. And that was that. We left the beach, defeated, with the bass still milling there, oblivious of anything we could offer them. It was a strange experience.

It was time to shift ground, and a phone call to Thaddeus O'Keeffe at Rosscarbery brought news of a wind there that was still sou'easterly. So off we went to West Cork. It was too late to fish that night, but a walk down to Owenahincha Strand proved that there was a fishable surf and brighter prospects. And then, in the morning, we had a bait crisis. We had ordered lugworm beforehand, but they turned out to be puny little creatures that would have to be a half-dozen to a hook to make any kind of show at all. We still had the remains of the ragworm and a few clams that were past their best, and these would have to serve.

We opened our campaign at the Warren Strand, the little beach on the side of the sand estuary at Rosscarbery. This often fishes well at the beginning of the tide, and so it proved on this occasion. Haggar caught a little one to start us off then I had a four and a six-pounder (we had set a size limit by this time – under 6lb went back to the water). Then, instead of fishing on where we were doing well, we thought we would have an hour on a different beach before lunch. Another fatal error. No fish there at all. Back to the Warren, then, for high water. A few school bass and big flounders, but the big bass had gone. That made two tactical mistakes already. And the wind was shifting east again.

It was the end of the beach fishing, right enough, and we had to face up to it. What to do with the remaining day or so of our long weekend? 'They've been catching codling at Cobh', said Brennan significantly, and at 10am next morning we were sitting in Ned Geary's boat, heading out past Spike Island to the mouth of Cork Harbour. We dropped anchor at No.2 buoy, and there were the codling, as planned, and some big dabs as well – enjoyable light fishing until the tide became too strong and we had to move back under the lee of Spike. Brennan, meanwhile, had taken out his big boat rod and baited up with half a small coalfish on a wire trace 'just to see what's down there.' What was down there was a 30lb tope that gave him a run for his money and the confidence to try again with the other half of the coalie. This was ignored until the day came to its end, the engine was started and the anchor about to come up. Then out screamed the check on the big reel again. Now, Roy Haggar hadn't taken a big tope before, so Brennan handed him the rod and invited him to deal with it. The tope made a few brisk runs, then changed into a skate that kept Haggar busy for a quarter of an hour until we gaffed it inboard – 90lb.

A good beginning and good end. No really blank days, and some good fish: the best sort of fishing weekend.

Clive Gammon, *Creel*, January 1965

Bass in the Fog

Today we were determined to get among them and teach them manners. The bass I mean. They had been shoaling strongly during the few days we had been fishing in Dungarvan Bay, and we had not enjoyed the success that we should have had with them. True, we had bloodied a few noses; I had six the day before – a nice run of fish averaging around 5lb the best making 7¾lb. Still, they were very finicky and not really inclined to take. The bay was full of fry – tiny sandeels and brit – which flashed and flickered in the sun, and peppered the calm surface of the water like light rain.

Bass would follow our lures right up to the boat without taking. It made no difference whether we worked the lines quickly or slowly. The bass would remain exactly the same distance behind the lures and sheer away on sighting the boat. We used small baits, medium baits and large ones. It made little difference. What fish we took we worked hard for, and perhaps that is the best way to catch them. You feel that you have earned your fish.

What really got under our skins was that there were so many bass. There were numerous shoals breaking the water all over the bay as the gulls screamed, wheeled, and dipped above them. In places the fish were so thick that it seemed impossible not to foul hook them on the retrieve. We came to the conclusion that fry were so plentiful that the bass were glutted from feeding on the morning tide, and the thing to do was to get up early and catch them when they were really feeding and not so fussy.

5.30am saw Hugh Stoker, John Casey and I groping our way down to the quay and at 6am we were afloat in John's 16-footer. Conditions were bad and the outlook bleak. A heavy fog was rolling in from the sea, and visibility ranged from 100 yards to absolutely zero. The fog, like so many sea fogs, was not very deep – only 60 or 70 ft high, for we could see the clear blue sky above. We held a brief council of war with the crew of another boat who were waiting for the fog to lift so that they too could have a crack at the bass. We decided that the strong summer sun would burn through the fog, and that we might as well make our way out into the bay and be on the spot when the visibility improved.

The outboard spluttered into life, shattering the stillness of the morning, and we were on our way. The sea was glassy calm and a beautiful and eerie luminosity pervaded through the fog. After a while we stopped and listened for the birds. When we heard them we tried to take a compass bearing and headed in the direction of the noise. Trying to find the gulls working in the thick fog was an impossible task. Frequently we would reach them just as they stopped working, to find them sitting on the water. They would take off as we approached, and disappear in the mist. Every now and then the fog would lift a little and we could see birds a quarter of a mile or even half a mile away working over the bass. We would set off post-haste in pursuit, only to find the fog closing in again like an impenetrable curtain. One particularly noisy outburst lured us right across the bay, past the shadowy boats from Helvic which were feathering for mackerel. We finally ran the flock down, only to find them resting on the rocky slopes of Helvic Head.

We felt slightly foolish as we headed back for the Black Rock in the middle of the bay and quite suddenly the sun burned through and the fog lifted. Then we saw them. Great flocks of fowl, their wings catching the sun as they worked over bass just north of the Black Rock. As we neared the rock, a great shoal of bass broke the surface in front of us and went under the boat. We pressed on, heading for the main shoals on the other side of the rock. There were birds everywhere, the air was thick with them, full of the beat of their wings and torn by their raucous cries. We cut the engine and the boat lost way.

We were among the bass at last. Great shoals of them on every side, breaking the water and turning it white as they ravaged the hapless fry. A shoal was heading towards the boat, making great swirls in the water and porpoising after the tiny bait. They were travelling at a rate of knots, and we could see their bluey black shapes edged with the white of their open mouths as they approached . We cast together and our triumphant cries rang out almost simultaneously as we each struck into fish.

There is nothing quite like a hefty bass taken in deep water on light spinning tackle. Your lure just stops dead as if it had come against a stone wall. Then the bass takes off and the reel sings out madly as the rod doubles over to the strain. With plenty of water under it, and with room to manoeuvre, the bass puts up a tremendous struggle, and like a true game fish does not give up until it lies belly up, exhausted. By the time it is in the boat your wrist and arm aches and, when bass are going well, fishing can prove to be very tiring work. When it came to boating a fish, it was every man for himself, as each of us was too occupied to lend a hand elsewhere.

The next half hour was really hectic, filled with the heady excitement that only shoaling bass can generate. We would cast, start to retrieve, and suddenly a fish was on. For some peculiar reason we were not hooking them properly. A bass would take, and after playing it for a few minutes it would get off. As the lure was being retrieved for another cast it would be seized again, that fish perhaps lost too, and yet another fish might take the lure before it reached the tip of the rod, so dense were the shoals. The bass were really savage, striking at anything that moved, and one fish threw itself clean out of the water to take my spoon as I whipped it across the top of the water when I thought I had missed the shoal.

The air rang with our cries of 'In' and perhaps a few minutes later with a crestfallen 'Out' and then 'In' again. The bottom of the boat was rapidly being covered by handsome shining fish. We had boated more than a dozen, despite our losses in the last half hour when John glanced at his watch and let out a startled cry – 'It's 9 o'clock!' That brought us all up suddenly. John had to open up his shop at 9am and here we were right out in the middle of the bay. There was nothing for it but to pack up and head for the quays as fast as possible.

Des Brennan, *Creel*, August 1965

BIBLIOGRAPHY

J. Adams, *Salmon and Trout Angling*, 1925

R. Allen ("Cosmopolite"), *The Sportsman in Ireland*, 1849

F.D. Barker, *An Angler's Paradise*, 1929

J. Bickerdyke, *Wild Sports in Ireland*, 1897

E. Craigie, *Irish Sporting Sketches*, 1894

J. Coad, *The Angling Excursions of Gregory Greendrake*, 1832

H. Davy, *Salmonia*, 1828

J.B. Drought, *A Sportsman Looks at Eire*, no date

W. Durand, *Wanderings with a Fly Rod*, 1938

T.G. Esmonde, *Hunting Memories of Many Lands*, 1925

N. Fallon, *Fly Fishing for Irish Trout*, 1983

N. Farson, *Going Fishing*, 1942

L. Gaffey, *A Freelance Angler in Ireland*, no date

    Freshwater Fishing in Ireland, 1949

C.W. Gedney, *Angling Holidays*, 1896

Lord Grey of Fallodon, *Fly Fishing*, 1899

A. Grimble, *The Salmon Rivers of Ireland*, 1913

S. Gwynn, *Fishing Holidays*, 1904

    Duffer's Luck, 1924

M. Headlam, *A Holiday Fisherman*, 1934

S. Heaney, *Death of a Naturalist*, 1966

J.W. Hills, *Summer on the Test*, 1924

T.C. Kingsmill Moore, *A Man May Fish*, 1979

W. Le Fanu, *Seventy Years of Irish Life*, 1893

G.D. Luard, *Fishing Fortunes and Misfortunes*, 1942

    Fishing Fact or Fantasy, 1947

A.A. Luce, *Fishing and Thinking*, 1959

W.H. Maxwell, *Wild Sports of the West*, 1850

A. Mainwaring, *Fishing and Philandering*, 1914

J. O'Gorman, *The Practice of Angling*, 1845

W. Peard, *A Year of Liberty*, 1867

M. Pritchard, *A Sporting Angler*, 1987

J. Reynolds, *A Life by the Boyne*, no date

C. Sinclair, *Coarse Fishing in Ireland*, 1947

W. Wilde, *The Beauties of the Boyne and Blackwater*, 1849

S.B. Wilkinson, *Reminiscences of Sport in Ireland*, 1931

Recommended reading from Merlin Unwin Books

THE FAR FROM COMPLEAT ANGLER
Tom Fort

Tom Fort, fishing correspondent for the *Financial Times*, travels to some exotic far-flung locations in search of trout, salmon, even dourado. He has fun with eels on the Test and takes his rods to Eastern Europe and Brazil. This is a wonderful collection of fishing travels, interspersed with some profound thoughts about the sport of fishing and written by a man with a sharp eye for the absurd and the funny.

Hardback **£16.99**

Few can match his effortless essay style. This book levers fishing writing out of a rut – The Field

AN ANGLER FOR ALL SEASONS
The Best of H.T. Sheringham

This author is considered by many to be one of the finest fishing writers of the twentieth century. This is a collection of his very best angling essays, written over a period of some 30 years. With equal gusto, he pursues carp, tench, chub, pike, roach, salmon and trout.

Hardback **£16.95**

His manner is wise and humourous, his style delicious in its elegance and wit - Financial Times

TROUT & SALMON FLIES OF IRELAND
Peter O'Reilly

A comprehensive guide to the best contemporary fishing flies for Irish waters. Includes trout, salmon and seatrout flies for rivers and loughs. Dry flies, emergers, wet flies, salmon hairwings, etc. This book, in its third printing, includes invaluable tips and advice from many of the flies' inventors. It is a must for all anglers in Ireland. With 26 colour plates illustrating hundreds of the best Irish flies. Hardback **£20**

Also available:
TROUT & SALMON FLIES OF WALES by Moc Morgan **£20**
TROUT & SALMON FLIES OF SCOTLAND by Stan Headley **£20**

RIVERS OF IRELAND
Peter O'Reilly

Completely revised, updated and with much new information, this deeply-researched guide to every trout and salmon fishing river in Ireland will now be even more useful to visiting and local anglers. This new edition includes websites of fishing organisations, details of local fishing guides and flytyers, important local tackle shops, details of disabled facilities, etc.

Hardback **£20**

FLYFISHING IN IRELAND
Peter O'Reilly

In this beautifully illustrated book O'Reilly describes the many techniques of river and lough fishing used in Ireland. From dapping on the great loughs, the duck fly, mayfly and murrough, to specialist methods like the Sheelin bloodworm and the Erriff-style slack water technique for salmon. This is a mine of information about fishing 'the Irish way' for trout and salmon.

Hardback **£20**

A HISTORY OF FLYFISHING
Conrad Voss Bark

With a delightful blend of wit and erudition Conrad Voss Bark tells the story of flyfishing, from the Macedonian 'plumes' of old to the hairwing streamers of today. He reviews the sport's formative protagonists: Juliana Berners, Robert Venables, Isaak Walton, Charles Cotton, Alfred Ronalds, George Kelson, Skues and Halford, Theodore Gordon, and many more.

Hardback **£25**   Paperback **£12.95**

An enchanting and learned book - The Field

CONFESSIONS OF A SHOOTING FISHING MAN
Laurence Catlow

Is it right to shoot and fish for pleasure? At the start of his sporting year, Laurence Catlow asks himself this central question. His sporting diary recording the high and lows of a sporting year in Cumbria often returns to this theme and in so doing tackles the controversial and highly topical issues in the fieldsports debate. Entertaining and disarmingly frank, Catlow presents powerful arguments in favour of shooting, fishing and hunting.

Hardback **£17.99** Paperback **£9.99**

If you are looking for a present for a friend who shoots or fishes, then you need look no further than this book
– Roger Scruton, The Times

All these books are available by direct mail, next-day despatch, from Merlin Unwin Books, 7 Corve Street, Ludlow, Shropshire SY8 1DB, UK.

Credit card orders on:
Tel (00 44) 1584 877456
Fax (00 44) 1584 877457

Or you can buy books via our website (www.countrybooksdirect.com) using our bank-approved, secure charging method.

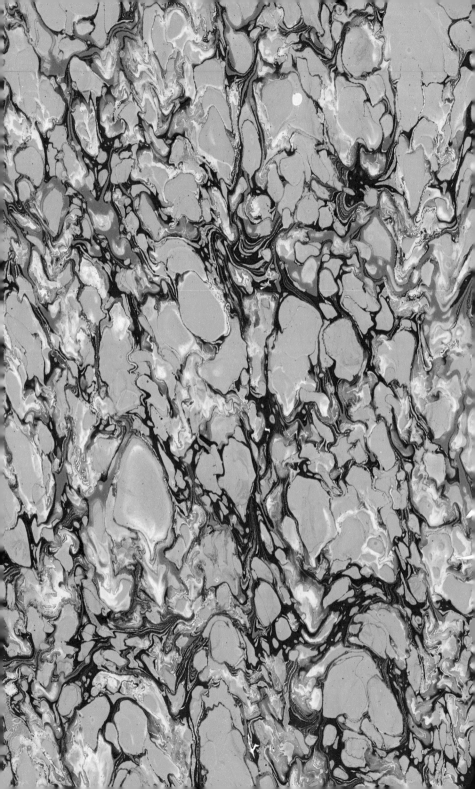